All Together in One Place

All Together
in One Place

Theological Papers from the

Brighton Conference on

World Evangelization

**Edited by Harold D. Hunter
and Peter D. Hocken**

 Sheffield Academic Press

VNYS BV 3755 .A44
1993 c.2

CYL501 · c.2

Copyright © 1993 Sheffield Academic Press

Published by JSOT Press
JSOT Press is an imprint of
Sheffield Academic Press Ltd
343 Fulwood Road
Sheffield S10 3BP
England

Production Editor	Typesetter
J. Webb Mealy	Robert Knight

Typeset by Sheffield Academic Press
and
Printed on acid-free paper in Great Britain
by The Cromwell Press
Melksham, Wiltshire

British Library Cataloguing in Publication Data

All Together in One Place: Theological
Papers from the Brighton Conference on
World Evangelism.—(Journal of
Pentecostal Theology Supplement Series,
ISSN 0966-7393)
    I. Hunter, Harold D. II. Hocken, Peter
    III. Series
    269

ISBN 1-85075-406-3

CONTENTS

PREFACE

The twentieth century has seen the birth and phenomenal growth first of what is now often called the Classical Pentecostal Movement, and, subsequently, of the charismatic movement and associated waves. Reaction to the Pentecostal movement in its first half-century was almost unanimously negative, principally expressing itself in the writings of behavioral scientists and of those Evangelical and Holiness leaders whose flocks were being reached by Pentecostal preaching. The vast majority of church leaders and theologians from the historic Churches, however, did not even seem to consider the phenomenon worth the attention of criticism. Accordingly, Pentecostals were judged by many to be emotionally disturbed, mentally limited, socio-logically deprived—more the object of pathology than of theology. Pentecostal claims to the illumination, guidance and power of the Holy Spirit were therefore dismissed *a priori* as inauthentic.

By the 1990s, Pentecostalism has come to be received much more generously. To cite just a few examples, theological dialogue has existed for nearly 20 years between the Roman Catholic Church and some Pentecostals; the Evangelical Lausanne II Congress at Manila in 1990 included a large Pentecostal and charismatic contingent; chairs of Pentecostal studies are being proposed in some Universities. Much of this change has no doubt occurred as a result of the spread of what the great Pentecostal leader Donald Gee called 'Pentecost outside Pentecost', that is, the charismatic movement bringing Pentecostal-type blessing and experience to Christians beyond the Pentecostal Churches. While the 1960s saw the beginnings of charismatic renewal among Anglicans and mainline Protestants, the late 1960s and 1970s saw a major renewal within the Roman Catholic Church, and the 1980s have seen a much greater welcome of this phenomenon in the Evangelical world.

The dramatic spread of the Pentecostal movement throughout the world has been another major factor in making other Christians wake up to its significance. It startled many when the enormous *World Christian Encyclopedia*, edited by David Barrett, determined that classical Pentecostalism was by 1980 the largest unit in the Protestant family. His statistics for 1985 identified 168 million believers as Pentecostal or charismatic. These figures lend considerable weight to the far-sighted designation of Pentecostal-type Churches being a third force in contemporary Christianity.

As a productive social and religious force within Christianity, the Pentecostal-Charismatic movement has clearly come into its own. What is less acknowledged is its potential contribution to the reflective, theological life of the international community of faith. It may be viewed as an interesting area for studies in church growth or in matters of missionary methodology, but it has perhaps not won its spurs in theology, Christology or even pneumatology.

It is against this background that the importance of the theological section of 'Brighton '91', an international congress on world evangelization held in Brighton, England July 8–14, 1991, must be judged. The leadership congress with the theme 'That the World Might Believe' was planned by the International Charismatic Consultation on World Evangelization (ICCOWE). The editors of this volume were given responsibility for organizing the theological stream. Of the 150 scholars attending, several were theologians, exegetes or historians of world renown who recognized the importance of the Pentecostal-charismatic phenomenon. Many were scholar-participants in these movements. Most striking was the diversity of nationalities and Church traditions represented: these ranged from Latin American Pentecostals, to a Coptic Orthodox bishop, from Scandinavian Lutheran to New Zealand Open Brethren, from African-American Pentecostal to Syrian rite Catholic. Particularly well-represented was South Africa, with scholars from most groupings in that troubled land.

The papers published in this volume represent a selection of those presented during the Brighton conference. Limitations of space as well as the more informal character of some contributions necessitated the choice of a selection, rather than a presentation of all, of the papers and responses. Unfortunately, the selection reduces the Brighton encounter's international breadth and its ecumenical range, which can however be sensed from the programme printed in the Appendix.

This unprecedented symposium attracted participants from many ecumenical and academic bodies, some in a representative capacity.

Thus there were representatives from the World Council of Churches, the National Council of Churches of Christ (USA), and the Graymoor Institute (USA); people were also present from the Latin American Council of Churches, the Latin American Theological Fraternity, the international Roman Catholic–Pentecostal dialogue, and the NCCCUSA–Pentecostal dialogue, as well as other more regional groups. With the exception of Oceania, all continents were represented by academic bodies concerned with Pentecostal-charismatic studies: the Society for Pentecostal Studies (North America), the Latin American Pentecostal Encounter, Pentecostal and Charismatic Research in Europe (East and West), Asian Charismatic Theological Association; the Society for Pentecostal Theology (South Africa), and the Association of Evangelicals of Africa and Madagascar.

It must be confessed that the media reaction to the conference, and perhaps especially to the theological section, was disappointing. The only serious reports to date have been in the North American monthly *Ecumenical Trends* (3, 4 [1992]) and the French bi-monthly *Tychique*, though shorter mention was made in *The Christian Century, Christianity Today* (both USA) and *La Croix* (Paris). It seemed hard for many commentators to grapple with the fact that significant theological work was being done and contacts made within the framework of a general conference easily perceived by the less-informed as yet another charismatic jamboree.

In fact, the setting of the theological stream within the general conference of Pentecostal-charismatic leaders was itself of real significance and benefit. Previous fears that there might not be much interaction proved to be totally unfounded. The six theological workshops open to the general conference were among the best attended, and many scholars took part in the plenary evening sessions of the conference. The welcome given to the scholars demonstrated that the leaders recognized both the need for serious theology and the importance of interaction between pastors, preachers and theologians.

Brighton '91 should lay to rest a number of misconceptions that still cloud academic and ecclesiastical circles, chief among them the notion that serious scholarly work is absent from the movement. This conference also illustrates why Pentecostalism is not correctly classified as a subcategory of Evangelicalism, and why not all charismatics are rightly described as Protestants. Another prejudice that dies hard is the assumption of endemic indifference on the part of Pentecostal and charismatic Christians towards social injustice. The contributions from South Africa with the presentation of *The Relevant Pentecostal Witness*, as well as the papers on liberation theology, tell a different— and encouraging—story. A session devoted to the sharing of information elicited several items of wider theological interest, for example, the proposal to endow chairs for the study of Pentecostalism at the Free University of Amsterdam and the University of Utrecht. Also announced was a new scholarly journal on Pentecostal theology and a monograph series from Sheffield Academic Press. An EPLA conference slated to convene in Brazil in late 1992 mentioned joint sponsorship by the WCC and CLAI.

The theological stream was particularly privileged to hear the Most Revd Dr George Carey, the Archbishop of Canterbury, and Professor Jürgen Moltmann of the University of Tübingen. Their presence together was a symbol of Church leadership and academic theology acknowledging and welcoming the contemporary work of the Holy Spirit among the people of God. There was virtual unanimity among the participants that this scholarly collaboration across continents and Churches must continue. The high level of interest in an ongoing network of scholars with a particular interest in Pentecostal-charismatic studies was shown in the replies to the professional data forms sent to all invited scholars. Copies of the completed forms were made available to all participants at Brighton, and produced immediate fruit in the gathering of special interest groups during the conference, such as the historians present and the specialists in Latin America.

The objectives for the theological stream, formulated in advance by the organizers, can continue to serve as the objectives for this ongoing theological collaboration and consultation. These objectives were formulated as follows:

1.   Awaken and deepen among leaders a sense of the importance, necessity and contribution of theological scholarship.
2.   Help theologians and scholars to have a heightened awareness of the concerns of Pentecostal and charismatic leaders.
3.   Increase understanding of each other's theological traditions and their relationship to the history and life of the churches.
4.   Contribute as only a world-wide conference can to a greater awareness of relationship between the Christian faith and the plurality of culture, and to participants becoming more attentive to the cultural components in their own theologies.

5. Stimulate ongoing international contacts between scholars in Pentecostal-charismatic studies, and opportunities for the growth of personal friendship between them.

6. Stimulate more scholarly research in the area of Pentecostal-charismatic studies, in particular among young scholars.

7. Facilitate greater awareness of relevant work being done in other places, continents and cultures.

8. Contribute to the world of theology by paying more attention to the contemporary work of the Holy Spirit in Pentecostal and charismatic movements.

Barriers of geography, language and denomination have made financial limitations to ongoing collaboration seem the least of worries. Every effort is being made to build on the contacts made at Brighton and to establish an ongoing network of scholars. It is too early to announce detailed proposals, though it clearly makes sense to encourage existing continental or regional societies and networks. Some of these however are not fully representative of the Pentecostal and charismatic movements, often lacking Roman Catholic and other 'mainline' Church scholars as well as those specialists who would not identify themselves as participants in these movements.

Ongoing scholarly collaboration across this wide range of ethnic, ecclesiastical and other barriers must surely be of major consequence for the future of these movements and their spiritual health. Not the least factor at stake is liberation from ethnic and racial narrowness and the ideological limitations that frequently accompany it. Readers of these papers who wish to have their names added to the list of interested scholars should write to one of the editors.

Peter D. Hocken
Harold D. Hunter

ACKNOWLEDGMENTS

The editors wish to express their gratitude to the following:

Dr John Christopher Thomas, Dr Steven J. Land and Dr Rick D. Moore for accepting this volume as part of the *JPT* Supplement Series, and Dr Thomas for his editorial help; Jeremy Woolen, for his art work for the cover design; Dr Cecil M. Robeck Jr, editor of *Pneuma*, for permission to publish the paper by Dr James Bradley, of which the major part had been previously published in *Pneuma* 13.1 (Spring, 1991); the Dixon Pentecostal Research Center in Cleveland, Tennessee for the accommodation provided to Dr Harold D. Hunter and the Mother of God Community in Gaithersburg, Maryland for the assistance given to Dr Peter D. Hocken.

The King's Library

ABBREVIATIONS

ACTA	Asian Charismatic Theological Association
CLAI	Consejo Latinoamericano de Iglesias
CPCRE	Conference on Pentecostal-Charismatic Research in Europe
DPCM	*Dictionary of Pentecostal and Charismatic Movements*
EPLA	Encuentro Pentecostal Latinoamericano
ICCOWE	International Charismatic Consultation on World Evangelization
ICCRO	International Catholic Charismatic Renewal Office
JES	*Journal of Ecumenical Studies*
JPTS	*Journal of Pentecostal Theology*, Supplements
LCL	Loeb Classical Library
NCCCUSA	National Council of the Churches of Christ in the USA
RPW	*Relevant Pentecostal Witness*
SJT	Scottish Journal of Theology
SPS	Society for Pentecostal Studies
WCC	World Council of Churches

LIST OF CONTRIBUTORS

Norbert Baumert is First chair of the Theological Committee for Catholic Charismatic Renewal of the German Bishops Conference. His publications include *Taglich Sterben und Auferstehen: Der Literalsinn von 2 Kor 4,12–5,10* and many small books and articles on biblical and spiritual topics.

Paul Bechdolff is a member of the National Council of the French Reformed Church and of the Directory of the Union de Prière.

James E. Bradley has published *Popular Politics and the American Revolution in England* and *Religion, Revolution, and English Radicalism*.

Roger Cabezas, author of various publications in Spanish, is active in Encuentro Pentecostal Latinoamericano, Consejo Latinoamericano de Iglesias, and Comision Evangelical Latinoamericano Educacion Cristiano.

Raniero Cantalamessa, formerly professor of history of early Christianity and head of the department of religious sciences at the University of Milan, is author of many books in several languages, including *Life in the Lordship of Christ*.

Dr George Carey, author of many books, was Principal of Trinity College, Bristol and Bishop of Bath and Wells before becoming Archbishop of Canterbury in early 1991.

Guillermo Cook, General Coordinator of Tercer Congreso Latinoamericano de Evangelizacion (CLADE III), is author of numerous articles and *The Expectation of the Poor: The Catholic Base Communities in Protestant Perspective*, and contributor to *Let My People Live: Faith and Struggle in Central America*.

Martinus L. Daneel is the Director of the Zimbabwe Institute of Religious Research and Ecological Conservation. Numerous publications include the 3-volume *Old and New in Southern Shona Independent Churches.*

Tormod Engelsviken, chair of the Egede Institute for Missionary Research, is author of the doctoral dissertation 'The Gift of the Spirit' and sundry books and articles in Norwegian and English.

Anthony Gbuji is Roman Catholic Bishop of Issele-Uku in Bendel State, Nigeria.

James R. Goff is author of *Fields White unto Harvest: Charles F. Parham and the Missionary Origins of Pentecostalism.*

Brian Hathaway, pastor of Te Atatu Bible Chapel, is one of the authors of *The Kingdom Manifesto* published by the Evangelical Fellowship of New Zealand.

Irving Hexham is author of the *Irony of Apartheid* and various articles on South Africa.

Karla Poewe-Hexham, is the author of *The Namibian Hereo,* which was based on eighteen months' field work during which she lived in the Black township of Katatura outside Windhoek in Namibia.

Nico Horn is author of *From Rags to Riches* and an executive member of Relevant Pentecostal Witness of South Africa.

Cheryl Bridges Johns is current president of the Society for Pentecostal Studies (1992–1993), a member of the NCCCUSA Faith and Order, and author of *Pentacostal Formation: A Pedagogy among the Oppressed.*

Theodore Jungkuntz, long time professor of theology at Valparaiso University, is author of *Confirmation and the Charismata.*

Wynand de Kock is the author of a UNISA dissertation entitled 'Geloof, Geloofsinhoud en Geloofsowtwikkeling'.

Japie J. Lapoorta is chair of Relevant Pentecostal Witness in South Africa and a member of the International Roman Catholic–Pentecostal Dialogue. His writings include 'Christian Commitment to the Poor and the Rise of Pentecostalism', published in *Azusa.*

Philippe Larère, former chaplain to technical colleges, is representative of the Bishop of Evry for ecumenical questions. His publications include *Baptême dans l'Esprit et Baptême d'Eau.*

Hubertus Lenz is a member of the theological committee for Catholic Charismatic Renewal of German Bishops Conference.

Jürgen Moltmann is the author of *The Theology of Hope, The Crucified God* and *The Church in the Power of the Spirit*, which, like volumes that have followed from the prolific pen of Professor Moltmann, have been translated into the leading world languages.

Derek Mutungu was head of the Scripture Union in Zambia before entering upon academic studies in London and Vancouver. Currently, he is finishing his ThM at Regent College, Vancouver, Canada.

Clark H. Pinnock, a respected Christian philosopher, has most recently added *A Wideness in God's Mercy* to his many publications.

Cecil M. Robeck is former editor of *Pneuma* (1984–1992), co-chair of NCCCUSA Faith and Order–Pentecostal Dialogue, member of the WCC Faith and Order Standing Committee and co-chair of the International Roman Catholic–Pentecostal Dialogue. Author of *Prophecy in Carthage*, he has contributed several articles to dictionaries and encyclopedias.

Luis Segreda has published in various Latin American journals.

Juan Esteban Sepulveda G., author of numerous articles in Spanish and English, is an Instructor of Pentecostalism in the Comunidad Teologica Evangelica de Chile. He is a leader in Encuentro Pentecostal Latinoamericano and Consejo Latino Americano de Iglesias.

Ronald J. Sider, author of several books, is executive director of Evangelicals for Social Action and co-editor of *Transformation: An International Dialogue on Evangelical Social Ethics.*

Miroslav Volf is an active member of the International Roman Catholic–Pentecostal Dialogue and the World Evangelical Fellowship Theological Commission. Author of numerous articles and the recent *Work in the Spirit: Toward a Theology of Work*, he is also on the faculty of Fuller Theological Seminary.

INTRODUCTION: THE IMPORTANCE OF THEOLOGY FOR THE CHARISMATIC MOVEMENT

The Most Reverend George Carey, Archbishop of Canterbury

Theology is as old as revelation itself. Indeed, in Genesis 3 it is arguably the case that the serpent appears to be a very competent theologian as he says to Eve, 'Has God said?' that is to say, 'Are you really sure, Eve, that you got it right? Did God really say that?'

Well, that might suggest that theology began with a massive 'own goal'. We have to admit that theologians have not always been popular people in the church. Listen to the poet Edwin Muir speaking of a new church being built. He longs for this new church to speak of the simplicity of the gospel. Verse six says:

> I look at the church again and yet again,
> And think of those who house together in Hell,
> Cooped by ingenious theological men
> Expert to track the sour and musty smell
> Of sin they know too well:
> Until grown proud, they crib in rusty bars
> the Love that moves the sun and other stars.

But, you know, we are all theologians. From the moment we start our personal walk with God, we start to theologize. The moment we are asked by the curious bystander, 'Why do you believe in Christ?' 'Why are you here at Brighton?', the answers we give are theological. Yet at a more profound level we are inescapably caught up in the theological enterprise. Let me offer three reflections why it is important for you at this conference.

First, theology is the task of understanding the Christian faith. Our tools are faith, experience, history and critical reason. In the Anglican communion, we talk of authority being dispersed among three important sources—Scripture, tradition and reason, with Scripture being the yardstick by which truth is acknowledged. As such, theology can be, and obviously ought to be, a marvelous handmaid of the church in helping us to work out our faith. For any movement that emerges in the church, theology acts as a control in the task of assisting whether a particular experience is an authentic Christian experience.

Second, the task of theology is to mediate between a faith and a culture. Its job is, or it should be, to explicate our faith so that we can talk in meaningful ways about the nature of Christian truth, about the person of Christ, and about the gifts and fruits of the Holy Spirit.

My third reflection is on the partnership there should be between theology and our experience of God. Genuine Christian theology cannot play a role merely as a bystander—watching other people get on with the game. The Roman Catholic theologian Jacques Pohier once remarked:

> Academic theology is like armor worn by knights at the battle of Agincourt. It is so heavy that it overwhelms the majority of those who take it on. Moreover, the weight of academic theology and the objectivity which it sets itself in order to prove that it is academic means that it talks a lot about God, but rarely of God.

So experience needs to infuse the academic process as academic study informs and underpins experience.

In this intermesh of theology and experience, Greek thought has so much to offer because it saw the outworking of this in terms of worship. Listen to two thinkers in particular. Gregory of Nazianzus said 'Theology is the son of God'. Didymus the Blind, a wonderful theologian, said, 'When you praise you theologize'. And again he says, 'All true theology is doxological'.

But let a young lady have the final word.

> Lucy finished cutting the bread. 'Lucy. Give me the hunchy bit', said Nina. 'Hunchy is NOT in the dictionary', said Cecilia. 'I want it on my plate and not in the dictionary', said Nina.

Speaking personally, I want it in both places!

Part I

THE SPIRIT GIVES LIFE: SPIRITUALITY AND VITALITY[*]

Jürgen Moltmann

All life that is born wants to grow. When a person is born, we speak of his or her birthday. When life begins, the senses are awakened. The child opens its eyes and sees the light. The child begins to breathe and feels the air. The child cries and hears the sounds. The child lies on the mother and feels the warmth of her skin.

Life, which we say is born anew by the eternal Spirit of God, wants to grow and gain its shape. Our senses are also born again. The illuminated eyes of understanding awaken to the knowledge of God. The liberated personality will judge its new powers of will in the instruction of life. The beating heart experiences God's love, is warmed by it to the love of life, and is made alive by its source. The experience of the Spirit of God is like the breath of air: 'God is continually breathing, as it were, upon the soul, and the soul is breathing unto God' (John Wesley). The Spirit of God is the vibrating and vitalizing energy-field of life: we are in God and God is in us; our life motions are experienced by God and we experience the life energies of God. In the free air of the eternal Spirit, the new life unfolds: in faith we measure the depth, the love, the width of the space—in hope the open horizons of the future. The Spirit of God is our life-power and our life-space.

Life is always specific, never general. Life is different everywhere, nowhere is it the same. It is female and male, young and old, disabled and not disabled, Jewish and Gentile, white and colored.

What does the Spirit of God have to do with these specific varieties of life? Are we not all the same before God: sinner and just, dying and born again, unholy and holy? Whatever we say in general about ourselves and other humans *sub specie aeternitatis*, the 'Spirit of Life' exists solely as Spirit of this or that life. The experience of the Spirit

---

[*] Paper translated by Marianne Martin and delivered in English.

of God is just as specific as the creatures which experience it and just as manifold as the experiencing creatures are manifold. Paul makes this clear on the simple procedure of the *calling*: 'Let every one lead the life which the Lord has assigned to him, and in which God has called him' (1 Cor. 7.17). Calling and giftedness, *klēsis* and *charisma*, belong together and are interchangeable. From this it follows that 'Every Christian is a charismatic' even when many do not realize their gifts. Gifts which one brings or receives stand in the service of his or her calling because by the call God reaches people and accepts them just as they are. God accepts people specifically, as man and woman, Jew and Gentile, poor and rich, and so on, and places their entire life in the service of God's coming Kingdom which renews the world. Therefore, when we ask about gifts of the Holy Spirit, we should not look for what we do *not* have but rather we must first of all recognize *who*, *what* and *how* we *are* in our being affected by God. What all believers are given, together and equally, is the gift of the Holy Spirit.

'The free gift of God is eternal life in Christ Jesus our Lord' (Rom. 6.23; Eph. 5.18ff.). What each one is given, unexchangeably and not mistakenly, are the different and diverse gifts of the Spirit: each her or his own! Diversity in unity and unity in diversity.

I first want to look at the Pauline doctrine of charismatic gifts with a special emphasis on the personal gifts of life. I will then ask about the competencies and limitations of life in the Spirit, and formulate unity in diversity in the community of the Spirit and in the participatory work for God's kingdom. Then I will ask from charismatic experiences, 'Who is the Holy Spirit and how is the vitalizing and fascinating power to be described?'

1. *The Charismatic Vitality of the New Life*

In 1 Corinthians 7, Paul speaks of the many who are called. All are called to God's peace but each is to retain an individual calling (1 Cor. 7.20). Just like the Lord called them, so they are to live as Christians. Under this, Paul counts being a Jew and a Gentile, a man and a woman, a free person and a slave. In light of social differences, he adds: 'But if you gain your freedom, avail yourself of the opportunity'. Otherwise the slave is to feel like a 'freeman of the Lord' and a free person like 'a slave of Christ' (vv. 21-23).

What the person is and brings along, becomes a gift through the

calling because it is received from the Spirit and placed in the service
of the Kingdom of God. Christian Jews should therefore remain Jews
and live according to the Torah. Christian Gentiles bring their Gentile
existence into the community. Being a woman is a gift and should not
be given up in favor of male ways of thinking and behaving. In social
conflicts, being a Christian begins where it reaches one person or the
other.

Why does Paul understand what one is and what he or she brings
along as a *gift*, although it concerns natural talents and everyday
realities? According to E. Käsemann, he wants to say with this that
Christ's domination reaches deeply into the profanity of the world.
Not only the special religious phenomena, but the entire physical and
social existence becomes a 'charismatic experience' to believers. In
addition to this, Paul bases his entire admonition on the charisma gift:
Whatever one does, one is to do 'in the Lord'. Only that which does
not come out of faith is sin, only what contradicts the love of the
neighbor is wrong. 'Life in the Spirit' is the presence and influence of
the Spirit in the lived life. No area is exempt from this. Everything
that the believer does and abstains from is done in the service of
following Jesus and is, therefore, the gift of the Spirit of Christ. With
this, then, also, the gauge of the gifts is set: 'in the Lord', as Paul says.
What can be placed in the service of his liberating reign, that is
charisma, is *gift*, which becomes the task: 'Here everything can
become charisma for me. It would not only be foolish, but rather also
a lessening of the honor of Christ who wants to fulfill everything, if I
wanted to remove the areas of nature and sexuality, of personal and
social behavior, from the sphere of his power'. Therefore Paul says:
'I know and am persuaded in the Lord Jesus that nothing is unclean in
itself' (Rom. 14.14). The entire life stands under the promise of the
charismatic gifting. Every Christian is in his or her individual manner
a Charismatic; they are not a few chosen or especially talented ones,
who deserve to be called that. The whole life and every life in faith is
charismatic because the Spirit 'will be poured on all flesh' in order to
make it alive. Individual strengths will become charismatic in the
relationships which form the common life process. They are often
only discovered and made conscious in these living relationships. 'The
charismatic doctrine is for him (Paul) the concrete presentation of the
doctrine of the new obedience. God makes the dead alive and builds
his kingdom through the conquering embrace of grace, there where

the demons ruled'. These are the gifts and the tasks for the reasonable service of God in the everyday life of the world, like Paul describes it in Romans 12. We call them the *everyday gifts of the lived life*.

If with this it is clear that through the calling into faith all individual possibilities and strengths are charismatically revived and are placed in the service of the liberating Kingdom of God, then we can go a step further and ask about the *special gifts* which are created anew through the Holy Spirit and which are only experienced in the *following of Jesus*. For Paul, these are most of all gifts and tasks in the building of *Christ's community* which testify to the coming kingdom. The community is the location of the 'revelation of the Spirit' for him. When one summarizes them, one finds the so-called *kerygmatic gifts* of apostles, prophets, teachers, evangelists, the exhorters, but also phenomena such as inspiration, ecstasy, speaking in tongues and other forms of expression of faith. There are *diaconical gifts* of deacons and deaconesses; those who care for the sick, give charity and care for widows along with individual phenomena such as healing, exorcising demons, healing of memories and other forms of help. Finally, there are the *cybernetic gifts* of the 'first ones' in faith, the chair, the shepherds and bishops but also the phenomena of making peace and the formation of the community. These tasks first arise with the existence of Christ's community and are, therefore, to be seen as special gifts and tasks of the Spirit. I would not call them 'supernatural' compared to 'natural' gifts of which I have just spoken, because in actuality believers place their natural gifts in the service of the community. But in the service of the community, they make something other than the usual in their life out of their talents. Boundaries here are just as flowing as actual life: talents related to the community and those talents which are practiced in family, work and society may not be separated. They do not exist under different laws. Being Christian is not divisible. The measure here, as there, is following Jesus. According to the Pauline doctrine of charisma, for the community of Christ, there is *only unity in diversity*, not in uniformity. Only diversity makes the living and viable unity possible, because when only 'birds of a feather flock together', the likes become completely indifferent to the likes and make themselves mutually superfluous. The acceptance of others in their otherness and the respect of their specialness is constitutive for Christ's community. Only the free abundance of the individually different gifts serve life and its liberation. Every limitation and uniformity in thoughts, words and works devastates the community and in the long run, becomes boring for other people. Only *unity in diversity* makes the community an 'inviting church' and a healing community in our uniform society. Life is plural and only in the new creation of life is it right. Whoever can not accept this becomes numb and dies.

Paul stands in the enthusiastic spring of young Christianity. The first communities apparently experienced an 'overwhelming wealth' of gifts of the Spirit. Therefore, he emphasized *unity*: 'there are varieties of gifts, but the same Spirit' (1 Cor. 12.4). Today we must rather emphasize freedom: there is one Spirit but there are many gifts. There is one God who creates everything with as many strengths as there are creatures. *Love* should unite the various gifts, says Paul, but *freedom* must set the various gifts free, we should say today.

With this, we come upon a critical question for Paul: Must the gifts be judged exclusively according to their functional value for the development of the community and the common life? 'To each is given the manifestation of the Spirit for the common good' (1 Cor. 12.7). Do not the gifts have their own value in themselves, aside from the functional value for the community? And do not the charismatic experiences have a value for the affected persons, aside from the 'common value'? With these questions, I want to attempt an unprejudiced treatment of the pros and cons of two special phenomena of the contemporary 'charismatic movement': speaking in tongues and healings.

2. *Speaking in Tongues*

It is a historical, undeniable phenomenon, that the Christian communities came to life with *speaking in tongues* as Acts 2 already reports of the first Pentecost. It is difficult to contest that renewing movements within Christianity were and are accompanied by such phenomena. It stands, finally, beyond doubt that Pentecostal and Charismatic communities today are expanding everywhere and not only in the countries of young churches but rather in old Christian countries as well. Because I have no special experience with this phenomenon, I can neither explain nor contest it. I can only describe it from the outside regarding its influence on those affected. I consider speaking in tongues such a strong inner grasp of the Spirit that its expression leaves the realm of understandable speech and expresses itself in an extraordinary manner, just as intense pain is expressed in unrestrained crying or great joy in jumping and dancing. A charismatic community answers God's revelation in word and deed with praise and prayer. New love and words, prayers which spontaneously stem out of the situation, spoken prayers, prophecies and testimonies, as well as a body language which is full of expression in the form of raised hands, clapping, kneeling, prostrating oneself on the floor before God and dancing—all these have become typical signs for gatherings in the area of charismatic renewal. Our German worship services are rich in sermonic thoughts and meditations, but poor in forms of expression and block every possibility for spontaneity. They are disciplined and disciplining gatherings for speaking and listening. But does the body of Christ really exist only of a great mouth and many little ears? It therefore has a liberating effect on us Europeans when in the pentecostal worship services of blacks in Africa and in the USA we see and learn of a body language other than that of sitting still with folded hands. I understand 'speaking in tongues' to be the start of loosening the tongues of speechless people as they express what they themselves experience and feel. Perhaps an analogy is to be seen in the Primal Scream therapy, although speaking in tongues goes beyond pure human possibilities. It is, in any case, a *new expression* for the experience of faith and it is a *personal expression*. Paul encourages us 'to desire' the gifts (1 Cor. 14.1), but most of all, to strive for prophecy (1 Cor. 14.2). With this, he means the personal, understandable witness in proclamation and pastoral care. He therefore considers speaking in tongues to be translatable in the Holy Spirit and sees its origin in God.

Prophetic speech is a special gift because it finds, in a personal or public *kairos*, the appropriate, binding and liberating word which says concretely at the right time what is sin or grace. One cannot deduce this appropriate word from a doctrine, nor can one psychologically experience it out of the situation, but one can develop a sensibility for the harmony of the appropriate word and the right time and open oneself for that which occurs. That our sermon-hearing congregation is barely able to give a personal witness also hinders our personal Christian life and the formation of personal conviction. For many, it is enough to belong to the Church, go to Church, and for the most part to be in agreement with her doctrine even when one does not know it well and it does not mean much to one. An awakening that is personally experienced, and faith that is personally brought to expression, is 'the charismatic experience' for which we are praying today. Before the German Churches and Bishops 'put the damper' on the charismatic movement, we should all give freedom to the Spirit, not only in worship services but also in our bodies which were, after all, to be 'temples of the Holy Spirit' (1 Cor. 6.20).

A critical question, however, must be directed to the neglect of gifts in the 'charismatic movement': where are the gifts of the 'charismatic movement'—where are the gifts of the 'charismatics' in the everyday life of the world, in the Peace Movement, in the liberation movements, in the ecological movement? If gifts are not given in order to flee from this world into a religious dream world but rather for the witness of the liberating reign of Christ in the conflicts of this world, then the 'charismatic movement' can not become an apolitical or even de-politizing religion.

3. *The Awakening of the Charismatic Experience*

Many people can do more than they believe themselves capable. Why? One believes oneself to be incapable of so many things only because one is afraid of being defeated. But those who withdraw themselves out of fear for the defeat or for the reactions of other people or for the loss of relationship and hide in themselves, never get to know their limits. Only when they want to go beyond their limits do they get to know and accept their limits. There are people who consider everything from the beginning to be impossible. 'It isn't worth it', they say. 'It will accomplish nothing', and 'I can't'. With this, they save themselves many conflicts but experience very little of real life. They remain anonymous to themselves. But there are other people who believe in the possible. Believers in the Synoptic Gospels proclaim 'All things are possible with God'. Those who trust feel 'All things are possible to those who believe'. They certainly experience defeats with this belief in possibilities, but they also experience the power to get up after defeats. Those who believe will become persons of possibilities. They will not limit themselves to prescribed social roles nor allow themselves to be defined by them. They believe themselves capable of more. And they do not tie other people down with prejudices. They do not define other people by their reality, but rather see them together with their future and hold their possibilities open for them. 'Love liberates from all images' (Max Frisch). It does not define, but rather sets free. When love gives trust then the other persons can grasp their good possibilities. Our charismatic possibilities are awakened through trust: through trust in God, through trust in oneself and through confidence in our neighbor. In these free spaces of trust, we also then believe ourselves to be capable of something.

Strengthening self-confidence entails the love of self. 'Love your neighbor like yourself', says the biblical commandment of humanity. It does not say: love your neighbor instead of yourself as Kierkegaard interpreted it. Love of your neighbor presupposes love of self. Love of self is the basis of a free life. We can test this: how can one who despises himself love his neighbor? How can one who cannot tolerate herself put up with her fellow humans? How can one who has no self-trust give others trust? Will not one who hates him- or herself and has not accepted him- or herself, also hate others? Self-hate is the torture of hell. True self-love has nothing to do with egotism. *Egotism* arises out of the fear of being short-changed. Only those who have lost themselves and cannot find themselves have this fear. Egotism leads to the struggle of all against all. Egotism is not self-love. This selfishness is only the reverse side of self-hate. Selfishness and self-hate are, however, only two sides of the same thing, the search for the lost self and the inability for self-love. If we encounter in faith the charismatic experience that God loves us unconditionally, then how should we hate what God loves so very much? God loves us just as we really are, not as we want to be or do not want to be. Self-trust based on trust in God, self-love based on God's love are the powers which our charismatic experiences awaken. In love and trust of our neighbors, we mutually concede to the experience of our good possibilities. The essential barrier of the charismatic experience of our life possibilities does not lie in active but rather in passive sin, not in desperately wanting to be oneself, but in desperately not being able to be oneself and, therefore, to fall short of one's own life out of fear of life and fear of death. The powers of the Spirit are present where belief in God drives away this fear of life and where the resurrection hope overcomes the fear of death. According to early Christian witnesses, the Easter joy about Christ's resurrection released the flow of the gifts in the communities. The pentecostal movement begins at Easter.

4. *The Healing of the Sick*

Healing of the sick is, next to the proclamation of the Gospel, Jesus'
most important witness of the approaching Kingdom of God. It is,
according to Matthew 10, a commission of Jesus' disciples and,
therefore, an essential part of the Apostolate of the community. The
experience of healing of physical and mental illnesses, therefore,
belongs to the charismatic experience of life. Healings are, in the
context of faith, signs of the rebirth of life. If the Spirit of God is
experienced from Easter as the Spirit of the resurrection of the dead,
then experienced healings are to be understood as anticipatory signs of
the resurrection of the dead and of eternal life. Just as eternal life
makes alive those who believe it, so eternal salvation heals those who
trust in it.

According to the Synoptic Gospels, the first thing people experienced about Jesus was the healing power of the divine Spirit.
Therefore, people in his presence were not revealed as 'sinners' as
with Paul, but rather as 'ill'. Out of the corners into which they had
been pushed, out of the deserts into which they had been set, out of the
shadows into which they had crept, the sick and the possessed come
forward and seek his closeness. In the closeness of Jesus, people are
not revealed according to the Greek ideal of the healthy spirit in the
healthy body but rather as sick, suffering and in need of help. In the
closeness of Jesus, humans show themselves not from their sunny side
but rather from their shadowy side. Why do the sick reveal themselves in his presence? Apparently, a life was experienced in him that
was of contagious healing power.

> That evening, at sundown, they brought to him all who were sick or
> possessed with demons. And the whole city was gathered together about
> the door. And he healed many who were sick with various diseases, and
> cast out many demons (Mk 1.32-34).

Demons are powers of disorder which appear in a personal manner.
They are characterized by their pleasure in torture. When the Messiah
comes, says an old Jewish hope, these spirits of torture will disappear
from the earth and humans will again be able to live healthily and
wisely. There were often miraculous healings in the ancient world.
They also take place today. But with Jesus they stand within the
horizon of his proclamation of the Kingdom of God: when God takes

possession of his power over his creation, the demons give way. When the living God comes and settles into God's creation, then all the creatures will be filled from God's eternal vivacity. Jesus brings the Kingdom of God not only in words that awaken faith, but also in healings that make healthy. God's Spirit is a power of life that permeates the body of humans and drives away the bacillus of death. The healing miracles of Jesus are 'kingdom miracles' (Christoph Blumhardt). In the uprising of the new creation of all things, they are in no way a 'miracle', but rather very natural, that which one must expect. Only when this eschatological hope is lost do those miraculous healings appear as miracles in an unchanged world. But in the frame of hope of the Kingdom of God, Jesus' healings are memories of hope. They give a basis to the present expectations about the Spirit of Jesus.

Because serious illnesses are forewarnings of death, so are healings of the sick to be understood as premonitions of the resurrection. 'We fight with death' in every serious illness. In every healing, we feel we have been 'given life again' and 'born anew'. In view of illness, the Kingdom of God means healing. In view of dying, the Kingdom of God means resurrection.

Jesus has not, however, healed all of the sick. In his hometown Nazareth 'he could do no mighty work' (Mk 6.5). Under what conditions could he heal and when could he not? In the case of a sick boy, it is a little disbelieving belief of the father: 'I believe; help my unbelief!' (Mk 9.23-27). The 'hemorrhaging woman' (Mk 5.25-34) takes her healing by herself. Jesus notices after the fact, 'that a power had gone forth from him'. 'Your faith has made you well', he said to her. The Gentile woman seeks help for her daughter; he, the Jew, refuses. As she reveals to him that the Kingdom of God does not end with Israel's borders, he says to her, 'Be it done for you as you desire' (Mt. 15.21-28).

Healing, therefore, occurs in the *interaction* between *Jesus* and the *expectation*, the *faith* and the *will* of the people. This means that these healings are contingent. They are not 'made', they occur where and when God wants it. There is no method for such healings because they are not repeatable and replicability is the presupposition for all methods. The healing of all ill is prayed for. Hands are laid on ill ones for healing which is to be obtained by prayer. In the case of psychosomatic illnesses, confessions of guilt and forgiveness of guilt are helps toward the healing of distressed souls and bodies. But then there is also work with the body for the healing of the soul. Torturing and burdening memories are also healed through the relaxation of tense bodies. Wherever illnesses are suffered holistically, healing concerns the whole human; wherever illnesses are suffered in disturbed interpersonal relationships, healing must also refer to the relationships in which and from which a person lives. Therefore, there is also a healing through love, through trust and through new community. Modern physical medicine has objectified healing so much that we only understand it in terms of health—and we see 'health' only as the restoration of a single organ's ability to function. Psychosomatic medicine alone gives us a generally understandable access to the healing experience of faith and takes the odor of peculiarity away from them.

Through what does Jesus heal? Of what does the healing power of his Spirit consist? In Mt. 8.17 we find an answer: '...and healed all who were sick'. This was to fulfill what was spoken by the prophet Isaiah, 'He took our infirmities and bore our diseases'. Jesus' healing power does not lie in his superpower over illnesses but rather in his *power of suffering*. He heals in that he 'carries' our illnesses; 'through his wounds we are healed' (Isa. 53.5). His passion and his sacrifice on Golgotha is the secret of his healing of the ill.

But how can wounded ones find healing in his wounds? Healing exists in the restoration of destroyed community and in the sharing and communication of life. Jesus heals the ill through the restoration of their community with God. He restores the ill's community with God through his solidarity with them and his representative role for them. In Christ, God became human and accepted limited and mortal humanness and has made it into a part of his eternal being God. He accepted it in order to heal. In the passion of Jesus Christ, God accepted the sick, weak, helpless and handicapped human life and made it into a part of his eternal life. God heals illnesses and sorrows in that God makes illnesses into God's suffering and sorrow into God's sorrow. In the image of the *crucified Jesus*, the ill and dying can recognize themselves because this one recognizes himself in them. Through his passion, Jesus brings God into the God-forsakenness of the sick and into the despair of the dying. The crucified Jesus embraces all sick life and makes it into God's life in order to communicate God's eternal life. Therefore, the crucified one is the source of healing as well as the comfort in suffering.

5. *The Gift of the Disabled Life*

Reports of the charismatic movement often sound like American success stories. Such a 'religion of success' finds no religious meaning in the pains, denials and handicaps of life. The Christian 'theology of the cross' does not fit into this 'officially optimistic society' nor into its religious optimism. Paul, however, not only experienced the 'power of God' in the strengths of his life, but also in his weaknesses: 'my power is made perfect in weakness' (2 Cor. 12.9). He, therefore, also exults in his weaknesses, the abuses, the needs, the persecutions, the fears which he had experienced. This 'suffering of Christ' which he personally experienced is proof to him of his apostolate and therefore of his gifts. 'For we are weak in him, but in dealing with you we shall live with him by the power of God' (2 Cor. 13.4). The 'Spirit of the resurrection' is present there where one experienced the shadow of the cross.

For this reason, Paul expects strong and weak ones, wise and foolish ones, educated and uneducated ones in the communities. No one is useless and without value, no one can be relinquished. Therefore, weak, foolish and uninformed ones have their special gift in the community of Christ. Why? All will be given equal form with the crucified one because the crucified one has not only taken on true humanity, but the entire misery of humanity in order to heal it. Every human life is life accepted by God in Christ and in it already takes part in eternal divine life.

'That which is not taken on, will also not become holy', says a principle of the ancient Church's Christology. But whatever has been taken on through the Son of God, become human and crucified, that is then already holy, good and beautiful in the eyes of God. It is important to recognize this today in those whom we call 'disabled' or handicapped in order to overcome this public and often very personal conflict between non-disabled and disabled in the community of Christ.

Disabled ones are not only hindered by the life of the able ones, but are often made into children through the welfare and care provided. In order to change this, it is necessary to recognize that *every handicap is also a gift*. The power of Christ is also made perfect in the handicap. We who are not disabled mostly stare only at that which is lacking or has been taken away from the person, and see 'disabled persons'. But when we forget about our value standards and look upon Jesus, we then discover the individual value and dignity of a disabled life and notice its meaning for our life together. Those who have experienced 'disabled persons' in their own families, as I have, know what meaning they have for the whole family, and they may have discovered what God says and does through the gift of these disabled persons. When what a person is and what he or she brings along is made into a gift through his or her calling, this includes his or her handicap. If the splendor of God's love falls onto a life with the calling, then it begins to shine. There are disabled, ill and deformed persons in whose faces this radiance is to be recognized.

Finally, according to Paul, the body of Christ does not need strong members but rather weak and disabled members, for God gives weak and disabled members the most 'honor and glory' (1 Cor. 12.22-24). Why? Because the body of Christ is the body of the exalted and of the *humbled* ones, of the resurrected and *crucified* one. In the amazing 'powers' of the Spirit, the *resurrection power* of God is revealed. In the pains, set-backs, handicaps and in the 'suffering' of the Spirit, God's *power of suffering* is revealed. There is, therefore, no good diaconia of the non-disabled to the disabled if they have not previously accepted and recognized the unconscious diaconia of the disabled to the non-disabled. *Communities without disabled persons are disabled communities.* In the Christian sense, a charismatic community is always the serving community since gift implies service. The large diaconical works of the Church are necessary, but what we need is the awakening of the *diaconical community* of disabled and non-disabled persons; a community which takes care of its disabled and ill themselves as far as possible.

6. *Each According to his Abilities—Each According to his Needs*

The charismatic community is a *unity in diversity* and a *diversity in unity*. Each as the Lord has called her or him, each as the Lord has assigned her or him. This is basically the formula of compensatory justice: 'Suum cuique' (Ulpian). This ingenious formula combines the

legal equality for all with the real diversities of humans: this hers—
that his. 'Each according to his ability—each according to his needs'
(Acts 4.32-35). This is the law of the true humane society.

The *power of unity* for humans who are so diverse and for their
gifts which are so manifold is, according to Paul, the *love* by virtue of
which believers are there for each other in order to be the body of
Christ together. He can also characterize this love as the *presence of
Christ* in which one should serve another (Eph. 5.21-22). At this
point, one should rather speak of the 'community of the Holy Spirit'
in which the gifted ones who are so diverse come together: There are
many gifts—but there is only one Spirit. And this unity of the Spirit is
the community between the believers who have been called and gifted
in diverse ways.

With this, all other guarantees of unity become relative: not the one
doctrine, not the one Pope, not the one faith, but rather the
community of the Spirit creates unity in the difference and diversity
of gifts. If there was no community of the Spirit in the diversity of the
gifts of the Spirit, then the other guarantees of unity of the Church
would also be powerless.

The power of unity is love. The *power of diversity* is freedom. The
community of the Spirit is the free space for the awakening and the
growth of various gifts of the Spirit. Mao's saying applies exactly to
the church of the Spirit: 'Let a hundred flowers blossom'.

To be a woman is a gift in faith, to be a man is a gift in faith. Each
her/his own and all together for the Kingdom of God. For the
'Kingdom of God' is nothing other than the *new creation of all things*
and the *rebirth of all that is alive*. The child of God is just as colorful
as the creation that we know. The Kingdom of God represents no
poverty, but rather an even greater wealth of creation. The Kingdom
of God does not destroy this creation—the Kingdom of God is much
more the *eschatological spring* of the entire creation. The charismatic
experience is, however, the experience that this life, which has
become old, unsuccessful and loaded with mistakes, will begin to
blossom again and will therefore be young again.

7. The Holy Spirit as the Power of Life and Space of Life

In closing, I ask about the charismatic experience of life in the Holy
Spirit: who or what is the Holy Spirit according to these experiences?

In charismatic experience the Spirit of God is experienced as *vitalizing* energy. Life begins to vibrate in the blessed closeness of God. We experience ourselves in the vibrations of the divine field of force. Charisma is, therefore, also identified as *dynamis* or *energeia*. The manner in which the Holy Spirit is charismatically experienced has been described over the ages as 'flowing', 'pouring' and 'glowing'. Inferred from these experiences, the Holy Spirit appears as the 'source of life', as the origin of the flow of energy, as light source for the glowing splendor. What kind of Spirit is this which 'is poured onto all flesh?'

The gifts of the Spirit are not 'creatures' of the Spirit because the Spirit itself is poured out in them. The 'water of life' which flows out of the 'source of life' is of the same quality as the source itself. The relationship of the one Spirit to the many gifts of the Spirit and of the one light to the many reflections is not the distanced relationship of the creator to the creatures but a much more intimate relationship. Through the Spirit, which is 'poured' onto all flesh, all flesh becomes spiritual. Through the Holy Spirit in our hearts, God's own self is 'in us' and we ourselves are 'in God'. In the Spirit experience, God is encompassingly *present* and no distanced *opposite*. This is a much more intimate community than the community between creator and created. It is the community of reciprocal inhabitation. In the Holy Spirit, the eternal God participates in our mortal life and we participate in God's eternal life. The reciprocal community is an enormous source of power.

The Holy Spirit, finally, brings the charismatically touched existence of humans to splendor. A radiation emanates from humans which gives their relationships a radiance. Earlier generations liked to represent this shining power of existence in picture as a *halo*. With this, they wanted to say that a charismatically moved and holy life again becomes the image of God and is illuminated by the divine splendor (*kābôd, doxa*) which reflects it. As Paul discovered 'the glory of God in the face of Christ' (2 Cor. 4.6), he described the Spirit experience as a 'bright light in our hearts'. Today we would speak of the *radiance* or the 'aura' of those who experience it. We also speak of the 'atmosphere' in a community which can be 'poisoned' or 'good'. There is a 'climate of trust' and a 'climate of distrust'. Each life has his and her own radiance. It arises out of that which keeps us busy and with which we work, but most of all through that which we 'fear and love above all things'. Other people become unnerved and distressed or made excited and alive by these unconscious auras. Life can radiate ambition and fear, it can radiate peace and quiet, and it can also radiate experiences of God. This divine shining power of existence remains unconscious to us and it must remain so because 'those who look at themselves do not shine'. But those who look at Jesus begin to shine in the light of the Holy Spirit.

A RHYTHM OF ADORATION AND ACTION:
A RESPONSE TO JÜRGEN MOLTMANN

Miroslav Volf

Jürgen Moltmann is known as a political theologian. The rumor is that political theologians are not interested in God at all but only in politics—they are dangerous politicians in theologians' clothing. The paper Jürgen Moltmann just read is proof to the contrary. Just think of its last sentence: 'those who look at Jesus begin to shine in the light of the Holy Spirit'. In the whole of Moltmann's theology, worship of God and political action go together. In the programmatic book of the mature Moltmann—*The Trinity and the Kingdom*—we find the following statement: 'There must be no theology of liberation without the glorification of God and no glorification of God without the liberation of the oppressed'.[1]

In my short response I will not try to play a teacher to my teacher by pointing out things Moltmann did well and things I think he could have done better. Neither do I think it would be appropriate for me to say what he often told me when I was his doctoral student: 'Machen Sie nur so weiter, Herr Moltmann'—continue in the same fashion Mr Moltmann. I will try instead to think in my own way of the connection between the worship of God and action in the world. In my book *Work in the Spirit: Toward a Theology of Work*,[2] I tried to do that from the side of action. Here I will do it briefly from the side of worship.[3]

1. J. Moltmann, *The Trinity and the Kingdom* (San Francisco: Harper & Row, 1981), p. 8.

2. New York: Oxford University Press, 1991.

3. This response to Jürgen Moltmann is a shorter version of a larger study entitled 'Worship as Adoration and Action' to be published as the concluding chapter of a book on worship by Paternoster under editorship of D.A. Carson.

I

Christian worship consists both in obedient service to God and in joyful praise of God. Both of these elements are brought together in Hebrews 13.15-16, in a passage that comes close to giving a definition of Christian worship:

> Through him let us continually offer up a sacrifice of praise to God, that is, the fruit of lips that acknowledge his name. Do not neglect to do good and to share what you have, for such sacrifices are pleasing to God.

Sacrifices of praise and sacrifices of good works are two fundamental aspects of the Christian way of being-in-the-world. They are at the same time the two constitutive elements of Christian worship: *authentic Christian worship takes place in a rhythm of adoration and action.* Why is this the case? What is the reason for this biformity of worship? In the following I will try to answer these questions.

First, why cannot worship consist simply of active life in the world? Why does adoration need to take place as a distinct activity besides action? Because God did not create human beings to be merely God's servants but above all to be God's children and friends. As much as they need to do God's will in the world, so also they need to enjoy God's presence. The center of Christian life consists in personal *fellowship* of human beings with the Son of God through faith. Adoration is a time when this personal fellowship, which determines the whole life of Christians—their relation to themselves, to their neighbors and nature—is nurtured.[1] This is the reason why human beings

> need periodic moments of time in which God's commands concerning their work will recede from the forefront of their consciousness as they adore the God of loving holiness and thank the God of holy love.[2]

---

1.   In the Eastern orthodox theology the summit of mystical life is sometimes perceived to consist 'in the personal encounter with Christ who speaks in our hearts by the Holy Spirit' (P. Evdokimov, *L'orthodoxie* [Paris: Desclée de Brouwer, 1979], p. 113).

2.   'The Oxford Declaration on Christian Faith and Economics', *Transformation* 7.2 (1990), pp. 1-8, no. 30. For the background reflection on this formulation see Volf, *Work in the Spirit: Toward a Theology of Work* (Oxford: Oxford University Press, 1992), pp. 136ff.

Second, why can we not make the adoration of God our supreme goal, and be satisfied to consider action in the world simply a necessary consequence of adoration? Because the world is God's creation and the object of God's redemptive purposes. Christian hope is not for the liberation of souls from the evil world, but for the redemption of human beings together *with* the world with which they comprise the good creation of God. The material creation is not a scaffolding that will be discarded once it has helped in the construction of the pure spiritual community of souls with one another and with their God; material creation represents the building materials from which, after they are transfigured, the glorified world will be made. This is why worship can never be an event taking place simply between the naked soul and its God. It must always include active striving to bring the eschatological new creation to bear on this world through proclamation of the good news and socio-economic action. Fellowship with God is not possible without cooperation with God in the world; indeed cooperation with God is a dimension of fellowship with God.

As Christians worship God in adoration and action they anticipate, under the conditions of this world, God's new creation. Through their action they seek to anticipate a world in which Satan will no longer 'deceive the nations', a world in which God will 'wipe away every tear' from the eyes of his people, a world in which peace will reign between human beings and nature. Through their adoration they anticipate the enjoyment of God in the new creation, where they will communally dwell in the triune God and the triune God will dwell among them (See Rev. 21–22). The eschatological bliss of God's people in the presence of their God and the eschatological *shalom* of God's world are two inseparable dimensions of Christian eschatological hope. It is this two-dimensional hope that makes Christian worship into a two-dimensional reality.

Adoration and action are two distinct aspects of Christian worship that are each valuable in their own right. The purpose of action is not merely to provide material support for the life of adoration. The purpose of adoration is not simply to provide spiritual strength for the life of action. When we adore God, we worship God by enjoying his presence and by celebrating his mighty deeds of liberation. When we are involved in the world, we worship God by announcing his liberation and cooperating with him by the power of the Spirit through loving action.

Christian worship is bivalent. But do its two components stand merely side by side or are they also positively related to one another? I will return to this question after I consider the relation between adoration of God and seclusion from the world.

II

I have argued that adoration is an activity distinct from involvement in the world. It would seem that as a distinct activity adoration requires distinct space and distinct time. If that is the case, are we not then back at the notions of sacred space and sacred time, which I have discarded earlier?

Does adoration need to take place in seclusion from the world? The answer to this question depends on where God is to be found. It is a consistent teaching of the Bible that God's presence is not limited to a particular locale. God is present in the whole created reality. No segment of it is secular in the sense that the transcendent God would be absent from it. All dimensions of life in the world have what one might call a sacramental dimension: they *can* be places of meeting God in gratitude and adoration.[1] This is why the New Testament can ascribe redemptive significance to such an ordinary event as the table fellowship among Jesus' disciples: a meal can be an occasion for an encounter with the risen Lord. Furthermore, if God is present in all of created reality, then the soul ceases to be the privileged place for meeting God. We do not need to turn away from the world and search into the depths of our soul to find God there. Adoration does not require seclusion—indeed it is provoked by the apprehension of God's presence and activity in the world.

Still the New Testament does speak of taking time to go to a 'secret place' (Matt. 6.6). The 'secret place' should not be confused with 'sacred space', however. It stands for the cessation of active involvement in the world, not for the exclusion of the profane reality of the world. Every place can be 'secret space', and every moment a time reserved for God. But if we want to escape the tendency to dissolve the holy into the secular, which seems to be a given with the

1. On the presence of God in creation in relation to worship, see A. Schmemann, *Sacraments and Orthodoxy* (New York: Herder & Herder, 1965), pp. 10ff.

affirmation that the holy is not restricted to particular places,[1] then we need to reserve special time for the adoration of God, whether it means going to the 'secret place' (as Jesus advised), spending a night in the mountains (as Jesus practiced) or gathering together in Jesus' name as a community of believers. The point of the talk about the *rhythm* of adoration and action is to preserve profane reality as a meeting-place with the holy God, not to reintroduce the division between sacred and profane.

But does not the very act of adoring God, wherever it takes place, involve turning away from the world toward God? Even if we affirm the possibility of meeting God in the profane reality, do we not reduce this reality to a mere vehicle for encounter with God? I will start answering these questions by noting the distinction between adoration and contemplation. As distinct from the modern way of knowing by which we manipulate things in order to grasp them, contemplation is a passive way of knowing by which we behold things as they present themselves to us (*theoria*). Its passivity notwithstanding, contemplation is a way of knowing *things and truths*, not persons. You can contemplate the works of a person, but you do not contemplate persons themselves; you know them by talking to them and letting them talk to you, by doing things with them. Seeing the persons (and touching them) is important, but only as a part of this conversation and of our activity which constitutes our common history.

Since God is neither an a-personal truth nor an aesthetic shape, contemplation is not appropriate as a way of relating to God. Adoration is. To adore God is not simply to behold the truth, goodness and beauty of God in a disinterested way, but to affirm one's allegiance to God by praising God for his deeds in creation and redemption. The contemplation of God's works (like beholding the grandeur of creation or meditating on the passion of Christ) is a presupposition of adoration. But to adore is not to look at God, rather it is to talk about and to God inspired by the works of God in the world. This, however, means that *turning to God in adoration does not entail turning away from the world; it means perceiving God in relation to the world and the world in relation to God.* The songs of praise to God are at the same time the songs about the world as God's creation and as a place which God will transform into a new creation. And the

---

1.   See P. Tillich, *Systematic Theology*. III. *Life and the Spirit, History and the Kingdom of God* (Chicago: University of Chicago Press, 1963), pp. 379-80.

songs about creation and redemption can be nothing else but songs about God the creator and redeemer.

Authentic Christian adoration cannot take place in isolation from the world. Because the God Christians adore is engaged in the world, the aesthetic Christian adoration of God leads to authentic Christian action in the world and the action in the world leads to adoration of God. Adoration and action are distinct, but nevertheless *interdependent* activities. So we need to investigate further the positive relationship they have to each other.

III

What is the significance of adoration of God for action in the world? We can answer this question best if we reflect on the nature of doxological language. At the one level, in adoration a person is stating what is the case; he or she is describing God's action (e.g. 'he has judged the great harlot [economic and political power Babylon] who corrupted the earth with her fornication') and God's character (e.g. 'his judgments are true and just' [Rev. 19.2]). There is no adoration without such description. But the actual point of adoration lies deeper than description. In thanking, blessing or praising God, people express their own personal relation toward the God they are adoring: joyous *gratitude* for what God has done and *identification* with God's character from which God's actions spring forth.

It is here that the significance of adoration for action becomes visible. First, by identifying with God in adoration one aligns oneself with God's projects in the world. By praising God who renews the face of the earth and redeems the peoples, one affirms at the same time one's desire to be a co-worker with God in the world. Adoration is the well-spring of action. Second, in adoration a person names and celebrates the context of meaning that gives significance to action in the world and indicates the highest value that gives that action binding direction. In the pantheon of the modern world, adoration identifies the God in whose name one engages in action. Without adoration, action is blind and easily degenerates into a hit-or-miss activism.

The dependence of action in the world on the adoration of God shows that the frequent disjunction found in cerebral and activistic Protestant circles between adoration and edification is inadmissible. As Psalm 119 shows, in the Old Testament the instruction in Torah could take place in doxological language. For Paul too, psalms, hymns and spiritual songs were precisely expressions of adoration and, at the same time, a means of instruction and admonition. Every authentic adoration is instruction, because it celebrates God's deeds and God's character, and expresses at the same time commitment to the God it celebrates. The inverse is also true. Every authentic Christian instruction is adoration. Instruction in faith which does not include (at least implicitly) adoration is deficient: it communicates knowledge without transmitting corresponding allegiance. Protestant theology (Evangelical theology included!) needs to learn from Eastern Orthodoxy on this point which, in addition to maintaining that there is 'no mysticism without theology', has stressed 'above all' that there is 'no theology without mysticism'.[1]

What is the significance of action for adoration? In order to answer this question we need to look briefly at the nature and the purpose of Christian involvement in the world. Christian action is nothing less than cooperation with God. As Genesis 2 vividly portrays, there is a partnership between the creating God and working human beings.[2] Just as Genesis portrays a farmer as a co-operator with God, so Paul thinks of missionaries as 'fellow workers of God' in God's field (1 Cor. 3.9). Whether it consists in evangelism or mundane work, human activity is a means by which God accomplishes God's purposes in the world. If God's deeds in the world open the hearts and mouths of people to praise God, then human action, which God uses to accomplish God's purposes, must do the same: the purpose of evangelism and good works is the well-being of the people and God's creation. And the integral well-being of God's world is the occasion for praise (see 2 Cor. 4.15; Matt. 5.16; 1 Pet. 2.11). Christian action in the world leads to adoration of God. Action establishes conditions in which adoration of God surges out of the human heart.

But there is also another sense in which action is a precondition to adoration. There is something profoundly hypocritical about praising God for God's mighty deeds of salvation and cooperating at the same

1. V. Lossky, *The Mystical Theology of the Eastern Church* (Crestwood, NJ: St Vladimir's Seminary Press, 1976), p. 9. For the same emphasis in the Catholic tradition see J. Cardinal Ratzinger, *Schauen auf den Durchbohrten: Versuche zu einer spirituellen Christologie* (Einsiedeln: Johannes Verlag, 1984), p. 18.

2. See on this Volf, *Work*, pp. 98-99; M. Hengel, 'Die Arbeit im frühen Christentum', *Theologische Beiträge* 17 (1986), p. 180.

time with the demons of destruction, whether by neglecting to do good or by actively doing evil. Only those who help the Jews may sing the Gregorian chant, said Bonhoeffer rightly in Nazi Germany. Only those who are truly concerned for the victims of economic, political, racial or sexual oppression can genuinely worship God. Without action in the world, the adoration of God is empty and hypocritical, and degenerates into irresponsible and godless quietism.

THE UNITY OF THE SPIRIT AND THE VARIETY OF CHARISMS: A RESPONSE TO JÜRGEN MOLTMANN

Raniero Cantalamessa

I

In his paper, Professor Moltmann has highlighted a fundamental point with which I completely agree: the importance of the cross as a criterion to discern the true power of the Spirit. One field in which this criterion proves very helpful is the awkward phenomenon of 'healings'. 'Jesus' healing power', says Professor Moltmann, 'does not lie in his superpower over illnesses but rather in his power of suffering. He heals in that he carries our illnesses' (p. 32).

This can be adopted, I think, as a general principle. In his infinite wisdom, God decided to overcome evil in all its forms, sin included, by suffering it, by taking it upon himself, instead of simply rejecting it and destroying it with his omnipotence. This is what happened once and for all when Jesus was crucified and what has to be continued in the life of the Church. In this light we can interpret what God said to Paul when he complained about his 'thorn in the flesh': My power is made more manifest in your weakness, than in your being miraculously delivered from all weaknesses (cf. 2 Cor. 12.9). I was struck by the statement: 'Communities without disabled persons are disabled communities' (p. 34), as was a charismatic community to which I recounted it, which is actually a community without disabled persons.

The Christian Pentecost comes from Christ's Paschal mystery and can never prescind from it. This, I think, is what assures a vital link between Christology and Pneumatology, making the stress on the Holy Spirit of modern Pentecostals and Charismatics very different from the one, say, of Joachim of Fiore.

The cross is what redeems charismatic enthusiasm. We know that religious enthusiasm has never had a good press throughout the centuries. It was already considered as something suspicious among the Greeks, when it was associated with Dionysos's cult and with the Bacchantes' immoderate displays. In ancient Christianity it was stigmatized because of Montanism, as it was during the Reformation period due to those Luther called 'the heavenly Prophets'. Ronald Knox has retraced this in a famous, though not very flattering, book entitled *Enthusiasm*.[1] If our charismatic and pentecostal experience is not to be an addition to this history, we must remain strictly united to the cross of Jesus and to his Paschal mystery.

Christian spiritual enthusiasm must be based on the cross, a cross-centered enthusiasm, so to speak. We can 'boast'—that is, raise our souls to a state of 'jubilant certainty' (H. Schlier)—but always, as Paul says, 'in the cross of Jesus Christ' (Gal. 6.14). St Paul, St Ignatius of Antioch and many others belonged to this category of 'enthusiasts'.

The Fathers of the Church adopted this ideal which they called the *sobria aebrietas*, the 'sober exaltation, or intoxication, of the Spirit'. In 1975, Pope Paul VI recommended the leaders of the Catholic Charismatic Renewal to take, as a programme and a motto for their movement, this formula which he quoted from St Ambrose: 'Laeti bibamus sobriam profusionem Spiritus', that is to say: 'Let us drink joyfully the sober abundance of the Spirit'. Enthusiasm, therefore, or exaltation is good, provided it remains sober, when the word 'sobriety' no longer means only a certain wisdom and moderation (as in Philo of Alexandria who invented the formula of *sobria aebrietas*), but also self-denial, humility, mortification of carnal pleasures. In a word, the cross.

I am grateful to Professor Moltmann for reminding us of such a relevant aspect. There is indeed a real danger of the 'theology of the cross' being reduced to a parenthesis in 'an officially optimistic society', and that 'the reports of the charismatic movement often sound like American success-stories' (p. 33). Fortunately this sort of excess is limited.

II

The point in Professor Moltmann's paper I wish to refer to as a Catholic interlocutor concerns the problem of unity and diversity in the Church. Professor Moltmann says that as St Paul needed to stress

1. *Enthusiasm: A Chapter in the History of Religion* (Oxford: Oxford University Press, 1950).

unity in his day, we need to stress freedom in our day. The Apostle says: 'There are varieties of gifts, but the same Spirit' (1 Cor. 12.4); we must say: 'There is one Spirit, but there are many gifts' (p. 26).

I agree that nowadays there is the problem of preserving the variety of gifts in the Church. As a Roman Catholic, I cannot help feeling directly challenged by this aspect since it is precisely what we Catholics are in most danger of neglecting where both individual persons and local churches are concerned. But we cannot deny that there is also another equally important problem which is this: how can we preserve the fundamental unity of the Spirit and the Church which, as we know, involves 'one faith and one baptism' (Eph 4.5), that is not just a simple subjective disposition to benevolence and mutual love?

In every Church, including mine, there are sad experiences of 'crazy charisms', of a diversity that is no longer richness but pure and simple carnal intemperance, which dishonors the very name of Christ. On what criterion should we base out judgment? We know the Apostle suggests the acknowledgment of Jesus Christ as Lord (cf. 1 Cor. 12.3), but we also know that we can make use of Jesus Christ and the Gospel for even the most absurd things. The criterion is right but someone must be authorized to use it, someone who, in cases where it becomes necessary to choose, can say: This is according to the Spirit of Christ, that is not according to his Spirit. This is what St Paul himself is doing (in 1 Cor. 12–14) and St John too (1 Jn 4.1–5.12).

Therefore, we are forced to ask ourselves: Does this authority or ministry exist in the Churches today? Who is entitled to exercise the 'discernment of spirits' at various levels in the Church?

No matter which point we start from, we are obliged to deal with the problem of charism and institution. An institution claiming it can survive without charisms is an institution doomed to fossilization and dead repetition; charisms claiming they can survive without any institution or authority are destined to harm themselves and the Church. This is not a matter of speculation but of daily experience. Undisciplined 'gifts' do not contribute to a Church that is 'joined and knit together' (cf. Eph. 4.16), but to a disjointed and disconnected body.

Personally I consider the relation between charism and institution as an aspect of the broader relation between law and love, freedom and obedience. Why did Jesus say: 'I have not come to abolish the law, but to fulfill it' (cf. Mt. 5.17), after he proclaimed the new commandment of love? And why did St Paul, in the second part of his letter to the Romans, give so many and sometimes such specific laws and regulations to the Christians, after he had proclaimed the end of the law in the first part of the same letter?

The explanation of the apparent contradiction would seem to be this: grace eliminates the law insofar as the law believes it can give life, that is to say, insofar as it claims to be the cause of justification. On the contrary, grace upholds the law insofar as it is a consequence of grace and a tangible expression of love. In the new covenant the law is at the service of love. The law in fact is 'issued for sinners' (1 Tim. 1.9) and we are still sinners. It is a support to our freedom still wavering as regards the good. It serves to discern God's will in practical situations. It also helps to orient the different gifts and individual freedoms towards a 'common good' that in this case is the upbuilding of the body of Christ (cf. Eph. 4.12). 'We were given the law'—St Augustine wrote—'so that we might seek grace, and we were given grace so that we might observe the law' (*De Spiritu et littera* 19.34).

The Holy Spirit is not granted to get rid of every law and precept, but rather to be able to put into practice the law and the precepts. This is the meaning of the prophecy of Ezekiel: 'And I will put my Spirit within you and cause you to walk in my statutes and be careful to observe my ordinances' (Ezek. 36.27).

What is said of the law can also be said, in a certain sense, of authority. The new 'law of the Spirit' (Rom. 8.2) makes us free to obey! In fact it frees us from ourselves; it frees us from internal and not only from external bondages.

I agree when Professor Moltmann says that it is not important to have 'one single doctrine, one single Pope or one single faith' (p. 35) in order to build 'one single Church'. I suppose, however, that by 'faith' he means the subjective faith of believers, not objective faith, or revealed truth—Paul's *una fides*—which I think must be recognized as an essential element of the 'one Church'. What is important is to have one Spirit and one love. For us Catholics, too, the 'soul of the Church' is not the Pope but the Holy Spirit!

Having excluded that 'one authority' is what makes, constitutes the Church intrinsically one, it remains to be seen if it is nevertheless a *conditio sine qua non* for the Church to live and manifest its oneness of Spirit and love. But perhaps by calling the unity of doctrine, authority, and faith 'relative' guarantees (p. 35), Professor Moltmann is pointing in the same direction and our positions do not differ so much from one another.

These remarks do not, therefore, contradict what Professor Moltmann has stressed in his paper. On the contrary I dare believe that they confirm it in a certain sense, since they lead us back, once again, to the great principle of the cross of Christ which is at the very heart of this discourse. Within the Church, charism and institution represent the two arms of the cross. Charism is often the cross of institution and institution is often the cross of charism and of charismatics. Nevertheless, they need each other and one would not be safe without the other. They must therefore accept each other in humility and love and work together for the glory of God and the upbuilding of the body of Christ.

PENTECOSTALISM AND LIBERATION THEOLOGY: TWO MANIFESTATIONS OF THE WORK OF THE HOLY SPIRIT FOR THE RENEWAL OF THE CHURCH*

Juan Sepulveda

Introduction

I was invited to share with the participants of this important conference 'a Pentecostal perspective on liberation theology'. When I began to reflect on the task, I soon realized that being a Pentecostal was not enough to assure a 'Pentecostal perspective'. In Latin America in general, the Pentecostal who has received academic formation has been educated in seminaries and universities, which are not Pentecostal, which gives one a quite broad theological outlook. That is precisely my case, since I received my theological formation in an ecumenical, academic environment, which, it goes without saying, was quite identified with the perspective of liberation theology.

Then, in order to assure a 'Pentecostal perspective', it seemed to me, that rather than a personal analysis of liberation theology, it would be more fruitful to look for a way to produce a dialogue between Pentecostalism and liberation theology through a comparative analysis of their fundamental theological intuitions. However, this is not easy. At least two obstacles arise immediately.

1. On the one hand in contrast to the extraordinary productivity of liberation theologians, which results in such a flood of

---

* Translated by J.M. Beaty. It should be noted that the following articles were released after the author's presentation at Brighton '91: A. Gaxiola, 'Poverty as a Meeting and Parting Place: Similarities and Contrasts in the Experience of Latin American Pentecostalism and Ecclesial Base Communities', *Pneuma* 13.2 (Fall, 1991), pp. 167-74; C.E. Self, 'Conscientization, Conversion, and Convergence: Reflections on Base Communities and Emerging Pentecostalism in Latin America', *Pneuma* 14.1 (Spring, 1992), pp. 59-72.

               publications that the task of keeping up-to-date is made difficult, Pentecostalism in Latin America, for understandable reasons, is characterized by its underdeveloped, or almost total lack of, theological production. Therefore, where is one to find 'Pentecostal theology', in a form that is more or less articulate?

2.   On the other hand, while one can find various references in the abundant bibliography of liberation theology which would permit one to document 'a perspective of liberation theology on Pentecostalism', the inverse is impossible. Except for some rare and commendable exceptions, there have been no serious debates and reflection on liberation theology among the Pentecostals.[1]

In order to remedy this situation, I have finally decided to attempt a dialogue between, or at least a comparative analysis of, the 'ecclesial subjects' in both theological perspectives, i.e. the Pentecostal congregations and the 'ecclesial base communities', which are also called 'popular Christian communities'.

After all, this juxtaposition does more justice to the idiosyncrasies of the theological perspectives in question. It is well known that Pentecostalism, more than a confessional doctrine or tradition, is a particular way of living or experiencing and proclaiming the Christian faith. The more widely known authors of liberation have also insisted, ad nauseam, that theirs is not a new 'school of theological thought' which has arisen from an academic environment, but an effort to articulate and systematize the new ecclesial experience ('a new way to experience the church'), which is being manifested in the emergence and proliferation of the ecclesial base communities all over Latin America.[2]

1.   One exception is an Encounter sponsored by the Hispanic sector of the Church of God (with offices in Cleveland, USA), under the title, 'Developing a Pentecostal Pastoral Model vis-à-vis Liberation Theology' (Saint Just, Puerto Rico, May 11–14, 1985). The position papers and results of this encounter were published in the *Revista Pastoralia* 7.15 (December, 1985) (published by CELEP, San José, Costa Rica).

2.   Cf. F. Castillo, *Iglesía Liberadora y Politíca* (Santiago: ECO, 1986). It is true that in its beginnings Liberation Theology was influenced by other kinds of movements that promoted the participation of Christians (priests and laity) in politics (for example the movement called 'Christians for Socialism') or the revolutionary

Since this decision has been made, one more clarification is in order, so that there may be a correct understanding of the reflections which follow. Latin American Pentecostalism is extremely diverse and heterogeneous. A central element of this diversity has to do with dissimilar origins. In very broad strokes, one is able to distinguish Pentecostalism which arose from local movements of revival, virtually simultaneously with the start of the movement in the United States, from Pentecostalism of missionary origin, which appeared later through work of churches, generally of North American origin and already quite institutionalized. While the first type, which is exemplified especially in the cases of Chile and Brazil, is characterized by a greater degree of 'incarnation' in the autochthonous culture and a lesser degree of doctrinal formalization, the second type manifests a greater cultural (and financial) dependency on its place of origin, and a high degree of doctrinal formalization. My reflections will focus primarily on the first type, which I have designated 'Crillo Pentecostalismo'.[1]

1. *The Common Origin in the World of the Poor*

Both 'Crillo Pentecostalism' (hereafter 'APCs'), and the 'Ecclesial Base Communities' (hereafter 'BECs'), arose and grew up among the poorest and most excluded sectors of society. Nevertheless, they arose in quite distinct moments of the history of the popular world. To assimilate these data is key for understanding their differences at the level of their vision of the ethico-political dimensions of the Christian faith.

On the one hand APCs developed during the first decades of this century, but with greater strength during the thirties and the fifties, in

option of some priests (for example, Camilo Torres). Nevertheless, the expression of Liberation Theology which has attained more acceptance in Latin America, as well as having a global impact, is the one articulated as 'the new way of being the church' as expressed in the BECs or popular Christian communities. It has also been these which have caused major concern in the Vatican, due to the challenge which they represent to the structures of the Catholic Church.

1.   To supplement the vision of the author about 'Crillo Pentecostalismo', see: 'Pentecostal Theology in the Context of the Struggle for Life', in D. Kirkpatrick (ed.), *Faith Born in the Struggle for Life* (Grand Rapids: Eerdmans, 1988), pp. 298-318; 'Pentecostalism as Popular Religiosity', *International Review of Missions*, 309 (January, 1989), pp. 80-88.

the midst of the 'poorest of the poor'. Sociological studies indicate that the 'typical clientele' of APCs in its formative period was found among the sectors which suffered a kind of 'social anomia', which was produced in part by their expulsion from the countryside by the crisis of the agrarian social structure and in part by their non-incorporation into the emerging urban industrial structure, which was still fragile and slow.[1] Consequently, they become part of the social sectors which survive by making works of handcraft, by street vending, by temporary employment and by simply begging. Such a social location bears the following characteristics:

1.   A condition of extreme poverty which, at the same time, causes a whole series of dramatic social problems, such as: instability in family relations, alcoholism, delinquency as one alternative for surviving, and so on.

2.   The non-availability, for this social sector, of real opportunities for social participation and community life. Up until the first half of this century, the political parties, as vehicles of democratic participation, had not gone beyond the limits of the middle class and the qualified worker class. Trade unions operated in the work-place, not in the 'neighborhood'. The Catholic Church and 'historical protestantism' likewise had their central focus in the middle class. For the poor, only the bars and the sport fields were left as meeting places.

3.   By being positioned in the so-called 'informal sector' of the economy, i.e. outside of the orbit of a 'salaried' stable position (patron–worker), the illusion is created in the poor that they alone have control of their lives and therefore, that their social condition is the fruit of their own responsibility or irresponsibility. Thus, they do not perceive their position as oppressed—one is poor because of one's own fault or perhaps because of determinations of fate.[2]

1.   Cf. C.L. d'Epinay, *Haven of the Masses* (London: Lutterworth, 1969); E. Willems, *Followers of the New Faith* (Nashville: Vanderbilt University Press, 1967). In this part I am following, fundamentally, the interpretation of Lalive d'Epinay.

2.   According to O. Labbé ('Consciencia de clase: Conclusiones en el caso Chileno', in *Dependencia y estructura de clases en América Latina* [Buenos Aires: Megápolis, 1975], pp. 263-70), the development of a social (or class) awareness in trade unions depends on the 'visibility' of the profits which occur in the salaried

These characteristics converge in an attitude toward life which is markedly pessimistic, hopeless and with a strong sense of culpability. Under these conditions, the poor expect nothing good from society. Rather, the latter represents for them a permanent threat of failure and meaninglessness. In this context, one's encounter with God, through the proclamation of the Pentecostal community, gives a new meaning for life, in spite of the meaninglessness of life in the world.

On the other hand, BECs have emerged and grown among the same social sectors, but in a substantially different time in their history, namely, the sixties. A combination of social, political and economic factors, which cannot be described here, has activated what Gustavo Gutierrez called 'the bursting forth of the poor into history'.[1] This was a matter of a progressive process of mobilization and awakening of social consciousness on the part of social sectors which before had been excluded from the whole process of social participation. It was a time of awakening of hope in the possibilities of social change and liberation. The ascendancy of BECs takes place in this larger context of the awakening of social consciousness and of the appearance of new possibilities for social participation.

Thus, while APCs were born into a social world marked by historical pessimism ('this world offers only perdition'), BECs are developing within a framework of effervescence of the hopes of change ('we are building the Kingdom of God'). It is true that such hopes suffered a hard setback because of the outbreak of a long period of military authoritarianism (Brazil 1954, Chile 1973, etc.). Nevertheless, they stayed alive under the guise of resistance, struggle for survival and defense of human rights.

Consequently, even though both ecclesial movements emerge with strength in the heart of the world of the poor, the differences between the historical moments notably marked the development of both theological perspectives. I do not pretend to affirm that the theology of one or the other is mechanically determined by its origin. What I mean is that both movements articulated answers from the faith to collective states of mind which were substantially different. Anyway, to the extent that APCs and BECs, joined by theological elaborations reflecting their experience, respond to the lifestyle of the poor, to

relation (worker–patron), and in politics of psychosocial and political 'mobilization'.

1.   Cf. G. Gutierrez, *Teología desde el Reverso de la Historia* (Lima: CEP, 1977).

their scarcities and needs, they have in common what Dr Miroslav Volf calls the 'materiality of Salvation'.[1] That is, for both movements, salvation is not a purely immaterial question; it is a concrete reality in the here and now of real life.

2. *The Experience of God*

According to my interpretation, the constitutive act of the APCs is the proposal of a direct and particularly intense encounter with God, which makes possible a profound change in the life of the person who experiences it. Reference to the Holy Spirit, which from a doctrinal standpoint is the characterizing mark of APCs, has to do fundamentally with the directness of the encounter. Through the Holy Spirit, God makes himself directly accessible to the believer who seeks him, thus eliminating every kind of external priestly mediation.

The importance and novelty of this possibility of a direct encounter with God is all the more evident if we remember all the barriers through which the simple people had to pass in order to have an encounter with God in traditional Christianity. In the case of Catholicism, it is a matter of mediation which is basically priestly. But to the extent that the priest is a carrier of a non-indigenous culture, and generally comes from a social setting alien to the world of the poor, it is also a cultural and social mediation. In popular Catholic religiosity, there are also the mediations represented by Marian devotion and reverence of the saints and spirits. In its theological discourse, Protestantism has always emphasized that Jesus Christ is the only mediator. Nevertheless, in practice, the Protestant missionary work in Latin America, and also in Asia and Africa, has imposed a mediation of culture. For anyone from those areas to have an encounter with God in response to Protestant preaching implies passing through a culture which was alien and different, and in many cases destructive to very profound and positive values of the popular culture. From this point of view, evangelization meant cultural domination. In the light of all these forms of mediation of the encounter with God, the APCs experience offers the possibility of a direct encounter with God, an experience which, furthermore, can be

---

1.   'Materiality of Salvation: An Investigation in the Soteriologies of Liberation and Pentecostal Theologies', *Journal of Ecumenical Studies* 26.3 (Summer, 1989), pp. 447-67.

communicated in the language of one's own culture.

On the one hand, reference to the Holy Spirit has to do with the intensity of the encounter. Through his Spirit, God practically invades the believer, dwells within him or her, filling one's life with a new sense of meaning. The ecstatic manifestations of the Baptism in the Holy Spirit (whether these are speaking in other tongues, crying, dancing, laughing or overflowing joy) constitute the language of this unspeakable experience. And it is the intensity, the power of the encounter, which makes possible the change in the life of the individual. It is not a matter of an immediate change in the objective conditions in the life of the individual, but in his or her subjectivity, that is, in the way one sees oneself and the way one sees life. The person feels that finally one is taking control of one's life, as the feeling of powerlesness and fatality, mentioned previously, is overcome.

In the BECs it is difficult to find any experience equivalent to that of APCs' conversion. In general, their members have not converted to Catholicism through the work of the BECs, but come rather from popular Catholicism. Nevertheless, it is also possible to observe a process—and by being a process, it is therefore less intense than in APCs—towards a more personal faith and a more direct relation with God. In BECs, believers learn to converse with God in their own words and to experience him as a Father and friend who is near. They discover that to talk with God, or to talk about God, neither the presence of the priest nor recourse to learned prayers are necessary. After this new experience of God, faith no longer means for them only adherence to a doctrine; it means a personal commitment to this God who is a loving Father, and, in obedience to his love, a change toward a more fraternal style of life in solidarity. As in APCs, this new experience of God is translated into new joy and ecclesial vitality. Also, BECs experience what we in the APCs call a 'living church'. Naturally, since it is a matter of an experience which is more in stages and less dramatic or 'traumatic' (as some designate APCs' experience), the cultural life of the BECs is somewhat less intense, but not less festive.

It is not far from the truth to maintain that behind this new experience of God in the bosom of Catholicism as it has developed in the BECs there is some influence of the nearness of God which is experienced in the APCs' congregations. The same can be said of the reflections which follow. In fact, Catholic scholars who study the emergence of BECs recognize this influence. Leonardo Boff quotes the following testimony from a pastoral document (Joint Pastoral Plan):

> Everything began by telling the testimony of an old lady: 'In Natal, the three Protestant churches were lighted and filled with people. We listened to their songs... and in the meantime our Catholic Church was closed, in darkness... because we could not find a priest'. A question was left unresolved: Does everything need to be stopped because there are no priests?[1]

3. *The Role of Popular Bible Reading*

Bible reading plays an important role in the development of APCs and BECs. The elitist appropriation of the Bible on the part of an illustrious clergy in traditional Christianity (Catholicism) is an excessive sacralization. Protestantism clings to an extremely rationalistic and scholarly reading of the Bible which also made it inaccessible to the common people. Both APCs and BECs represent a revolutionary process of recovering the Bible for the common people, which has had an impact only to be compared with that of the translation of the Bible into German by Martin Luther.

In Pentecostalism, preaching of the Bible in public places by the shoe repairer, the housewife, the ex-alcoholic, and so on, has represented, graphically, to the surprised astonishment of the learned and Catholic common sense, this recuperation of the Bible for the common people. The assertion of the right to use the Bible and to proclaim it is, further, the most concrete manifestation of the destruction of the barriers (points of mediation) in one's relation with God. Believers have the conviction that it is the Holy Spirit who helps them have a correct understanding of the biblical message.

The importance of the Bible in the APCs' experience is extra-ordinary. For many, the Bible has been their first contact with the printed page. For all practical purposes, they learned to read by using the Bible. In the midst of a world where so many things are lacking, a world of social and cultural exclusions, this relationship with the Bible has profound significance for the common people. It is as though they were saying: 'I am poor and ignorant, I don't have anything. But I have it all, the Word of God.' This is how the Bible is transformed

---

1. *Eclesiogénesis: Las comunidades de base reinventan la iglesia* (Santander: Sal Terrae, 1980), p. 13.

into a point of mediation (bridge) between APCs and reality. All reality is seen through the lens of the Bible. The Bible is what gives meaning and consistency to reality. What is not biblical does not merit our attention.

For their part, the emergence of BECs was, in many cases, the development of what at the beginning were 'Bible study circles' or small community groups for the reading and study of the Bible, focusing on the problems of daily life.[1] It was through these groups that a strongly popular interest in the Bible arose for the first time in the bosom of the Catholic Church in Latin America. Once again the poor reclaimed their right to read the Bible, with the conviction that the Holy Spirit and community discernment (sensitivity) would give light for the correct understanding of the sacred text. Catholics generally recognize—even though it may be in private—their debt to Protestantism, especially APCs, as being the most effective means of putting the Bible into the hands of the common people.

A superficial comparison of these two ways produces the impression that in both cases the type of Bible reading which is being done is radically different. In APCs, the movement is solely from the Bible to life. In technical terms the process is always exegetical, even when it is a matter of a rustic exegesis, generally literal and non-critical. By contrast, in BECs the movement is only from life to the Bible. In technical terms, this is a process which is fundamentally eisegetical. In practice this means that in APCs the Bible is read, interpreted and proclaimed in total abstraction from the problems, tensions and questions of real life, thus falling into a 'spiritualization' of the biblical message. For their part, BECs seek in the Bible a mirror to see themselves, searching for a theological justification for their social struggles, and thus falling into a 'politicization' of the biblical message.

Even though this putting of the matter, at least as a tendency, is partially correct (at the level of conscious awareness), a more rigorous analysis shows that APCs also read the Bible from the point-of-view of people's own life. In both cases the self-understanding which is derived from living, i.e. its subjectivity, grants them the keys for biblical hermeneutics. The great difference in how the Bible is read by the two movements is generated precisely by their particular moments of birth. If permitted an expression lacking scientific

1. Cf. C. Mesters, *Colección Círculos Bíblicos* (Petrópolis: Editora Vozes, 1973), as an example of the experience of the Bible Circles of BECs.

precision, the 'collective states of consciousness of the poor' for the two movements were fundamentally different, as was affirmed in the first section of this study.

In neither case is an abstraction from life made. What happens is that in each case Bible reading responds to a different subjectiveness. What, indeed, is certain is that the biblical interpretations which appear as valid in the founding moments of a movement tend to become the norm and close themselves off from new questions which later arise from the surrounding reality. It is necessary that both APCs and BECs admit this risk, in order to avoid falling into a fundamentalism, whether of the right or of the left. In order to enrich both expressions of popular Bible reading, the establishment of a dialogue between these two experiences is necessary. In this way the circularity of the hermeneutical process could be guaranteed.[1]

4. *The Understanding of the Church as Community*

The development of APCs, at least in its formative stage, bears a vision of the church as community whose principle of structure or organization is the charismata. The church does not conceive of itself as an institution built on a hierarchy, but rather as an association or place of meeting of the converted. In spite of the amount of institutionalization which the Pentecostal churches of today may have, the institutional feeling of tradition and historic continuity is absent in their self-understanding. As far as self-awareness goes, the actual origin of APCs goes back directly to the time of the New Testament, to the day of Pentecost, thus putting nearly two thousand years—and especially the last two hundred years—in parenthesis.

On the one hand, the church is experienced as a 'healing community'. In the testimonies of pentecostal conversion it is very easy to discover that a change of life, in addition to the intense experience of God, seems to be closely related to the discovery of a community with open arms. Persons who had experienced abandonment, loneliness and powerlessness found in the pentecostal group a community which accepted them and made them one of their own, without conditions. This warm welcome which APCs freely offer to people has a strong healing power. When one feels that the whole community is praying

1. In order to understand the 'hermeneutical circle' in Liberation Theology, see J.L. Segundo, *Liberation of Theology* (Maryknoll: Orbis, 1976).

for one, that everyone has an interest in one's salvation, that everybody is happy to see you, the person who is lonely, sick, or suffering from low self-esteem experiences a great reversal in self-understanding. Immediately one feels important, that life is worth living, that God really does love one because the community manifests concretely the reception as a 'brother or sister'. Thus, the person recovers the meaning of living, overcomes loneliness, and often this experience is confirmed by overcoming physical illnesses.

The church is experienced as a 'missionary or priestly community'. The person who is incorporated into a pentecostal community by conversion receives, and is recognized as having from then on, a gift or charisma with which one will begin to take part in the carrying out of the evangelizing mission of the church. In this way, APCs put into practice in a very radical manner the concept of the 'universal priesthood of believers'. All aspects of the life and mission of the church are conceived as a community task in which all members, even the newest, participate with their gifts and individual abilities. All functions, from proclamation of the Word in the service or preaching on the street to tasks of 'greeter' or usher who takes the offerings, the same value is assigned as to apostleship. The role of the pastor is rather that of organizer, or a community leader who has no priestly prerogative, except to administer the sacraments (baptism and Lord's supper). But these, due to their infrequency, have a lesser value beside the importance of daily services and the task of evangelization, where no difference is made between pastor and laity.

BECs have developed an ecclesial way of life which is truly community-centered, where the charisma (gift) is also the organizing principle. It has already been stated that one factor, among others, which motivated the emergence of BECs was the lack of priestly vocations. Lack of priests caused the Catholic Church to give more responsibility to the people in the pastoral task. Thus, without desiring it, a process was begun which today represents an enormous challenge to Roman Catholic ecclesiology.

In fact, as it has been affirmed by Leonardo Boff, one of the best known liberation theologians, who in recent years was strongly questioned by the Vatican, BECs represent a true 'reinvention of the church', an ecclesial restructuring from below, from the lay people, through the exercise of charismata which God grants to all believers, not only to priests.[1] For Boff, this has meant the rediscovery of the pneumatic dimension of the church, over against the excessive Christomonism of traditional ecclesiology.[2] Thus in liberation theology, as well as in APCs, there has been a profound rediscovery of pneumatology, of the action of the Holy Spirit in the church and in the world.

There are two important elements that are different in the experience of the BECs, which in my judgment represent a great challenge for pentecostal communities. In the first place, BECs and liberation theologians who have systematized their experience have not been transformed into a schismatic movement in the bosom of the Catholic Church. They have been able to maintain a creative tension between what Boff calls the christological and the pneumatological dimensions of the church, between continuity and change, between unity and renewal. In his suggestive analysis of New Testament criteria for discerning the authenticity of charismata, Boff affirms that a true charisma of the Holy Spirit is never divisive, it always brings edification to the communion, unity in the diversity.[3]

The other element of difference which is worth pointing out is the non-sectarian character of the BECs. Perhaps owing to having inherited the parochial structure and likewise the absence of a 'traumatic' conversion experience which radically separates the before and the after, BECs maintain a fluid relation with the 'civic community', with the neighborhood, without this becoming a threat to ecclesial vitality nor to a militant sense of Christian commitment. Because of the counterpart to the reasons just mentioned, a tendency is found among APCs towards community sectarianism (in the strictly sociological meaning of the term), which excludes itself from the 'civic community', which in my judgment limits its potential to evangelize.

It would be extraordinarily rewarding for APCs to study and to let themselves be enlightened by these aspects of the life of the BECs, in order to overcome the habit of attributing their scandalous and frequent divisions to the action of the Holy Spirit and being puffed up over sectarianism.

1.   Boff, *Ecclesiogénesis, passim*.
2.   Cf. *Iglesia, Carisma y Poder* (Santander: Sal Terrae, 1985). See also J. Comblin, *Tiempo de Acción* (Lima: CEP, 1986), and *The Holy Spirit and Liberation* (Maryknoll: Orbis, 1989).
3.   *Iglesia, Charisma y Poder*, pp. 227-62.

5. An Analysis

The principal conclusion of this study is that there is much more in common between Crillo Pentecostalism and liberation theology than is generally recognized. Images, which are frequently conditioned by ideological prejudices, make these two movements appear as essentially opposed, facing each other in enemy trenches in the struggle for liberation. As these caricatures are overcome, it is possible to discover in both movements two expressions of the work of the Holy Spirit to renew the whole church of Jesus Christ. And then, it is possible to find common ground for dialogue, which doubtless will produce mutual enrichment.

To approach the pentecostal experience without prejudice can help liberation theology reassess its perhaps too structured vision of the reality of the poor in Latin America. The pentecostal experience reveals needs and problems of the 'popular subjectivity', to which it has not given much attention. Not all aspirations for liberating the poor come from political awareness. However, as some theologians recognize, in the experience of BECs there are notable influences of pentecostal communities. To admit this fact in a more open way could be a good step toward the thawing of existing prejudices.

As it has been indicated throughout this study, pentecostalism also has much to learn from the life of BECs, from their biblical work, from their relation to the neighborhood, and from the value they place on ecclesial unity.

In spite of the fact that significant experiences of encounter and dialogue already exist between pentecostal communities and BECs in some neighborhoods in Chile, in Brazil and surely in other countries, these are exceptional cases. A multiplication of these is seen as quite difficult due to the strong 'ideological bombardment' which feeds and reproduces prejudices and caricatures. One must recognise that one of the sources of feeding these prejudices are Pentecostal Churches of North American origin and the so-called 'electronic church', which is too conditioned by the now obsolete ideology of the cold war and national security. Yet, any type of ecumenical dialogue is hindered by the orientation of Vatican decisions, particularly as these are reflected in appointments of bishops.

It is to be hoped that such an important encounter , 'he one now taking place in Brighton will, with the help of the Spirit, contribute to the destruction of prejudices and toward respect for the cultural, historical and also ecclesial identity of the nations.

A RESPONSE TO JUAN SEPULVEDA

Hubert Lenz

Professor Moltmann told us that 'a faith community without handicapped members is a handicapped community'. Latin American liberation theology gives us the new insight that 'a Church without the poor is a poor Church'. I must admit that I lack sufficient contact with the poor, and the Brighton Centre and the Metropole Hotel are not places where the poor live. Leonardo Boff, one of the leading Catholic liberation theologians in Brazil, lives and works in the *favelas* for nearly six months of each year. Boff and his friends probably know the situation of the poor better than any of us.

Lic. Sepulveda made a distinction that was new to me, between the Pentecostal churches imported from North America and those which have developed from among the poor in South America (i.e. APCs). Many liberation theologians are very critical towards the Pentecostal-charismatic groups and communities. A major reason is that the CIA supports these groups while at the same time being critical of liberation theology and all the pastoral works and political efforts which arise from it. Liberation theology is seen by the CIA as subversive and something that must be kept in check.[1] If Lic. Sepulveda's distinction is correct, then a useful and enriching dialogue between the charismatic movement and liberation theology should be easier.

In such a dialogue liberation theology would address a theme not raised in the paper, the question of *structural sin*. Not only can individuals be sinful, but also structures. This can be seen in the political and economic structures within particular countries, and the relations and dependencies between countries. A clear example can be found in the current 'debt-crisis'. Change is necessary not only for

1. Cf. *Totaler Krieg gegen die Armen: Geheime Strategiepapiere des amerikanischen Militärs* (ed. and commentated by U. Ucharov *et al.*; Munich: Chr. Kaiser Verlag, 1989).

individuals but also for the structures created by society. The German theologian J.B. Metz has repeatedly tried to express this easily forgotten truth when he said: 'The world trade prices are not irrelevant to the kingdom of God'.

Good relations with others are not just a question of charity, as pious people may think, but also of justice. The poor should not be dependent upon our generosity; rather they have a right to be supported by us, who are richer, in order to live with dignity. The Catholic Church has taught this throughout more than 100 years of social teaching.[1]

The basis of this teaching is the Church's view of the human person as an individual as well as a social being. As the Old Testament prophets wrote, our personal relationship with God must never be separated from our relationship with our neighbour. The strength and calling of the APCs and the charismatic renewal is undoubtedly in the emphasizing of the centrality and richness of a genuinely lived relationship with God. All socio-political movements are in danger of overlooking this dimension. The opposite however is true of spiritual movements, which are in danger of short-changing the social dimension of their faith. Liberation theology and charismatic renewal represent two aspects of Christian life, which must neither be separated nor opposed to one another. Being a Christian never means just 'God and I' or 'God and the Soul'.

From a charismatic viewpoint, a dialogue with liberation theology or other political theologies could ask whether enough importance is given to our experience of God and our relationship with God, when there is such a strong emphasis on the social and human dimension of Christian life. We must look more closely to see whether or not there is a vast difference in the solace given by the two approaches. According to Lk. 11.13 there is only one real comfort: God, that is, the Holy Spirit. This solace, which consists of our relationship with the Trinity, remains forever while social progress is, unfortunately, always fragile.

Charismatics quite correctly emphasize the importance of an experience of the Holy Spirit. Lic. Sepulveda placed particular emphasis on the immediacy of our relationship with God, not without

1. Particularly in the encyclicals of Pope John Paul II: *Laborem Exercens* (1981), *Sollicitudo Rei Socialis* (1987) and *Centesimus Annus* (1991).

being critical of the Catholic Church. Despite some false impressions and misunderstandings, this is also the view held by the Catholic Church.[1] However, Catholic theology speaks of 'mediated immediacy'. A direct relationship and mediation do not exclude each other. Is not Jesus our mediator to the Father, and the Holy Spirit our mediator with the Father and the Son? Are not the Scriptures, that are so important for us, and the 'community of believers' classical forms of mediated immediacy? Catholics do not see the official ministry, as bishops, priests and the like, as a substitute or go-between for the personal relationship of believers with God. I neither gloss over the existence of wrong practices nor deny that criticism from APCs is justified.

In his reference to the social context of the 'home-grown' APCs in South America, Lic. Sepulveda points towards the beginnings of an integrated view of Christian faith. The theme of mediation will be important both for reflection on charismatic renewal and for ecumenical dialogue. I am pleased that he mentioned the lack of a sense of institution and of history in the APCs. Are we not building on the foundations laid down by our ancestors as well as being enabled through the Holy Spirit to enter into a direct relationship with God and pray 'Abba, Father?' (Gal. 4.6).

The poor are just as important in mediating our faith. We cannot know the quality of our love from prayer alone. Our relationship with the poor tests how genuine and how deep this love is. Jesus made his last judgment dependent upon how we meet the poor, the prisoners and the needy (cf. Mt. 25), and we are asked very clearly, 'How can you love God whom you do not see, if you do not love your brother whom you do see?' (1 Jn 4.20).

A true experience of the love of God, emphasized by charismatics, is shown through a love of the poor. Mother Teresa, during a talk in Germany, asked the question: 'Do you know the poor in your town?' The great Catholic theologian Hans Urs von Balthasar speaks of the 'sacrament of the brother' besides baptism, eucharist and the other sacraments.[2] Those of us in the charismatic movement should always

1. John Paul II has written 'not only priests...lay people as well are personally called by the Lord, from whom they receive a mission on behalf of the Church and the world' (*Christifideles Laici* [1988], no. 2).

2. H.U. von Balthasar, *Die Gottesfrage des heutigen Menschen* (Vienna: Herold Verlag, 1956), pp. 205-23.

be open to the questions put to us by liberation theology, because it is not the strong, but rather 'the weak whom God has chosen' (1 Cor. 1.27). Therefore Jesus speaks to each one of us: 'I was sick, I was homeless. I was naked; have you seen me and loved me in this situation?'

A RESPONSE TO JUAN SEPULVEDA

Brian G. Hathaway

Introduction

I first need to acknowledge my limitations in responding to this paper. Living in a country like New Zealand, with its Westernized culture, well away from the type of socio-political issues that affect the Church of Latin America, is not the best place to assess the interaction between Pentecostal and liberation theology communities. To seek to lift this paper out of its particular setting and then evaluate it is open to considerable distortion. It would probably be true to say that many New Zealand theologians are somewhat critical of both Pentecostalism and liberation theology of the Latin American kind.

My second limitation is that I do not have access to the literature cited at the end of Pastor Sepulveda's paper.

A. *Comments*

1. *Dialogue*

I applaud the attempt to produce dialogue between Pentecostalism and liberation theology. A very important point which clearly shows the underlying difference between the two is the disparity between the breadth and depth of theological material issuing from both movements. This fact of course makes dialogue somewhat difficult.

2. *World-Views*

The difference between the more pessimistic world-view of the Pentecostals (*Pentecostalismo Criollo* or PC) and the more optimistic world-view of the BEC (Base Ecclesiastical Communities) is of course reflected in other areas of the Christian Church and often stems from a view of eschatology. Such differing world views are also common in my country. A more pessimistic world-view often being held by those from pentecostal/evangelical backgrounds and a more optimistic world-view by those involved in what could be called the 'liberal' wing of the Church—those involved with social justice.

3. *Experience of God*

As a charismatic I am forced to ask questions about the difference in the experience of God between those of PC and BEC. The profound conversion experience and encounter with the Holy Spirit of many Pentecostals impacts all areas of their life and is at the heart of charismatic renewal and Pentecostalism. Such an experience is clearly seen in the lives of our Lord's disciples and of many of the converts to Christianity recorded in the pages of Scripture. I wonder if this really does equate to the process occurring in BECs outlined in the paper.

On the one hand, is the warming up process occurring in BECs due to a more thorough educative process and could not PCs learn from this? On the other hand, would a radical conversion experience in BECs speed up the process occurring in them? I readily admit that this reflection may indicate my more conservative Protestant heritage but I am forced to ask the questions: Are there any charismatic BECs, and if so what do they look like? Are there any PCs that have the same commitment to social justice as the BECs, and if so what do they look like?

4. *The Role of the Bible*

The danger of spiritualizing the biblical message on the part of the PCs and politicizing it on the part of the BECs highlights the hermeneutical problem. This is a problem that many movements have been faced with. However, that two quite dissimilar movements are reading and studying the Bible seems to be especially significant. One would assume that the best context for this to happen more effectively would be within a community where the operation of spiritual gifts is encouraged. Here we clearly see the need to bring together the strengths of these two movements—the strength of a community wrestling with socio-economic issues as seen in the BECs and the ministry of the Holy Spirit as demonstrated in PCs.

5. *The Church as Community*

Those of us outside of the Roman Catholic Church have often pondered the incredible diversity that can be maintained under the umbrella of Rome. We have been horrified at the frequent divisions that have occurred in Protestantism and deeply disturbed at the frequency of division within the Pentecostal ranks. One has to ask serious questions as to the roots of this persistent and pernicious problem within Protestantism. Maybe it is linked to Sepulveda's encouragement of PCs to 'study and allow themselves to be enlightened by the living aspects of the BECs, so that they can overcome this habit of attributing their scandalous and frequent divisions to the work of the Holy Spirit'. It seems that new movements which break away and become independent of the founding movement are particularly susceptible to spiritual pride and arrogance. Such attitudes often lead to isolation. Despite the barriers to dialogue, is it not possible for local informal discussions to take place between PCs and BECs?

B. *Areas Requiring More Reflection*

There are two polarizations that urgently need correcting. It seems to me that these polarizations are not only seen in the discussion between PCs and BECs as demonstrated in Latin America but also in other areas of the Christian world.

1. *The Polarization between Individualism and Community*

There is a need to balance the vertical dimension ('loving the Lord our God with all our heart and soul and strength and mind') with the horizontal ('loving our neighbour as ourselves'). The vertical, with its emphasis on evangelism, personal salvation, forgiveness of sin and relationship with God, is correct but not complete. The horizontal, with its emphasis on social concern, the poor and social justice is also correct, but not complete in itself. Pentecostalism needs an increase in the involvement in the community. It needs to gain a much deeper identification with the poor and their struggle. It must allow Scripture to be read from the 'underside of history'. This is especially so where Pentecostals take their theology from North America and embrace ideologies such as the 'prosperity gospel'.

2. *The Polarization Regarding the Nature of Evil*

The emphasis found in liberation theology on institutional sin as seen in social, political and economic areas of society needs to be balanced with that of personal sin and the influence of the demonic. On the other hand, God's salvation is bigger than just my personal salvation. His intention is to redeem everything to himself. If sin has penetrated all aspects of human life and society, then God's grace must be more persuasive and penetrative than sin. We need to adopt a view of the work of Christ that can embrace both salvation from personal sin and salvation from social sin.

3. *A Theology of the Kingdom of God*

Embracing a theology of the Kingdom of God seems to be a way forward. Not only will it permit us to embrace the strengths of PCs and BECs but also other strands of what have sometimes been seen as opposing theological viewpoints. A theology of the Kingdom of God embraces both the individual and the community, personal and social sin. God is bringing about his Kingdom, and restating a concept of the Kingdom of God goes beyond the limitations of liberation theology (which reduces the kingdom) and Pentecostal theology (which limits the kingdom). This concept was the central expression of our Lord's ministry while on earth. If the various streams of the Christian Church across the world would study and dialogue over the implications of this model, particularly in regards to controversial or polarizing issues, I believe great benefit would be realized.

Conclusion

In fact the chasm between PCs and BECs is not so different from that which we have seen in Western countries between, on the one hand, Pentecostal, charismatic and evangelical groups and on the other hand those more 'liberal' groups who espouse the causes of social justice. The term 'social gospel' to many Christian groups in the West is still anathema. Several movements in the West have been seeking to bridge this gap. These include the Lausanne movement and the Kingdom and Spirit consultation.[1] This process must continue if we are to learn from each other and recapture a vibrancy and breadth in Christianity that will challenge the three emerging world systems of secular humanism, eastern religion and resurgent Islam.

1.   For the Kingdom and Spirit consultation, and papers presented at its 1988 and 1990 meetings, see *Transformation* 5 (October–December 1988) and 7 (July–September 1990).

CHARISMATIC CHURCHES AND APARTHEID IN SOUTH AFRICA

Karla Poewe-Hexham and Irving Hexham

The study of charismatic Christianity is fraught with controversy. North American and European charismatics are accused of being cult members. In Latin America, Korea and South Africa they are frequently associated with right-wing political groups and social reaction. Predictably, such reactions come from investigative journalists, political activists and theological writers.[1] All of these approaches are valid in their own right. What is unacceptable is for theological or journalistic writers to present their work as though they were social scientists, thereby wrongly applying the authority of social sciences. Although respectable social scientists are highly critical of the Charismatic movement, in general most recent studies of note by social scientists have tended to take a more positive attitude toward the Charismatic movement.[2] This paper looks at Charismatic Christianity in South Africa on the basis of interdisciplinary, longitudinal social research using techniques derived from anthropology, history and sociology.

Charismatic Christianity is particularly controversial in South Africa.[3] Mainliners, evangelicals and Pentecostals are quite willing to

1. See F. Conway and J. Siegelman, *Holy Terror: The Fundamentalist War on America's Freedoms in Religion, Politics and our Private Lives* (New York: Delta, 1982); J. Haven, *Faith, Hope, no Charity: An Inside Look at the Born again Movement in Canada and the United States* (New Star Books, 1984); P. Pattison, *Crisis Unawares: A Doctor Examines the Korean Church* (Sevenoaks, Kent: OMF Press, 1981).

2. M.M. Poloma, *The Assemblies of God at the Crossroads: Charisma and Institutional Dilemmas* (Knoxville, TN: University of Tennessee Press, 1989); H. Newton Malony and A. Adams Lovekin, *Glossolalia: Behavioral Science Perspectives on Speaking in Tongues* (Oxford: Oxford University Press, 1985).

3. For example, most of the articles in the *Journal of Theology for Southern Africa* 69 (December, 1989) entitled *Right Wing Religious Movements* deal with

retell stories about excesses. For example, in 1987 we were told by a well known Christian leader that Tim Salmon of the Pietermaritzburg Christian Center had helped a right-wing candidate defeat Graham Macintosh, a well known Christian MP in the 1987 General Election. When we interviewed Salmon he denied this and explained that as a Christian he felt it was his responsibility to encourage his congregation to think intelligently about the election. Therefore he arranged a meeting in his church where both candidates were given the opportunity to speak. Later, we met Macintosh who confirmed Salmon's account of the incident.

1. *Faith for the Fearful?*

Our longitudinal data, based upon extensive research among members of new Charismatic churches in South Africa, suggest a complex picture quite different from that popularly conceived. There are some disquieting elements and many encouraging ones. Many people, however, refuse to accept our findings because they regard Elda Susan Morran and Lawrence Schlemmer's book , *Faith for the Fearful?*, as the benchmark against which all other studies are to be measured.[1] Apparently based on solid sociological evidence, it claimed to show that Charismatics who joined new independent churches were reactionary neurotics. These findings were widely reported in the press.[2]

reactionary religious groups such as the Gospel Defense League. Yet in the midst of this special edition is an article by P. Gifford ('Theology and Right Wing Christianity') which specifically identifies a number of Charismatic and evangelical groups as right wing.

1.   E.S. Morran and L. Schlemmer, *Faith for the Fearful?* (Durban: Center for Applied Social Sciences, 1984). The book arose out of a study commissioned in 1982 by the ecumenical organization Diakonia which is largely financed by the Roman Catholic Church. Usually these reactions were verbal ones. T. Soeldner reflects them in 'Charismatic Churches and the Struggle against Apartheid: A Dispute', *The Christian Center* (January 4–11, 1989), p. 18. We were told to read *Faith for the Fearful?* to 'understand' South African Charismatics by such diverse people as Archbishop Hurley, Michael Cassidy and Professor David Bosch. The book was used as the basis for a major interdenominational conference on Charismatic churches organized by Diakonia in November 1984 and subsequently cited in by various church bodies, e.g. *Report of the General Synod of the Presbyterian Church of Southern Africa* (Johannesburg: Presbyterian Church, 1986), p. 39.

2.   Cf. *The Natal Mercury*, 17 November, 1984, and *The Sunday Tribune*, 18 November, 1984.

Unlike earlier negative evaluations of new Charismatic churches, this book did not look like the work of a disgruntled theologian or rival church leader concerned about the loss of members of his congregation to another church.[1] Instead their findings, like the following, seemed to rest on scientifically validated sociological data and, therefore, could not be easily dismissed.

> Survey results showed... some suggestion that the new churches are appealing to people with problems or particular personality types, i.e. those who tend to be anxious, neurotic, or 'hysterical'...[2]

Politically the implication of this was said to be that

> new church charismatics are more politically conservative than their established church counterparts... Their aversion to the social gospel is not neutral and amounts to support of the status quo...[3]

If these findings are correct, and if, as the authors claim, the teachings of new Charismatic churches encourage and actually increase such tendencies, then the case against the Charismatics would be damaging. It is not surprising then that many people unfamiliar with the social sciences accepted the word of these authors on the authority of their claim to be presenting valid sociological evidence. However, careful examination of the book shows that the entire study is fundamentally flawed.

The basic problem is methodological. The entire study is based on a sample of eighty people. Of these, fifty belonged to what the authors call 'established churches' and were drawn from an undisclosed number of congregations belonging to five different denominations. Twenty members of the established churches claimed to be Charismatics and the rest were traditionalists who had little sympathy for Charismatic religion. The only 'new church charismatics' actually interviewed were thirty members of the Durban Christian Center.

Yet the book repeatedly talks about 'membership in the new churches', 'new church charismatic respondents', 'the new churches', and 'new church charismatics' as though a large number of congrega-

---

1. Cf. T. Verryn, *Rich Christians Poor Christian: An Appraisal of Rhema Teachings* (Pretoria: Ecumenical Research Unit, 1983); *Daily News*, 25 March, 1982; *Sunday Express*, 17 July, 1983; *Sunday Tribune*, 31 July, 1983.

2. Morran and Schlemmer, *Faith for the Fearful?*, p. 170.

3. *Faith for the Fearful?*, pp. 171, 179.

tions were involved in the study.[1] It is very easy, therefore, to miss the fact that all of the evidence presented about 'new church charismatics' comes from a sample of thirty people belonging to one congregation, the Durban Christian Center.

Confusion is increased because after explaining the nature of their sample, an entire chapter is devoted to discussing the history, organization, membership and finances, and so on, of six new charismatic churches in the Durban area. This information is totally unnecessary. It wrongly creates an unconscious impression that these sociological data are based on a survey undertaken in all six churches by only once conceding that the survey was undertaken at the Durban Christian Center alone.[2]

Further, the impression that the authors were working with a large sample is reinforced by the use of percentages in all their tables.[3] It is, of course, normal to work with percentages, and the approach used would be acceptable if the sample was not a mere thirty people and if it had been based on probability sampling. A non-random sample of thirty is far too small to allow for statistically valid inferences. Yet instead of admitting this the authors argue that because:

> the sampling could not be rigorous...the key focus group had to be sampled by means of a rough quota sample based on broad estimates of the social profiles of the new church group.[4]

Again, many non-specialists may think the use of technical terms and sociological jargon about 'sampling', 'focus group', 'rough quota sample' and 'broad estimates of the social profiles' bespeak reliability. Nevertheless, as Herman J. Loether and Donald G. McTavish point out in *Descriptive and Inferential Statistics,*

> Although non-random techniques are often more economical and convenient than random sampling techniques, these advantages are outweighed by the disadvantage of being unable to estimate sampling error. Therefore, the use of non-random techniques by sociologists should generally be discouraged.[5]

1. *Faith for the Fearful?*, pp. 64, 67, 170, 171.
2. *Faith for the Fearful?*, p. 47.
3. In fairness it ought to be noted that at the bottom of each table they add 'n = 30 n = 20 n = 30', but to most readers unfamiliar with sociological data this information is meaningless.
4. Morran and Schlemmer, *Faith for the Fearful?*, p. 46.
5. H.J. Loether and D.G. McTavish, *Descriptive and Inferential Statistics: An*

Before conclusions stated in *Faith for the Fearful?* can be accepted, several things need be considered. First, even if the survey results were statistically valid they would not allow for generalizations beyond membership of the Durban Christian Center. Such statistics would not apply to members of other new Charismatic churches in Durban or in the rest of South Africa. The evidence presented, at best, applies to one specific church. Second, dealing specifically with political issues implies a clarity which can not be sustained. Compared with established church respondents, members of the Durban Christian Center seem to support the Government. This finding is misleading because it does not take into account ethnic background and/or educational level of the people interviewed.

The Durban Christian Center has a relatively large number of members from traditional Afrikaner backgrounds. As a group, Afrikaners have been more indoctrinated than English-speaking South Africans to believe in apartheid and unquestioning support for the government. A knowledge of the ethnic background of respondents is necessary because a political statement by an Afrikaner may be radical in comparison with the views of other Afrikaners, but conservative when compared to the views of English-speaking South Africans. One cannot simply compare a mixed ethnic group including people with English and Afrikaans backgrounds against a homogeneous one drawn from established, English-language churches, whose membership, while not necessarily liberal, is certainly anti-Nationalist in the first place.

Equally important is the fact that in drawing conclusions from their data the authors did not take into account educational attainment when political attitudes were discussed. Thus while 35% of the established church traditionalists held university degrees, only 3% of Durban Christian Center members had one. Since education plays a large role reducing prejudice, any comparison between the two groups which does not factor in educational achievement is meaningless.[1]

Introduction (Boston: Allyn & Bacon, 1980), p. 424. For an excellent discussion of sampling, see E. Babble, *The Practice of Social Research* (Belmont: Wadsworth, 4th edn, 1986), pp. 136-77. Here it is pointed out that to the extent quota sampling is useful it depends on a very carefully constructed matrix which takes into account many factors that were ignored by Morran and Schlemmer (cf. p. 175).

1. Morran and Schlemmer, *Faith for the Fearful?*, p. 48. For a good general discussion of this issue, see R. Stark, *Sociology* (Belmont: Wadsworth, 1989), pp. 290-328, esp. p. 296.

An important but neglected finding of *Faith for the Fearful?* is that 'none of the sample groups was found to be particularly racist' and that membership of the Durban Christian Center 'apparently increased tolerance' of other races.[1] These findings did not fit the authors' argument and were curtly dismissed: 'These "non-racist" findings are confusing in view of the fact that the majority of new church charismatics...vote Nationalist'.[2]

According to their data, 53% of Durban Christian Center members professed to vote Nationalist compared with 17% of traditionalists in established churches. However, the area of Durban that houses the Christian Center is located tallied 57.27% of whites who voted Nationalist in the 1984 election.[3] So the finding is neither surprising nor quite as bad as they are made to appear. According to data used in this study, Durban Christian Center members are less likely to vote Nationalist than their secular neighbors. But, this significant finding was not mentioned by the authors of this study.

Comparison with white South Africans in general, 60% of whom are Afrikaners, rather than members of English-speaking churches in particular, reveals further possible evidence that membership of the Durban Christian Center had an ameliorating effect. According to a national poll published in 1984 by Market and Opinion Surveys,[4] only 58.5% of whites were prepared to accept Blacks in their churches. Yet 87% of Durban Christian Center members answered that they would 'willingly admit blacks to my church or club as personal friends'.[5]

What is more, these people backed up their words by attending a church which the authors of *Faith for the Fearful?* concede was integrated.[6] This admission points to another misrepresentation of the Durban Christian Center found in the book, which states, 'the new churches have a predominantly white membership (80%)...' Yet in another place, they reveal that only 70% of the congregation at the

1.   Morran and Schlemmer, *Faith for the Fearful?*, pp. 79, 82.

2.   *Faith for the Fearful?*, p. 79.

3.   *SA Barometer Election Focus* (Johannesburg: John Mark Associates, 1989), p. 32.

4.   Market and Opinion Surveys, P.O. Box 755, Durbanville, 7550, South Africa, Nr. 3/84 (November, 1984), p. 11.

5.   Morran and Schlemmer, *Faith for the Fearful?*, p. 78.

6.   *Faith for the Fearful?*, p. 78.

Durban Christian Center were white.[1] The rest were Black. What is equally telling is that nowhere do they indicate the number of Blacks attending the established churches in their sample. Thus while the Durban Christian Center may not seem particularly integrated, it is extraordinary when compared with other churches in South Africa, where more churches attended by whites have no regular Black members.

The Anglican church, to which we belong, is theoretically integrated in South Africa. But it is very difficult to find congregations attended by whites where there are more than a few Blacks. Certainly, in our experience we have never attended a South African Anglican church where more than 5% of its regular congregation was Black. Against this record the achievement of the Durban Christian Center, where 30% of its members were Black, looks positively amazing. Clearly, when judged against other churches and whites generally, members of the Durban Christian Center look far more liberal than *Faith for the Fearful?* suggests.[2]

2. *Africa Shall be Saved*

A quite serious criticism of Charismatic Christianity is found in the work of Paul Gifford who has published one book and several technical papers on the topic. His inaugural article, 'Africa Shall be Saved',[3] was touted to be a study of Reinhard Bonnke's work in Zimbabwe. Regrettably, his evidence appears to have been obtained through casual interviews, attendance at a few revival meetings and indiscriminate reading of charismatic literature from the bookstall at Reinhard Bonnke's 1986 meetings in Harare.

The bulk of the article consists of an extended analysis of the theological content of thirteen sermons preached by Bonnke and his

1.   Morran and Schlemmer appear to have gathered their data in 1983, although they never give exact dates. When Irving Hexham first visited the Durban Christian Center three years later, about 60% of the congregation were Black. One of the pastors claimed that when the *Faith for the Fearful?* survey was carried out at least 50% of the population were Black. In 1987 and 1988 we not only checked attendance figures but also made video films to record the extent of integration in this church.

2.   Other criticisms could be raised, including the ambiguous wording of many of the questions used, but this would take too much time.

3.   P. Gifford, 'Africa Shall be Saved: An Appraisal of Reinhard Bonnke's Pan-African Crusade', *Journal of Religion in Africa* 17.1 (1987), pp. 63-92.

associates. Although Gifford's bias against the theology he discovers in these sermons is undisguised, this part of his paper makes interesting reading.[1] Gifford approaches these sermons as a trained theologian without taking into account the dynamics of preaching.

For example, Gifford says, 'Bonnke's exegesis seemed rather odd...'[2] in his interpretation of Mk 15.33-34. But, in fact, the argument of Bonnke cited by Gifford is to be found in traditional commentators using either Mark 15.33-34 or parallel passages. Admittedly, Bonnke's language is that of an evangelist, but the point he makes is one frequently made by commentators like Calvin and Matthew Henry. Bonnke could at worst be criticized for perpetuating historic modes of exegesis now abandoned by more enlightened theologians.

The second part of the article is an account of the Bonnke crusade written in a way that suggests empirical research and sociological observation. Reinforcing the impression that this part of the study is sociological in nature is Gifford's appeal to the work of May de Hass[3] and the general tone of the discussion. The problem here is that while Gifford clearly did some fieldwork, it was that of an untrained amateur who simply wrote about what he observed, without being aware of the need to verify observations by standard sociological and anthropological techniques. It should be noted, however, that Gifford never claims to be writing as a social scientist and that he quite clearly states that his criticisms are theological.

Gifford followed this with *The Religious Right in Southern Africa*, where he describes the first three chapters as 'mainly historical and sociological'.[4] Out of 118 pages, only 17 of them are devoted to Southern Africa. The rest contains an assortment of charges about the CIA and a right-wing American conspiracy to subvert Africa and the Third World.[5]

Although Gifford provides extensive documentation to back up his claims, the works cited in the first three chapters are little more than journalistic political and theological polemics. A careful examination of his footnotes show that out of 256 references in these chapters only

1.   P. Gifford, 'Africa Shall be Saved', pp. 67-68.

2.   'Africa Shall be Saved', p. 70.

3.   'Africa Shall be Saved', pp. 83-84.

4.   P. Gifford, *The Religious Right in Southern Africa* (Harare: Baobab Books, 1988), p. ix.

5.   Gifford, *The Religious Right*, pp. 13-24, 27-31.

10 are to writings by sociologists, 10 by historians, and 18 by theologians. In other words, a mere 38 out of 256 references are to serious academic works. The rest are newspaper and magazine articles, journalistic books and popular religious literature. Interesting as these references may be, they hardly qualify in a scholarly study of Charismatics.

The only section of this book which appears to be based on empirical research is ch. 3, where Gifford uses material from six interviews and gives evidence of having visited a number of religious groups. Problematic here is the small number of interviews and the fact that they were all with key individuals in organizations he considered significant. No attempt at a systematic study of these organizations seems to have been made nor any solicitation of rank and file members. Further, no details are given of the method used in interviewing or of the way he approached any of the groups to make his observations. In other words, these interviews and observations are unscientific reports of informal conversations and impressions. As such, they have no validity in generalizing about Charismatic Christianity in Southern Africa.

Ironically, faulty methodology undermines the most vocal condemnation of Charismatics in Southern Africa by established academicians. In-depth interviewing is hard work. Attending churches over a lengthy period of time demands commitment. Using scientifically valid research techniques such as probability sampling is costly and time consuming. Although such components are requirements for academic excellence, it would appear that the serious study of charismatics places too many barriers before those aspiring to publish articles and books.

Strongly negative evaluations often rely heavily on selected charismatic publications, many of which originate from outside South Africa. While this may be helpful for some purposes, reading a book or magazine is very different from the systematic study of a social movement. To draw conclusions about South African Charismatics, or any other dynamic social group, from their literature does not reflect the true dynamics of the movement. It is essential to observe what people actually do, rather than simply analyzing books they may or may not read. Apart from anything else, the impact of the book on its readers may be very different from what its author intended.[1]

1. A good example of this can be seen in the history of J. Bunyan's *The*

A common rejoinder goes something like this: 'but we know charismatics; we have met them'. However, eavesdropping on dialogical meetings and church functions hardly qualifies as a systematic study worthy of recognized anthropological and sociological methods. We freely admit that anyone who reads South African charismatic literature will discover a highly conservative morality which takes a traditional, evangelical view of the relationship between Church and state vis-à-vis Romans 13. The result is an apparently naive trust in the goodwill of the government which gives a clear signal of unreserved support for government actions.

Books such as Derek Morphew's *Principalities and Ideologies in South Africa Today*, and his more recent major study *South Africa: The Powers Behind*,[1] are not easily located. Once in the hands of a researcher, the palms may turn sweaty on encountering the literalist charismatic talk about 'evil spirits' and 'demons'. However, when the prism of certain scientific prejudices is removed, stringent opposition to apartheid becomes evident.

Modern theologians may easily discount literal devils and may find such primitive talk distasteful. Nevertheless, when a charismatic represents South Africans as 'oppressed by the demon of apartheid', this is more far reaching than the calculated language of mainline Christians who speak of 'evil structures of South African society'.

It is true that many White South Africans have stood firm against apartheid and through church organizations, like the SACC, have attempted to reach Blacks. Such efforts should by no means be undervalued and deserve admiration. Regrettably, when placed in the context of involving the whole congregation, most of these efforts are shown to be no more than tokenism. Individuals and church leaders have made strenuous efforts to overcome apartheid, but no one can claim that rank and file members of mainline churches have persisted in resisting apartheid.[2]

Pilgrim's Progress. Cf. C. Hill, *A Tinker and a Poor Man: John Bunyan and his Church 1628–1688* (New York: A.A. Knopf, 1989), pp. 373-80.

1. D. Morphew, *Principalities and Ideologies in South Africa Today* (Tygerpark: Cape Fellowship Ministries, 1986); and *South Africa: The Powers Behind* (Cape Town: Struik, 1989).

2. This point is well made by C. Villa-Vicencio in his *Trapped in Apartheid: A Socio-Theological History of the English Speaking Churches* (Maryknoll, NY: Orbis Books, 1988).

In the early 1970s and 1980s, we attended various 'integrated' cele-brations and other 'meetings' organized by mainline churches and church related groups to break down racial barriers. With the excep-tion of some successes like the South African Christian Leaders Assembly (SACLA) organized by African Enterprise, most of these self-conscious attempts to integrate the races were failures.[1] By con-trast, our extensive scientific analysis bears out the view that South African Charismatic churches are changing attitudes by their activities at the grass roots level.

1.   For an account of SACLA and critical discussion, see *Journal of Theology for South Africa* 29 (December, 1989) (SACLA Edition). The best account of African Enterprise is to be found in M. Cassidy, *The Passing Summer: A South African Pilgrimage of Love* (London: Hodder & Stoughton, 1989). There are, of course, some remarkable exceptions such as Koinonia Southern Africa, but these are few and far between.

A RESPONSE TO KARLA POEWE-HEXHAM AND IRVING HEXHAM

Nico Horn

Introduction

Since the last cornerstone of apartheid—the Population Registration Act—has been repealed (17 June, 1991), it seems more relevant to speak of racism rather than apartheid. This will aid the attempt to see our ordeal from an international perspective, perhaps prodding the international community beyond decrying faceless apartheid into examining their own racism.

The Hexhams speak to the political caricature of charismatics constructed by academicians and mainline churches subsequently publicized by the press. I dealt with the unscientific methodology of Morran and Schlemmer in *From Rags to Riches*, and engaged the work of Gifford in a newspaper article, then publicly (during a response period following his 1991 lecture on right wing religion at the Council of Churches of Namibia).[1]

The Hexhams argue that the prosperity teaching is compatible with the African world-view. However, Concerned Evangelicals (hereafter CE) and Relevant Pentecostal Witness (hereafter RPW) have been forthright in their condemnation of this theological trend in South Africa.

> We are concerned that some of these groups are blatantly capitalistic and materialistic. They preach the gospel of prosperity, claiming that this 'blessed' capitalism is from God by faith if one believes the Scriptures, confesses them and claims possessions (material) desired! What a false God of Materialism. This sounds like real idolatrous mammon![2]

1. N. Horn, *From Rags to Riches* (Pretoria: Unisa, 1989); 'Moenie Vinger Wys Nie', *Beeld* (July, 1990). Gifford appeared before the Council of Churches of Namibia in July, 1991.

2. *Evangelical Witness in South Africa: Evangelicals Critique their own Theology and Practice* (Johannesburg: Concerned Evangelicals, 1986), p. 32.

RPW links up with the Azusa Street revival and God's involvement with the poor and oppressed to prove that the prosperity gospel has no place in Pentecostal or charismatic thinking.[1]

The Hexhams rightly state that it is not correct to link all charismatic churches with the prosperity message. The different streams of the Charismatic Movement are often linked only in the sense they are all part of what Pentecostals and Charismatics see as the renewal of the church. In South Africa, one can easily delineate several charismatic groups with completely different approaches to both Christian practice and theology on the one hand, and politics on the other.

Vast differences exist, in particular, between the theological approach of 'faith' churches and 'restoration' churches. Faith churches are connected, in the main, with the International Fellowship of Christian Churches (IFCC) and are thereby in close fellowship with the mega Rhema Bible Church, led by Ray McCauley in Randburg. There are, however, growing faith churches with no formal ties to IFCC or the Rhema Bible Church. Rhema and McCauley have always acknowledged an indebtedness to North American leaders like Kenneth Hagin and Kenneth Copeland. Restoration churches interact most with the house church movement in the United Kingdom and are influenced by Wimber and Paulk of North America. Some restoration leaders submit directly to the British 'apostles' Bryn Jones and Terry Virgo.

The Hexhams seem to deal primarily with faith churches, especially Rhema and Durban Christian Center, but turn to the writings of Derek Morphew (a restorationist) when arguing for the political relevance of South African Charismatics. Progressive South Africans make a clear distinction between multiracial churches and non-racial churches. Although both groups have integrated memberships, multiracial churches do not have blacks in leadership, whereas non-racial churches share all aspects of church life—including leadership positions—among blacks and whites.

There are exemplary non-racial communities in the charismatic category, among them being the Covenant Community at Bizweni, Somerset West. Kobus Swart has created an authentically non-racial church with two black pastors and several other blacks heading

1. *Relevant Pentecostal Witness* (Durban: The Relevant Pentecostals, 1988), p. 3ff. See also Lapoorta and Horn in *Azusa* 1.1 (1990) (Durban: The Relevant Pentecostals).

subdepartments. The majority of these churches are in the restoration fold, while most faith churches reach a plane no higher than multi-racial. After the Rustenburg Conference, CE and RPW met with IFCC and Christian Ministers Network (CMN is a restoration oriented group). Progressive Pentecostals and Evangelicals quickly discerned the theological difference(s) between the two streams. One delegate observed afterward that IFCC people are moving toward non-racialism and political justice in spite of their theology, while the Restorationists are coming to grips with the political consequences of their theology.[1]

Alan Scotland, a member of Bryn Jones's team, concurs with this assessment.[2] When the apostles and prophets of Covenant Ministries initiated socio-political action, they were severely criticized by their South African related churches. However, when they considered con-textualized implications of the reign of God and life in the kingdom, most of them could not avoid political questions. Derek Morphew warns that even the distinction offered above can be confusing.[3] He points to the possibility of being more aligned with Ray McCauley in his views of socio-ethical issues than to some leaders in CMN. It seems nevertheless inappropriate to quote Derek Morphew and other Restoration theologians when dealing with the political role of faith churches. Unqualified use of the term Charismatic may prove too elastic when discussing the influence of theology on a political system like apartheid.

Another aspect of the Hexham presentation to be noted is the lack of reference to the growing non-denominational charismatic churches

1.   Personal telephone conversation with Maharaj (Windhoeck–Durban, May, 1991). The Rustenburg Conference was convened by Dr Louw Alberts, unofficial church advisor of the state president, and Revd Frank Chikane, general secretary of the South African Council of Churches. Most of the mainline and large Pentecostal-Charismatic churches attended the conference. The Rustenburg Declaration, con-demning apartheid, was adopted on the final day. CE is a movement of progressive Evangelicals, Charismatics and Pentecostals opposing apartheid. The movement evolved around a document responding to the Kairos Document. The Relevant Pentecostal Witness is a movement of progressive Pentecostals and Charismatics. The movement took shape around a document of the same name released in 1988 as a Pentecostal-Charismatic response to the Kairos Document.

2.   Personal conversation with Alan Scotland at Ansty, Coventry.

3.   Personal telephone conversation with Morphew (Windhoek–Cape Town, June, 1991).

under black leadership with very little or no relation to large, white charismatic churches. Joseph Kgobo's Life from Africa is certainly worthy of attention. Kgobo is a former cadre of Umkhonto we Sizwe ('Spear of the Nation'), the military wing of the African National Congress. Although Kgobo has loose ties with several Charismatic groups and is a part of the CMN, he is very critical of the theology and practices of white charismatics. A scientific research of charismatics and their socio-political views is not complete without at least a peep 'through the eyes' of black Charismatics.

The fact that Morran and Schlemmer and Gifford overstate their case does not mean there is no credibility to the accusation that right wing politics influenced some charismatic churches. Moss Nthia[1] points to the fact that Rhema and other Charismatic churches played an active role in Casa, a well-known right wing Christian group in South Africa. I treated the right wing image of Casa in *Vrye Weekblad*.[2] In short, while advertising to be a progressive anti-apartheid movement, as late as November 1989 they encouraged President De Klerk to maintain the ban on political organizations that had not forsaken violence. Recalling that President De Klerk unconditionally lifted the ban on political organizations and lifted the state of emergency only two months later, it is clear that Casa played a negative rather than a positive role in dismantling apartheid.

Both RPW and CE[3] point to the right wing language of charismatics and evangelicals who fought communism in the same way as did the

1. M. Nthia, 'Right Wing Christian Groups', *Azusa* 1.1, pp. 5-10. See also Leach, Lapoorta, Balcomb and Horn in *Azusa* 1.1 for more examples of explicit politically right wing involvement by charismatics. Consider Chikane's response to McCauley's insistence that Nelson Mandela must state openly that he is a Christian and that he should sever his ties with the South African Communist Party. Cf. I. Van der Linde, 'Ray McCauley. Van Mnr. Republiek Tot Johannes Die Doper in 'n Synerspak', *Vrye Weekblad* (January 19–25, 1991).

2. N. Horn, 'RPW En Kasa', *Vrye Weekblad* (26 January, 1990). De Klerk wanted to unban political parties unconditionally—Casa urged him not to do so until they forsake violence; De Klerk wanted to place a moratorium on capital punishment—Casa asked him to keep it intact; De Klerk wanted to repeal the state of security unconditionally—Casa urged him not to do so until all violence has stopped; De Klerk wanted to repeal *all* apartheid laws—Casa was satisfied to ask him to go on with reform. See also *Natal Witness*, 1984.

3. *Evangelical Witness in South Africa*, p. 32; *A Relevant Pentecostal Witness*, p. 8.

'pre-De Klerks': they concentrated on personal sins and omitted corporate sins of racism and oppression. It must be stated that Ray McCauley has positioned himself away from his former right wing image. Although tensions remain between McCauley and progressive Pentecostals-charismatics-evangelicals, he is gaining credibility daily.

RPW members voice concern that this change is simply one facet of Ray McCauley's dynamic personality and his ability to adapt to new situations and challenges. This does not mean that they question his bona fides, but they do feel that as long as the new insights of McCauley and other leaders are not reflected in their theology, less sincere charismatic leaders will simply jump on the bandwagon without the experience of a change of heart. It could also be possible for charismatics in the faith movement to lose their prophetic relevance the moment right wing politics regains credibility and power.[1]

The widespread absence of black leaders is an inflammatory issue. While critical blacks point to the absence of black leadership in white-led multiracial churches, white charismatics state their willingness to share leadership with blacks, provided that it does not bear the marks of tokenism. However, it must be pointed out that even moderate white charismatic leaders like Kobus Swart of Bizweni and evangelist Gerald Kennedy see the absence of black leadership in most multiracial churches as a sign of racial prejudice.[2] Closely linked with this point is accusation that the white charismatic leaders are often paternalistic in their approach towards black pastors in their own ranks. At the meeting between IFCC and CMN on the one hand and RPW and CE on the other, prominent black Christian leader Ceaser Molebatsi accused Ray McCauley of this.[3]

Oppressed people of South Africa took specific actions which led to the fall of apartheid. It was not a mere change of heart in the white community which convinced the Nationalist Party to change its path. There is no doubt that the disinvestment, boycott (cultural, athletics, etc.) and sanction campaign was *the* factor that brought apartheid to

1.   Relevant Pentecostal Witness General Annual Meeting 1991, *Reports by J. Lapoorta, R. Maharaj and T. Balcomb on Meeting between IFCC, CMN, CE and RPW* (Durban: The Relevant Pentecostals, 1991).

2.   Personal telephone conversation with Kobus Swart (Windhoek–Somerset West, May, 1991); Personal telephone conversation with Gerald Kennedy (Windhoek, May, 1991).

3.   *Reports on Meeting between IFCC, CMN, CE and RPW.*

its knees. Charismatic churches have almost without exception rejected disinvestments and sanctions. By so stating, one cannot unilaterally condemn charismatic churches. Sanctions and disinvestments pose a difficult ethical issue. Many politicians and Christians accepted the value of sanctions and disinvestments, but could not support the campaign because they feared ruination of the South African economy.

In 1988 the Mass Democratic Movement initiated a defiance campaign. Thousands of black people defied apartheid laws all over the country. Initially the police and defense force tried to stop thousands of peaceful demonstrators from entering 'whites-only' amenities like beaches, parks, libraries and leisure resorts. The defiance campaign was rejected by most of the white Pentecostal and faith churches on the grounds that Christians are commanded to submit to civil authority. However, many restoration oriented charismatic churches and leaders actively participated in the campaign. If faith leaders participated in the campaign, it was in spite of their theology, while restorationists expect Christians to move ahead with the restoration of all things, including politics and government.

The fact that law and order continued after Namibian independence, that whites stayed in the country, and that the United Nations' supervised elections took place peacefully played a major role in the dismantling of apartheid. It is not coincidental that President De Klerk announced his new political vision only two months after the Namibian elections. The independence of Namibia has never been an issue among charismatics and perhaps very few faith churches supported it.

The paper by the Hexhams can be commended as a contribution to the ongoing debate between charismatics and assorted academicians. They are correct to argue that charismatics, including the faith movement, have done more than any other dominant white religious group in South Africa to normalize race relations. Pentecostals and mainline Christians are the last people who have the right to point fingers at the charismatics.

However, like all of us, charismatics cannot stop here and think their obligation complete to elevate the oppressed in South Africa. Charismatics need to listen carefully to the voices of their estranged brothers and sisters. Leaders such as Ray McCauley and Derek Morphew are to be commended for starting this journey. It is my prayer that the relationship between RPW and CE on the one hand and IFCC and CMN on the other will grow in understanding and love under the power of the Holy Spirit. Nkosi Sikelel iAfrika!!

A RESPONSE TO KARLA POEWE-HEXHAM AND IRVING HEXHAM

Wynand J. de Kock

It is a great opportunity for me to be able to respond to this paper. Little is required to convince a South African Pentecostal to respond to a paper on this topic presented by non-South Africans at an international gathering of Pentecostals and Charismatics. Add to this that the authors are observers and not themselves participants in the movement, and one can quickly discern that the dynamics are right for a lively and, I hope, a fruitful discussion.

It seems to me that the authors attempt to do the following four things. First, they describe Charismatics and their critics in South Africa. Second, they place methodological and ethical questions on the table for discussion. This is done in approximately forty pages (in the first draft), followed by another seventeen pages in part two on the same problem. Third, the authors seek to construct an ethical code for social research, a direct result of which would be a more equitable treatment of Charismatics in social research. Fourth, this extensive prolegomenon gives way to an interpretative analysis of quantitative and qualitative data which results in a preliminary profile of Charismatics in South Africa.

This lengthy analysis may be formulated in a thesis-statement as follows: that the Charismatic churches in South Africa are playing a role in the formation of a new culture in South Africa, by providing the opportunity for exposure to and interaction with people from different racial backgrounds.

There are several things for which I would like to express appreciation to the authors, not least of which is their effort to ensure that social analysis of the Charismatic movement is conducted in a professional and unbiased fashion. Also to be affirmed is the preliminary profile of Charismatics which based on my experience is generally true. Unfortunately, time constraints prevent me from identifying additional constructive aspects. Rather, I believe that it will be more profitable to identify the areas of major concern or areas where I want to push the discussion further.

My concern is with the interpretation of the quantitative and qualitative data. First, I must admit that I am a bit puzzled that in the otherwise extensive discussion of the geographical distribution of Charismatic churches, the authors are strangely silent about the Charismatic movement in the Orange Free State (OFS), a province significant both in size and its ethnic composition. It is apparent from their paper that they are aware that a strong Charismatic fellowship exists in Bloemfontein, the capital of the Orange Free State whose pastor is Johan Volmalter. Does this mean that the authors believe that the Charismatic movement in the OFS is numerically insignificant, or that their contribution to the struggle against apartheid is negligible?

My second concern in the quantitative and qualitative analysis is the authors' preoccupation with 'mega' churches and successful affluent leaders. We are never told why 'mega' churches are apparently considered to be representative of the movement and why smaller fellowships are excluded from consideration. Such an approach tends to skew the analysis from the very beginning. This is in part due to the fact that large churches in S.A. often are *not* community based because they draw their constituency from all over the cities. It would be interesting to know how such churches would compare with smaller community based fellowships regarding social involvement.

In a similar vein, the authors' limited leadership sample, comprised primarily of either 'privileged' whites or blacks who were able to break through the middle class barrier, also presents a problem. This procedure is flawed in that it excludes from consideration the voices of those who have not traditionally been allowed to speak, but from whom we have much to learn on the topic. It perpetuates the myth that when one has heard from leaders in a position of privilege, one has heard from the people. An example of this is the way in which the missionary exploits of representatives of this group are merely assumed, with no attempt to verify their 'success' by means of data gathered from the townships themselves.

Still another weakness of the qualitative and quantitative analysis is the authors' failure to identify the differences between the two main groupings of Charismatics in S.A., including their failure to explain their origins. If the researchers had pushed further on this topic, they would have discovered that the two groups are less compatible than they assumed. The opinion of Dr Derek Morphew, obtained in a personal interview, demonstrates this point. Morphew remarks that the IFCC and the CMN could not work under the same umbrella since they are different in three areas.

a.   Theologically: IFCC is theologically in line with Kenyonism, while CMN is more in line with evangelical tenets of faith. The CMN is also being influenced by John Wimber and Terry Virgo. Morphew recently criticized Kenyonism as a modern manifestation of gnosticism in *The Spiritual Spider Web: A Study of Ancient and Modern Gnosticism* (Associated Christian Ministries, 1991). The IFCC also tends to be more dispensational in its eschatology, while the CMN is, thanks to the influence of Virgo, Wimber and others, more interested in 'Kingdom Theology'.

b.   Politically: The IFCC has aligned itself with the powers that be. The CMN could not do so because of its ties with pro-gressive black leaders.

c.   Structurally, the IFCC churches tend to be more hierarchical while the CMN is moving away from this leadership style (May, 1991).

Because the researchers fail to distinguish between the two groups in this way, they also fail to see that the groups may respond differ-ently to the situation in S.A. It would be very interesting to know: What is the actual eschatology of the two groups? How does this affect the praxis (socio-political involvement) of the two groupings? What are the political affiliations of the two groups?

A final concern with the analysis of the authors has to do with their preliminary profile of Charismatics. While the profile is helpful in many ways, there is no attempt to translate its results into language which addresses the particulars of the South African situation.

Before identifying issues for further discussion or reflection, I would like to make an observation about the relevance of this paper as a whole. It strikes me that this paper is quite outdated.

A primary reason for this is that the research concerns itself with the Charismatic church(es) in S.A. prior to 1989. But we have lived 'light years' in South Africa since 1989, and the terrain has changed almost daily. I would lift up two events as examples. First, on

February 2, 1990, president F.W. de Klerk informed the country and
the world of his intentions to dismantle apartheid, an event that caught
the liberation movements and churches off guard. A second example
of change was the Rustenburg Conference which brought all churches
together. At this conference, churches confessed their sinful participation in apartheid. It is significant to note that a joint confession of
sin was made by the two Charismatic associations and it reads as
follows:

> We recognise our guilt in that our opposition to Apartheid did not go far
> enough, nor was it effectively expressed.
>
> Our statements and convictions were often not put adequately into
> practical action.
>
> As a result we were often silent when our sisters and brothers were
> suffering persecution.
>
> We confess that our silence in these areas was in fact a sin and that our
> failure to act decisively against all forms of Apartheid made us party to an
> inhuman political ideology.
>
> We, therefore, confess our failure and repent of our sin and declare our
> complete rejection of all forms of racism and the evil and unjust system of
> Apartheid. Please forgive us.
>
> Further, as part of the family of God, we declare our resolve to play an
> active and positive role in ensuring that all people will receive an equal
> opportunity to take part in all forms of political, economic and social life
> in a post-Apartheid South Africa (CMN Circular, 1991).

This confession implies that the contribution of the Charismatic
churches is less, in their own eyes, than the authors would suggest.
I close with the following questions:

1. Were Charismatics in predominant Afrikaans areas (i.e.
    tribalized Afrikaners) more reluctant to commit themselves
    to social action than Afrikaners in predominantly English
    environments?
2. Do the researchers consider 'mega' churches as representa-
    tives of the Charismatic movements in South Africa, and if
    so, why?

3. Is it accurate to use the title 'Charismatics' for the two associations only? What about Charismatics in mainline churches and Roman Catholic Charismatics or even 'Pentecostal Charismatics'? How have these Charismatics responded to the South African situation?

AFRICAN INDEPENDENT CHURCH PNEUMATOLOGY AND THE SALVATION OF ALL CREATION

M.L. Daneel

Ever since the beginning of this century African Independent Churches (AICs) have taken root, proliferated and shown phenomenal growth throughout the continent, particularly in sub-Saharan Africa.[1] Because many of these churches originated through a variety of schismatic processes within Western oriented mission churches (either large scale schisms or individual defections), they were often characterized negatively as 'separatist', 'parasitic', 'nativistic' or 'sectarian' movements.[2] In Christian terms they were considered either non-Christian movements whose members should be approached as objects of mission or evangelism (to be baptized or rebaptized into mission church folds), or marginally Christian because of their alleged syncretism, and therefore not properly belonging to the mainstream of Christianity— the so-called 'mainline churches'.

In contrast to these one-sidedly condemnatory views I wish to point out that despite obvious limitations (notably the lack of a written theology) and with the exception of those movements which deliberately move away from a Christian position,[3] I consider the AICs on the whole to be *integral to the mainstream of Christianity*. Most of them accept and apply Scripture as literally and fundamentally

---

1. D.B. Barrett, *Schism and Renewal in Africa: An Analysis of Six Thousand Contemporary Religious Movements* (London: Oxford University Press, 1968), pp. 78-79; M.L. Daneel, *Quest for Belonging: Introduction to a Study of African Independent Churches* (Gweru: Mambo Press, 1987), p. 25; N.I. Ndiokwere, *Prophecy and Revolution: The Role of Prophets in the African Independent Churches and in Biblical Tradition* (London: 1981), p. 281.

2. H.W. Turner, 'A Typology of African Religious Movements', *Journal of Religion in Africa* (1967), *passim*; Daneel, *Quest for Belonging*, pp. 28-29.

3. Turner, *African Independent Church* (2 vols.; Oxford: Oxford University Press, 1967); Daneel, *Quest for Belonging*, pp. 35-36.

normative. Belief in a triune God, the reign and closeness of a creator father, the saviourhood and mediation of Christ and the pervasive presence of an indwelling Holy Spirit, together with the regular or intermittent practice of the sacraments of baptism and holy communion, are common and key features of these churches.[1] Their enacted theology, moreover, represents a sensitive and innovative response to Africa's existential needs and must be seen as a central—if not the most important and authentic part—of African theology. Consistent with this view is the assertion that the AICs constitute an integral and legitimate part of the universal church and that their response to the gospel, their belief systems and missionary strategy are well worth considering in a context such as this conference where the world-wide evangelistic outreach of Christ's church is focal.

One need only consider the current growth and size of some of the AICs to realize their significance. In South Africa alone an estimated 5,000 AICs represent between 30 and 40 percent of the total black population. The Zion Christian Church (ZCC) of Bishop Lekhanyane with its millions of adherents all over South Africa is probably growing faster than any other church in the country. Among the Northern Sotho-speaking people, for instance, where the ZCC has its headquarters, the growth rates of the various churches in the period 1970–80 were as follows: Independent Churches 173.8 per cent; Roman Catholic Church 83 per cent; and Dutch Reformed Church 59.9 per cent. Most other churches grew at a rate below the 43.7 per cent of the Northern Sotho population growth rate.[2] Among the three groups showing significant growth, the Independent Churches far outstripped the others.

In Zimbabwe the Independents in many of the rural areas represent 50 per cent or more of the Christian population.[3] The larger Spirit-type churches, such as the African Apostolic Church of Johane Maranke, the Zion Christian Church of Bishop Mutendi and the Ndaza (holy cord) Zionist movement together have several million

1. Daneel, *Quest for Belonging*, pp. 223-24, 250-51.
2. J.J. Kritzinger, *Die onvoltooide sendingtaak in Lebowa* (Pretoria, 1982), p. 65.
3. See e.g. the statistical analysis of church growth in the Chingombe chiefdom, Gutu district, in M.L. Daneel, *Old and New in Southern Shona Independent Churches*. II. *Church Growth: Causative Factors and Recruitment Techniques* (The Hague: Mouton, 1974), ch. 1.

adherents. The Kimbanguist church in Zaire is the largest independent church of the continent with more than eight million members. In West Africa the Aladura churches represent a vast and still growing movement.[1]

For classification purposes a distinction can be made between the Pentecostally oriented Spirit-type prophetic churches and the so-called 'Ethiopian' or non-prophetic groups.[2] Some observers also distinguish a third messianic category, where a prophetic leader usurps the position of Christ and poses as a black messiah.[3] This, however, can be a highly misleading classification. Despite some messianic trends it rarely happens that prominent prophetic leaders deliberately attempt to supersede the mediatorship of Christ by posing as Christ figures.[4] It is more appropriate to speak of iconic leadership in those cases where prophets closely identify with the Christ figure in an attempt to illuminate dramatically and contextually the salvific gospel message.[5]

Significantly, the vast majority of AICs, in southern Africa at least, are of the prophetic type. They reveal definite Pentecostal traits, in that the Holy Spirit features prominently in their worship and daily activities. 'Jordan' or adult baptism is directly related to the conversion experience. Spirit-induced faith healing and exorcism become focal in Christian living. The Spirit, moreover, is believed to manifest itself through the visions, dreams, prophecies and/or glossolalia of the believers. It follows that numerical growth, geographical expansion and the development of church headquarters at the holy cities—the 'Zions', 'Moriahs' or 'Jerusalems' of Africa—are attributed directly to the activity of the Holy Spirit.

Although in many respects this characterization is equally applicable to Western Pentecostalism, there are essential differences. These should become apparent in my discussion of a few important pneumatological tenets underlying the practices of the Spirit-type AICs. But

---

1.   Turner, *African Independent Church*.

2.   M.L. Daneel, *Old and New in Southern Shona Independent Churches*. I. *Background and Rise of the Major Movements* (The Hague: Mouton, 1971), chs. 4, 5; *Quest for Belonging*, pp. 38-39.

3.   B.G.M. Sundkler, *Bantu Prophets in South Africa* (London: Oxford University Press, 1961), p. 323.

4.   Daneel, *Quest for Belonging*, pp. 189-90.

5.   B.G.M. Sundkler, *Zulu Zion and Some Swazi Zionists* (London: Oxford University Press, 1976), p. 309.

this is not in the first place a comparative study of Western and African Pentecostalism. On the contrary, I shall merely sketch briefly the AIC experience of the working of the Holy Spirit. The admittedly limited pneumatological profile which emerges, both in its historical contextuality and in its relevance for an interpretation of salvation, may present a challenge and/or inspiration for the ongoing missionary task of the universal church.

In probing for the essentials of AIC pneumatology I am engaged as a fellow Independent coming from a Protestant (Dutch Reformed) background. In the course of many years of identification with and participation in the life of the Shona Independent Churches in Zimbabwe I have become part of that movement. Consequently my observations and insights are based mainly on the AICs of Zimbabwe. Special attention will be given to the two largest Spirit-type churches in that part of the world: Bishop Samuel Mutendi's ZCC and Apostle Johane Maranke's vaPostori. Since both these founder leaders have passed away and have been succeeded by their sons, I wish to present this paper in truly African fashion, that is in commemoration of two of the outstanding missionary spirits of our continent. By now they belong to the Christian cloud of witnesses, so their message to the world church is essentially the one they proclaimed so fervently to their followers: salvation in Christ and renewal through the Holy Spirit to the four corners of the earth!

1. *The Holy Spirit as Saviour of Humankind*

Before they founded their own churches, Bishop Mutendi and Apostle Maranke were members of the Dutch Reformed and Methodist churches respectively. Both of them were attracted by the Pentecostal features of the Independent Churches they came across,[1] both in South Africa (Mutendi) and Zimbabwe (Maranke). As a result the work of the Holy Spirit featured prominently in their campaigning activities right from the start. Their ministries were preceded by call-dreams, visions and spells of Spirit-possessed speaking in tongues, which both of them considered to be the visible manifestations of a missionary mandate received directly from God.

In the ZCC Rungano (the handbook of Mutendi's church) the

---

1. Daneel, *Old and New*, I, pp. 287-88, 315-16.

leader's first important sermon in 1923 in the Bikita district is
described as follows:

> He stood up and preached with great power from Luke 3, as he was told
> to do by the prophets...Many believers were possessed by the Holy
> Spirit. The people present got frightened and some of them ran away,
> saying: 'That man arouses [vengeful spirits which destroy cattle]'...
> Some people laughed when they saw the others getting possessed by the
> Spirit...From that day Mutendi never stopped preaching the Word of
> God, and he was greatly strengthened by that same Spirit.[1]

Johane Maranke's visionary spells are recorded in his *Umboo utsva
hwavaPostori* (New Revelation of the Apostles). He is said to have
received directly from God two books which he could only understand through the inspiration of the Holy Spirit and not through the
education he had received at the European mission station. The contents of these books held the message of eternal life (*sadza risingaperi*:
literally, porridge, i.e. food, of eternal life), and it is this message of
salvation for human beings which became focal in Johane's sermons.
In his visions Johane saw himself like a Moses figure, leading his
followers from many countries through hostile terrain and fires to a
safe, heavenly destination. The host of followers was likened to the
sand on the shores of Lake Nyasa in Malawi.[2]

The ministries of both these prophetic leaders were characterized
by awareness of the lostness and sinfulness of humanity and the urgent
need for conversion and baptism as a means of avoiding God's judgment through entry into his kingdom. God himself was the one
responsible for drawing people into his kingdom (Jn. 6.44). The Holy
Spirit was the main agent directing the judgment prophecies against
sinners and unaware ministers in mission churches, the healing
miracles in and around baptismal pools or rivers, and the building of
new communities of the kingdom. The prominence of and dependence
on the Spirit are clearly portrayed in the song which the vaPostori of
Johane have sung ever since the inception of their church near Mutare
in eastern Zimbabwe in 1932:

1.   Zion Christian Church, *Rungano* 19; Daneel, *Old and New*, I, p. 294.
2.   *New Revelation*, pp. 2-3.

Everywhere we see people who do not know Christ,
They are lost, that is why they sin,
Our mighty God send the Holy Spirit to those who do not have it.
God bless Africa and hear our prayers; God bless it!
Come Holy Spirit, come Holy Spirit, come Holy Spirit!
Bless us your servants.

In both movements the Holy Spirit provides the full charter for the new church. All the laws and customs of the church, the innovations and deviations from Western Christianity, are justified by attributing them directly to the inspiration and command of the Holy Spirit. In a sense therefore the Spirit legitimates the exodus from the religious house of slavery, the reign of the white mission churches. Salvation takes the form of black liberation from foreign institutions where the full benefit of the gifts of the Spirit was allegedly withheld from black converts. The reaction to missions during this first phase of new AIC formation finds its most poignant expression in the allegation that white Christianity dropped the banner of the Holy Spirit and that this banner has now been picked up by Africans, the black, rejected (by whites) house of Ham. Consequently the black race of Africa—the neglected, the poor and the oppressed—are now the exalted and the elect, called by the Holy Spirit to spread the true message of salvation throughout the continent.

How was this to be achieved? Both leaders responded to the challenge by designing their churches as missionary institutions in which the sacrament of holy communion was to become the launching pad from which wave upon wave of Zionist and Apostolic missionaries was sent forth to preach the good news of salvation to their fellow Africans.

Bishop Mutendi developed his church headquarters as a 'holy city' where he conducted at least three Paschal celebrations annually, each culminating in holy communion. In preparation for the sacrament Mutendi used to preach about the great commission (Mt. 28.19), encouraging his followers to prepare themselves, like Christ's disciples, to 'go forth and make disciples of all the nations'. In his treatment of Mt. 28.19 Mutendi seldom dwelt on the actual meaning of the words, 'all the nations', and he rarely defined the actual object of missionary endeavour. Instead he gave the text a specific Zionist connotation by relating it to such texts as Isa. 62.1: 'For Zion's sake I will not hold my peace, and for Jerusalem's sake I will not rest'. In addition he would protest against the half-hearted response of some of his followers to the church's mission by citing Rom. 11.25 which deals with the hardening of the Israelites' hearts.[1]

Following the climactic celebration of holy communion, the ZCC teams of missionaries would set out on properly planned two- to three-week campaigns all over Zimbabwe and sometimes beyond its borders. Meanwhile the congregation at Zion City engaged in daily intercession for the campaign. Upon the return of the emissaries, their reports on conversions, healings, establishment of new congregations, church growth, and so on, were preached to the people at Zion City. Thus the entire church participated actively in a variety of ways in fulfilling its missionary mandate.

Johane Maranke interpreted his calling as an Apostle not in terms of building a holy city, but in setting a personal example—together with a band of fellow Apostles—as an itinerant missionary. For just over thirty years, from the founding of his church in 1932 until his death in 1963, he travelled—on foot, by ox cart, then by bicycle, and ultimately in a Landrover—preaching the gospel, converting people and establishing new congregations. In his church the annual 'Pentecost' ceremony—in commemoration of the Holy Spirit's institution of the movement—became the pivot of spiritual renewal and missionary outreach. Here, too, the ritual of holy communion was the overriding statement on Christ's Saviourhood, triggering waves of Apostolic evangelizing activity. Apart from campaigns throughout Zimbabwe, Johane regularly travelled south as far as the Transvaal, westwards to Botswana, east to Mozambique and north to Zambia, Malawi and far up into Zaire; overall he and his fellow preachers converted and baptized hundreds of thousands of people.[2]

Johane's ministry as a travelling missionary was—quite remarkably —undertaken on the basis of an agrarian subsistence economy. Budding Apostolic congregations all over Zimbabwe and in the surrounding countries, consisting mainly of relatively poor peasant families in rural areas, supported—both economically and spiritually—what they considered to be the salvific movement of God's Spirit in their midst.

In both Mutendi's ZCC History and Johane's *New Revelation*, salvation, conversion and baptism into the kingdom in preparation for eternal life (in the sense of the Holy Spirit drawing individuals to

1. M.L. Daneel, 'The Missionary Outreach of African Independent Churches', *Missionalia* 8.3 (1980), p. 107.

2. Daneel, *Old and New*, I, pp. 327-31.

repentance) are set against a background of God's imminent judgment. This remains focal in both Zionist and Apostolic evangelistic outreach. During the 1960s I accompanied some of the ZCC missionaries on their campaigns. Their appeal for individual conversion was direct and blunt. 'To those who do not believe God's Word', the Revd Ezekiah proclaimed,

> there will be gnashing of teeth on the day of judgment... My friends, we have not come to put up a show or to show you how to dance, but to warn you of the coming danger... Even love between people on this earth comes to an end. My friends, let us believe what the Bible says in order to be saved... *Pindukai! Pindukai! Pindukai!* [be converted].

In Ezekiah's sermons the destructive power of God's judgment was always expressed in terms of the biblical deluge, the destroying sword of Ezekiel 33 or the pit of fire (*gomba romwoto*). Such destruction could only be avoided by seeking shelter in God's kingdom, symbolized in this existence by the Zionist Church and, in the African context, likened to a maize granary (*dura*). The real purpose of ZCC evangelization, then, is to gather people into the *dura raMwari*—the granary of God, where they would be safe from eternal damnation. It is to this end that the missionary activities of Mutendi, the 'man of God', and the mighty stir of the Holy Spirit is directed.

Ezekiah's elucidation of the granary concept highlighted the eschatological tension between the partly realized kingdom and the one yet to come. On the one hand there were the this-worldly benefits of church affiliation, and of Zion City as a shelter against racial discrimination, illness, witchcraft, and the like. On the other hand suffering (e.g. the persecution of Zionists) remains, 'for we have not here an abiding city, but we seek after the city which is to come.' (Heb. 13.14). Ezekiah's frequent use of this text to emphasize the apocalyptic, futuristic character of God's kingdom meant that his campaigning sermons—like those of his fellow missionaries—centred more on the eschatological 'not yet' than on the 'already' of God's kingdom.[1]

Here we have a significant indicator that AIC pneumatology, as perceived in the prophetic churches, is not confined to this-worldly salvation, despite strong trends in this direction (see below). Ever since the inception of these two churches, the good news of their

---

1.   Daneel, 'Missionary Outreach', pp. 112-13.

missionary proclamation implicitly upheld the eschatological tension between an incarnate Christ present in the prophetic leader and the work of the Holy Spirit here and now, and the yet to be fulfilled eternal salvation of human beings.

2. *The Spirit as Healer and Protector*

Although the healing ministry of Christ featured strongly in the proclamation and practice of both Zionist and Apostolic churches from the outset, it was only in the 1940s and 1950s that there was a shift of the pneumatological focus. During this period faith-healing colonies were established at Mutendi's Zion City in Bikita and at the homesteads of several Apostolic healers in the vicinity of Johane's headquarters in the Maranke chiefdom. In both instances the dwindling of mission church influence, the powerful drive towards genuine contextualization of church practice, and the amplification and diversification of the main leader's prophetic task through the activities of a host of subordinate prophetic healers operating daily in the healing colonies, contributed to change. Church life started revolving to a large extent around faith healing. Healing interpreted in its widest sense (i.e. not only of physical maladies, but also of the 'illness' of oppression, racial discrimination, lack of job opportunities, conflicts between spouses, family members, factions, etc.) became the most potent recruitment instrument in these churches.

Healing and protection against evil forces now manifested more than anything else the pervasive presence of the powerful Spirit of God. Speaking in tongues became the prelude to all prophetic diagnostic sessions, during which the Holy Spirit would reveal to the prophet the cause of the patient's illness. All symbols used during healing rituals, such as holy water, paper, staffs and holy cords, symbolized the power of the Holy Spirit over all destructive forces. 'Jordan' baptisms increasingly became purificatory, healing and exorcist sessions during which the power of the Spirit to expel all evil was persuasively evident. Witness preaching about successful healing became focal, and in Mutendi's case Zion City started to represent an African Jerusalem in which the triumphal reign of Christ, through the Holy Spirit, permeated every activity. In a sense the Holy Spirit had turned the Black Zion of Africa into a haven for the afflicted, the lost, the poor, the widows, orphans and social misfits.

Increasingly the liturgy of these prophetic churches reflected their preoccupation with healing. The very songs sung during daily prayer, Bible reading and healing sessions challenged all comers to consider God's acts of transforming human brokenness into wholeness. At Zion City one frequently hears the following words, sung jubilantly:

> Come and see what Jesus does,
> Come and see what Moyo [Mutendi] here performs.
> Come from the East and look
> You from the West, come and observe what Zion does.
> You who are sick, to Zion for treatment come!
> Come and see!
> You epileptics, come and be healed,
> Come and see what Jesus does.
> The other day we were with him
> Last night we were in his sight
> Last year we were with him
> Even today he's with us
> Come and see what Zion does!

A close scrutiny of the *diagnosis* and *therapy* of prophetic healers reveals both parallels with and deviations from traditional divination and healing practices. It is at this level, so crucially important to both healer and patient, that there is a continual dialogue between contextualized Christian and traditional African world views. Here an intuitive and unwritten, yet very real African theology takes shape. Here, too, AIC pneumatology finds its existentially most meaningful expression.

a. *Diagnosis*

All prophetic consultations start with prayer and speaking in tongues, to recognize and establish in the mind of the patient(s) the presence of the Holy Spirit as the source of revelation. Yet to the casual observer the prophet's obvious concern—much like that of the *nganga* (traditional doctor)—with the personal causation of illness (be it ancestral spirits, vengeful spirits or witchcraft) appears to be sufficient evidence of a return to the old order and a warning against syncretism. Significantly, however, the prophet claims an entirely different source for his extra-perception, namely the Holy Spirit of the Bible, as opposed to the *nganga* who relies on divinatory slabs (*hakata*), ancestral or *shavi* (alien) spirits for divination. This does not mean that all prophetic claims in the name of the Holy Spirit are valid or genuine. But the prophetic insistence on the direct involvement of the Holy Spirit reflects an important departure from traditional divination. For prophetic diagnosis, unlike traditional divination, is not aimed at satisfying the demands of the afflicting spirits. Instead, through revelations inspired by the Christian God, the prophet seeks to take the thought world and experience of the patient seriously and to introduce, at an existentially important level, the healing and salvific power of the Christian God.

A sure sign of the Christian prophet's more critical approach, compared to that of the *nganga*, is his general qualification of the afflicting spirit, once it has been identified in terms of traditional conflict patterns, as a demon or evil spirit which must be opposed. This is a far cry from the early observations of Sundkler, who suggested that in Zulu Zionism in South Africa the inspiring Angel or Spirit visiting the prophet-healer was in reality the ancestral spirit itself;[1] also the statements of Oosthuizen who saw prophetic concern with the spirit world as a reversion to ancestor domination at the expense of genuine Christianity.[2] To the Shona Zionist and Apostolic prophet, however, the work of the Holy Spirit excludes any form of ancestor worship or veneration. Compromise solutions are only prescribed in family conflicts when patients are pressurized by non-Christian relatives to produce sacrificial beasts to appease afflicting spirits with legitimate claims in terms of customary law. In such instances the threatening spirit is exorcised by the prophet-healer in the church context, while traditionalist relatives conduct an appeasing ancestral ritual on their own. Thus the liberating power of the Holy Spirit is ritually acknowledged and family conflicts are resolved in order to create the best possible circumstance for successful therapy.

b. *Therapy*
After the diagnosis of illness, the similarity between *nganga* and prophetic activity ceases. Both trace the origin of disease to a disturbed society. Both recognize the disruptive effect of evil powers unleashed in interhuman relations. But they ward off these powers differently. While the *nganga* seeks a solution which accedes to the conditions of the spirits, prophetic therapy is based on belief in the

1. *Bantu Prophets*, p. 250.
2. G.C. Oosthuizen, *Post-Christianity in Africa: A Theological and Anthropological Study* (London: C. Hurst, 1968), p. 120.

liberating power of the Christian God, particularly the Holy Spirit, which surpasses all other powers and is consequently capable of offering protection against them.

In an attempt to restore disrupted social relations the *nganga* advocates ancestor veneration in the case of neglected ancestors, and the expulsion of evil witchcraft or vengeful *ngozi* spirits through magical rites. To the Zionist and Apostolic prophet the ancestral claim to sacrificial veneration is inadmissible on biblical grounds. Once identified (as an ancestral, alien or witchcraft spirit) the afflicting agent is qualified by the healer-prophet as a demon or *mweya yakaipa* (evil spirit). In true Christian tradition the prophet prescribes only one solution: exorcism of the demon in the name of the triune God! This is done by means of whichever one of a variety of dramatic exorcist rituals is applicable. Sometimes the spirit is virtually 'drowned' in Jordan water; or it may be tied down with holy cords or chased away by condemnatory curses. All such activity is designed to demonstrate vividly the Holy Spirit's triumphal power over evil. Even where a compromise solution is found to satisfy non-Christian relatives, the overriding aim of prophetic therapy remains the incorporation of the patient, or preferably the whole family, into the 'new community' of Zion or the Apostles, which in terms of the healer's convictions offers the best prospects of physical and spiritual security and well-being.

The extent to which therapeutic treatment of this nature enhances the image of the church as a healing and more specifically as a protective institution is clearly reflected in the observation of Elias Bope, a young epileptic who was treated for many years in Mutendi's Zion City. He said:

> My cousin and a vengeful [*ngozi*] spirit are conspiring to cause my downfall. I was carried here in a totally debilitated state. That same day I was baptized as a protection against the *ngozi*. The baptismal water [of 'Jordan'] was blessed with prayer beforehand to make it more potent for the *ngozi's* expulsion. At present I drink the hallowed water regularly and undergo the laying on of hands daily. Sometimes during fits of possession [presumably epileptic seizures] Bishop Mutendi treats me with his holy staff, which contains great power. This power [of the Holy Spirit] is

from on high. Here at Moriah I am protected against the *ngozi* spirit, and
for the time being I remain here, because I am shielded from the destructive attempts of my cousin.[1]

The question is whether this shift of focus in AIC pneumatology does
not lead to a one-sided and limited understanding of salvation. It
stands to reason that in the prophetic healing colonies salvation can
easily be identified with healing, since it includes the restoration of
harmony in interpersonal relations, as well as physical and material
well-being, in a society marked by conflict, suffering and deprivation.
In theological terms this tendency can be described as an overemphasis
on this-worldly progress, on a realized eschatology. God's kingdom
must take on concrete form here and now! The Spirit saves and uplifts
humankind in this existence through his prophets, the totality of whose
activities is a sure sign of God's blessing on his African Zion or
Apostles.

Several theologians have criticized this trend in the AICs. Mention
is often made of a secularistic or materialistic distortion of eschatology. Oosthuizen, for example, maintained that in all 'nativistic'
religious movements (which would include the Shona prophetic
churches) the objective is material well-being—an Africanized utopia
in which Christ plays no role and where the black messiah effects
health, fertility and material progress for his disciples.[2] The profoundly felt need for liberation from physical and social suffering
makes the message of a future salvation a stumbling block. Full salvation must be available now. Consequently, according to Martin,[3] the
prophetic quest is for healing rather than redemption. In this version
of salvation the eschatological tension between the 'already' and 'not
yet' of God's kingdom lapses. Because the future kingdom is to be
taken by force—as Martin[4] and Oosthuizen[5] put it, there is a 'seizing'
and a 'snatching' of the future—the prospect of eternal life and the
hope of Christ's second coming is lost.

In my view, however, empirical reality does not warrant such a

1. M.L. Daneel, 'Charismatic Healing in African Independent Churches',
Theologia Evangelica XVI/3 (1983), p. 39.
2. Oosthuizen, *Post-Christianity*, p. 96.
3. M.-L. Martin, *The Biblical Concept of Messianism and Messianism in
Southern Africa* (Morija: Lesotho Book Depot, 1964), p. 158.
4. Martin, *Biblical Concept of Messianism*, p. 160.
5. Oosthuizen, *Post-Christianity*, p. 97.

harsh judgment. The manifestly heavy emphasis on Spirit-inspired realization of God's kingdom in this existence, in the case of the Shona Zionists and Apostles, does not lead to a so-called 'snatching of the future'. The shift of pneumatological focus resulting from the Zionist and Apostolic preoccupation with healing and protection is not absolute. One should rather speak of an extended, more comprehensive and holistic interpretation of salvation, which at no point excludes the kind of conversion or missionary proclamation described above. The themes of a futuristic kingdom and ultimate eternal salvation for individual beings keep recurring in the Zionist and Apostolic sermons preached in their holy cities and healing colonies. Pneumatologically, the work of the Holy Spirit comprises both eternal salvation for a redeemed humanity and a concretely experienced wholeness and well-being in this existence for those who place themselves in faith under his healing care. Hence the good news of eternal salvation is not superseded but acquires concrete and understandable contours through healing in this troubled and broken existence.

3. *The Spirit of Justice and Liberation*

In the prophetic movements the activity of the Holy Spirit has never been conceived of as restricted to spiritual matters or healing. At an early stage Bishop Mutendi entered the political arena by opposing the colonial administration on educational, land and religious issues, for which he was detained several times. To his followers he became a Spirit-led Moses figure, champion of the oppressed. Like Shembe of the Zulu Nazarites in South Africa, Mutendi drew many chiefs and headmen into his church. Through regular advice to these tribal dignitaries and the appointment of Zionist prophets in their tribal courts, the Zionist bishop managed to secure considerable influence in tribal political affairs. During the 1950s and 1960s many of the Zionist chiefs openly stated that the power of the Holy Spirit, represented by supportive prophets, enabled them to maintain some form of just rule and balance amid the complex and conflicting demands of white colonial rule and the rising tide of black nationalism. They also considered the role of prophetic court counsellors to be crucial for fair trials, both in the administration of customary law and in harmonizing these laws with Christian principles in a changing situation.

As a descendant of the royal Rozvi tribe, Mutendi, in the context of his impressive 'Zion City', also appealed to the sentiments of tribal leaders who had not forgotten the past glories of the once powerful Rozvi dynasty. Mutendi represented the supratribal unity which had once been the backbone of a great nation. In addition to Zionist religious connotations, his popular title ('man of God') had distinct political overtones to many of his followers. Zion City became a safe spiritual anchorage for tribal dignitaries, a place where they could discuss the pressing issues of boundary disputes, unruly tribesmen and even intimidation by extremist politicians. Here a message of liberation could evolve. It was not a message which promised easy solutions or revolutionary change in the political constellation, as if sudden freedom from bondage would be ushered in by divine power. Basically it meant the presence of Mwari in his Spirit, which could liberate chiefs and headmen from fear and anxiety, enabling them to deal more effectively with the issues confronting them.

Just as Christ failed to introduce a messianic order which would satisfy Jewish nationalistic aspirations, Mutendi did not promise another Rozvi confederation or a Zionist empire which would overthrow white rule. But throughout his life he set an example to the chiefs of how one could realistically cooperate with the rulers of the day without loss of dignity and how one could fearlessly resist unjust legislation or action even if it did not always bring about the desired results. In a sense his Zion City became to the chiefs a halfway house between white local government and African nationalistic factions, a refuge where they could participate in the subtle resistance of their people to the imposition of foreign influence without entirely jeopardizing their position in relation to the white administration on which they depended financially. As Isaiah Shembe did for his 'Israelites' in South Africa, Bishop Mutendi presented his Zionist followers not with an indifferent, remote deity, but one who, through the power of the Spirit, manifested his involvement in the totality of life (politics in particular) as 'a God who walks on feet and who heals with his hands, and who can be known by men, as God who loves and has compassion'.[1]

Possibly the most dramatic episode of Spirit involvement in Mutendi's resistance to colonial rule was the Rozvi–Duma boundary dispute in Bikita, which came to a head in 1965. Mutendi's Zion City itself was situated in the disputed area and he organized the Rozvi chief's opposition to the District Commissioner's decision which

1.   Sundkler, *Bantu Prophets*, p. 278.

favoured a rival Duma chief's claim. Ultimately, when all else had failed, Mutendi sponsored and initiated legal action in the high court against such formidable colonial opponents as the Bikita District Commissioner, the Provincial Commissioner of the then Victoria Province and the Minister of Internal Affairs. The outcome was predictable. Mutendi had become too prominent an adversary to the administration, and the state machinery was set in motion to destroy the Rozvi bishop's power base.

I lived in Zion City at the time. The spiritual mobilization of the entire community during the months of uncertainty and stress while the 'man of God' did battle was a moving experience. Sermons became more intense. Regular prayer meetings were held on behalf of those involved in the struggle, and in a host of prophecies the Holy Spirit was considered to give guidance on future action which would lead to justice and liberation. But liberation in this instance did not mean the preservation of Zion City. Liberation meant suffering and loss. Liberation to the 'man of God' implied not compromising, overcoming fear, and, at the cost of the most prized achievement of a lifetime—a 'holy city' symbolizing African achievement—standing up and protesting against impossible odds.

As the Zionist chiefs and headmen rallied round their leader during a Paschal celebration before the court case, one of them, Chief Ndanga, preached as follows:

> Let those with the strong hearts stand up and stand by his [Mutendi's] side. Let this man build our hearts so that we will be humble people. Africa has started to listen to the voice of Mutendi... Allow this chief sent by God to examine your hearts. Praise him because he works through the spirit of Jesus!

Bishop Mutendi himself on the same occasion called his followers to be courageous:

> Fear not and do not be offended when people accuse you falsely. He who does not stay amongst the proud is blessed. The police and the prophets [i.e. the administration and the church] should first consider the word of God before setting about their tasks, if they want to perform well. In Zechariah 8 God says: 'I am back in Zion, the City of Jerusalem, therefore it will not be destroyed any longer'. We take these words to support us. This Jerusalem of ours will not be destroyed! Zion is small but strong. It will never die because it belongs to nobody but God.

These were prophetic words, inspired by the Spirit of liberation. Only as the message was translated into the ensuing events at Zion City did its real significance become evident. For it was Mutendi himself who, in the aftermath of bitter defeat, was liberated by the Spirit he propagated from bitterness, indecision and even from his ties with the settlement in Bikita. His vigour in leading a large contingent of Rozvi kinsmen and Zionist followers to settle in a remote area in Northern Gokwe, far away from his original sphere of influence, gave real meaning to his publicly declared conviction that Zion would not die, because it belonged to God. Like Moses of old, the aging bishop arranged the exodus of his people. In the course of only a few years another Zion City was erected in the far north of Zimbabwe, and the Zion Christian Church, instead of fizzling out, showed an increasing growth rate.

During the same period in the late sixties, the Apostles of Maranke voiced the mood of black nationalism in even more aggressive antiwhite statements than the Zionists. Here the interjections during sermons were not 'Peace in Zion' or 'Joy be with you all' but, challengingly and stridently, 'Peace to us Africans!' and even in some cases 'Peace to Africans only!' Feelings of naked resentment surfaced in the repeated accusations that the white race had killed Jesus and that the whites, in their oppression of the blacks, had deliberately repressed the message and benefits of the Holy Spirit.

At the Pentecostal festivities of the vaPostori near Mutare in April 1966, the following messages were preached:

> The true witnesses of Mwari were buried by the Europeans, until God gave them the task of witnessing to us, the Apostles of Africa. They killed Jesus and the early Apostles because they wanted to eliminate the Church of the Holy Spirit. So God decided to send the Church of the Holy Spirit to our race in Africa. Peace to Africa!

> The houses of Shem and Japheth were blessed long ago. Now we, the descendants of the house of Ham, are blessed! We are blessed because the prophecy of Isaiah, 'I will send them a leader of their own race', has come true. God sent us black people a leader to do the same things that were done by Moses in Egypt. My brothers, let us obey the message which a black man of Africa has brought us. A donkey does not low like an ox. Therefore we shall not follow the instructions of the Europeans, but of our own black messenger.

Racial bias and concern for a unique supernatural mandate for the Apostolic church, free from white interference, are evident in these sermons. One should remember that they were delivered on the eve of *chimurenga*, the Zimbabwean liberation struggle, when anxiety and uncertainty were rife and intimidation and detentions were becoming more frequent. Basically the Apostolic preachers aimed at reassuring their people. They were using the church as a place to vent their frustrations at white rule and were virtually claiming the work of the Holy Spirit exclusively for their cause of liberation.

It should be noted that the Zionist and Apostolic movements during the 1960s officially maintained a certain aloofness from politically organized violence and subversion. Bishop Mutendi even dissociated the ZCC from the then banned political parties ZANU and ZAPU. Nevertheless, these churches gave full expression to African nationalist sentiments. They became the propagators of equality between the races, the dignity of black Africans and their ability to rule themselves. In doing so, they sharpened the concept of a just God who sided with the oppressed and who, through his Spirit, could be counted upon to inspire the poor and the dispossessed in their struggle for the lost lands. At this stage, therefore, the prophetic contribution to political liberation, particularly in the rural context, lay in providing what was considered to be a sound, scripturally based legitimation and justification of the struggle.

Against this background it is not surprising that Zionist and Apostolic prophets increasingly played a key role at the war front as *chimurenga* escalated in the form of a bush war throughout Zimbabwe in the 1970s. Much like the traditional spirit mediums, who were providing the guerrillas with mystical ancestral guidance, prophets were also moving around with the fighters at the front, prophesying to them in the name of the Holy Spirit about enemy movements and related security matters. Thus the diagnostic and revelatory services of the prophets became a significant factor in the determination of guerilla strategy as the fighters improvised their tactics from one situation to the next. On the one hand, the senior ancestral spirits, as 'guardians of the land' (*varidzi venyika*), directed the fighters in their battle for the lost lands through their spirit mediums (*masvikiro*). On the other hand the Holy Spirit, also acting as a kind of 'guardian of the land' against the white intruders, was directing the forces of liberation through his emissaries, the Zionist and Apostolic prophets. Much depended on the predilections of Christian and non-Christian guerilla commanders whether they favoured traditionalist or prophetic guidance. Many of them made use of both, cross-checking the one against the other.

Apart from the 'fighter prophets' operating at the front, there were others who stayed at their church headquarters or healing colonies, from where they provided the guerrillas with information, pastoral support, faith-healing services and the like. Stressed or wounded fighters at times lived at healing colonies, or in secret caves nearby, in order to receive regular prophetic treatment.

Possibly the most important *chimurenga* function of some prophets was their assistance in 'community-cleansing' operations during *pungwe* meetings. There they had to help the guerrillas to determine who were the sell-outs, the traitors to the cause. Much of this work took place in the traditional idiom of tracing wizards. Invariably collaborators of the Rhodesian army, or villagers involved in attempts to poison or expose guerrilla fighters, were branded *varoyi*. Ritual affirmation of accusations, either through ancestral or Holy Spirit revelations, was required before cleansing, through execution or other forms of punishment, could take place. Thus the Holy Spirit of the prophets was publicly seen to act radically and judgmentally against the opponents of *chimurenga*.

The role of prophets in the *pungwe* courts could raise critical questions about arbitrary judgments, executions and the possible misrepresentation of the work of the Holy Spirit. In fairness, however, one should consider that it was in this very context that the Spirit invariably revealed himself to suspect members of the community as a life-giving and protective force. In a number of case studies I have established beyond doubt that prophets were often also instrumental in preventing executions whenever it was apparent that villagers were merely using the *pungwe* to project their prejudices and animosities in order to get rid of people they resented. In cases where wizardry accusations during *pungwe* sessions merely reflected tensions and internal village conflicts, prophets elicited public confessions from suspects, the background to which demonstrated to the guerrillas and village elders that they were not dealing with war offences. In numerous cases suspect villagers were actually ordered to go and live in prophetic healing colonies, where the scrutinizing, revelatory and disciplinary power of the Holy Spirit could, over a period of time, bring the culprits into line with the requirements of society at the time. Hence, by appealing to the ultimate authority of the Holy Spirit, prophets managed to introduce an element of moderation and sanity, often at grave personal risk, into *pungwe* situations where flaring emotions and the need for revenge in a war-torn society could easily claim innocent lives.

Judging by these prophetic activities one surmises that the pneumatology evolved by the Spirit-type churches during *chimurenga* was one of a warring Spirit, deeply immersed in a just cause, inspiring the fighting cadres to overthrow the oppressive rule of an alien enemy, as well as do combat with the enemy within their ranks which could devastate innocent lives if left unchecked. During the war the theology of liberation—unwritten, yet spontaneously enacted by the Independents— led to a closer identification of the concepts of salvation and political liberation. Yet the quest for political and socio-economic liberation at no point obscured the prophetic vision of God's saviourhood in terms of eternal life. Whereas the perception and experience of the Spirit's direct involvement in the achievement of peace and improved living conditions in this existence were certainly broadened and deepened, this did not obscure the good news of future salvation. On the contrary, the indications are that during the liberation struggle numerous AICs intensified their quest for conversion and eternal life. Quite a number of guerrilla fighters and people who sought refuge in the prophetic healing colonies were actually evangelized by the prophets whose assistance they sought. To such converts prophetic Spirit manifestations certainly meant both liberation from unjust rule and individual salvation, the culmination of which still lay in the future.

Despite religious revival and church growth during the war years, there were also signs of retrogression. Paradoxically, intensified concern with a liberating Spirit was in many instances countered by a submerged or diminished Christology in both AICs and mainline churches. The reason for this was that a renaissance of traditional religion caused many of the bush fighters to oppose Christianity. Some of their units destroyed or closed down church buildings. They saw Jesus as the white man's god, the epitome of oppressive rule. Consequently they operated under the slogan, *Pasi na Jesu!* (down with Jesus!). Many of the church leaders and congregations who continued to profess their faith in Jesus Christ publicly had their Bibles and vestments burnt by the guerrillas. Some were martyred, while others were forced to go underground. Many church leaders today frankly admit that during the war years they continued to preach about Mwari the Father, the one God who was known in Africa long before Christianity came, and that they prophesied or acted in the Spirit; but that they seldom spoke about Christ for fear of being branded traitors to the cause. The war years, therefore, present us with a chequered picture which defies easy generalization, but a picture which, for all its complexity, does not erase the predominant image of God's liberating Spirit operating in his black prophets throughout the war.

4. *The Earthkeeping Spirit*

In the post-Independence period in Zimbabwe, starting in 1980, the AICs increasingly turned their attention to development projects. Fambidzano, the ecumenical council of Independent Churches (present membership about 90 churches) raised funds for quite a number of churches to erect community development and vocational training centres, to develop small-scale industries such as carpentry and clothing manufacture, and engage in agricultural and water projects. Here, too, the Independents saw the Holy Spirit featuring prominently, in this instance inspiring socioeconomic progress. Having delivered his people from political bondage, the Holy Spirit was now increasingly seen as the liberator from poverty and economic despair, as one intimately involved, through the Fambidzano and other churches, in nation building. Development projects and even educational training centres at AIC headquarters—such as the multi-million dollar college which Bishop Nehemia Mutendi (son and successor of the late Samuel Mutendi) erected at Zion City—increasingly became the hallmarks of God's blessing on his people. This was not an entirely new development. It was rather a broadening of a pneumatological trend already manifest, namely that the Holy Spirit's function as healer and life-giver encompassed everything relating to human well-being. The Spirit was also the healer and protector of crops. Through a host of symbolic, supplicatory rites he could be persuaded by the faithful to safeguard or multiply their agricultural produce.

As was argued before, the perception of salvation undergirding this pneumatology does not exclude faith in a redemptive future for believers, or a heavenly eternity beyond this existence. Nevertheless, a strong focus on this-worldly salvation which includes Spirit-led improvement of the quality of this life—whether in terms of spiritual, cultural or socioeconomic progress—is unmistakable. A pragmatic anthropocentric trend is also discernible. After all, it is human beings who are saved, individuals who make progress through schools, community development centres and agricultural projects, and oppressed people who are liberated from unjust rule. The totality of creation is indeed holistically considered, as the prophetic appeal to God for good rains, bumper crops and prolific cattle breeding indicates. But pragmatism leads to exploitation! And African holism does not of necessity imply a world view which altruistically incorporates all of creation in the humanly perceived salvific work of God. So in the AICs—as elsewhere in the church—human self-centredness and the tendency to emphasize a personalized soteriology at the expense of the cosmic dimension of salvation easily lead to a triumphalist attitude—one which plays down human stewardship over nature, prioritizes human liberation and, by implication, promotes unjust and destructive overexploitation of a suffering creation. In a sense therefore the AICs, notwithstanding their peasant environment and holistically contextualized liturgies, share with the rest of Christianity a limited and incomplete perception of the grace of God, a grace which encompasses the entire creation as a gift from God. All of us together have somehow proved unworthy of this gift and we must all confess that 'the ruin of nature and the denial of God go hand in hand, because both over-exalt human beings'.[1]

It is against this background that we of the AICs in Zimbabwe are endeavouring to reinterpret and develop a praxis-related pneumatology on the basis of existing belief systems. For example, while seeing the Holy Spirit as saviour, healer and liberator, we are moving away from a predominantly personalized and therefore exploitative soteriology towards a more universal, cosmic and—by implication—altruistic approach which proclaims and promotes justice, peace and salvation for all of creation. Such a comprehensive pneumatology will hopefully characterize AIC theological trends in the 1990s and beyond.[2] The main difference from the historical pneumatological

1. J. Carmody, *Ecology and Religion: Towards a New Christian Theology of Nature* (Ramsey, NY: Paulist Press, 1983), p. 79.
2. M.L. Daneel, 'Towards a Sacramental Theology of the Environment in

trends is that some of the incentive for change derives from external, more specifically Western-related sources, such as my own participation in the AICs concerned. In other words, Western theologies of the environment or of ecological liberation (e.g. those of Moltmann, Carmody and Granberg-Michaelson) are being reinterpreted, adapted and blended with AIC prophetic praxis in a mutually enriching learning process, instead of all development being determined solely by spontaneous prophetic praxis as in the past. In this respect ecumenical interaction is complementing prophetic contextuality and exclusivism, underscoring in the process AIC recognition of their integral relatedness to the universal church. This realization, however, does not detract from the fact that current developments in pneumatology still basically reflect the local church's response to deeply felt needs or crises, as happened during the liberation struggle. In this instance, peasants in the communal areas are increasingly faced with overpopulation, overgrazing of lands, soil erosion, diminishing crop returns on overextended soils, deforestation and the related problems of desertification, scarcity of firewood and spoilt water resources.

How do the prophetic movements respond to this crisis? In my opinion the prophets are starting to conceive of and respond to the Holy Spirit as the earthkeeping Spirit. Increasingly the guidance of the Spirit appears to point to the healing and restoration of nature as a vitally important part of his salvific work. As this conviction grows—an experience which I share with and propagate among the AIC prophets—the churches are being mobilized into ecologically liberating action. I shall attempt briefly to sketch the current profile of such action and some of the more pertinent theological convictions behind it.

First of all, the prophets have been critically watching and assessing the conservationist work of AZTREC (Association of Zimbabwean Traditional Ecologists), a body consisting of traditionalist spirit mediums, chiefs and ZANLA ex-combatants. Founded in 1988 as a sister organization of an institute, ZIRRCON (Zimbabwe Institute of Religious Research and Ecological Conservation), of which I am the director, AZTREC aims at extending *chimurenga* from the sociopolitical arena to ecological conservation—tree planting, wildlife conservation and the protection of water resources. As happened during the struggle for political independence, the implementation of projects

African Independent Churches', *Zeitschrift für Missionswissenschaft und Religionswissenschaft* 75.1 (1991), *passim.*

to liberate nature from destruction is inspired by the guardian ancestors of the land and the traditional oracular deity, Mwari. At present the prime objective is afforestation of communal lands where the threat of desertification is greatest.

At AZTREC's initiative several nurseries have been developed in Masvingo Province. Since 1988 more indigenous seedlings have been grown than ever before in Zimbabwe. Mobilization of rural communities has resulted in the planting of 5,000 trees in 1988, 150,000 trees in 1989 and more than 500,000 during the 1990–1991 rainy season. Rural committees were formed by peasant villagers to take responsibility for all the woodlots: planting ceremonies, fencing, watering of trees, protective measures and so on. Thus the largest earthkeeping movement in Zimbabwe was developed at grassroots level over a relatively short period of time—its success deriving from ecological commitment rooted in traditional religion and philosophy.

Not to be outdone by AZTREC, yet taking their cue from AZTREC activities, the AICs have recently formed the Association of African Earthkeeping Churches (AAEC). Some 35 churches have already joined. A constitution has been drafted and an executive, with a salaried general secretary, is already in charge. The new movement has similar ecological objectives to AZTREC, the main difference being that earthkeeping activities are based on Christian principles evolved in the AIC context. A situation has therefore developed in which ZIRRCON, besides being the nerve centre, provides funding, policy-making and organizational services for two sister organizations—the one traditional, the other Christian, but both aimed at the liberation or restoration of nature in terms of their respective religious traditions. Attempts are made to establish meaningful interaction between AZTREC and AAEC at all levels, resulting in sustained interfaith dialogue on common religio–ecological goals.

In the second place, the immediate practical consequence of forming the AAEC has been the development of several church nurseries for exotic fruit and indigenous trees at or near prophetic church headquarters. Plans for large-scale tree-planting operations by participant churches during the next rainy season are already underway. The unfolding 'battle of the trees' in the churches is being interpreted in prophetic circles as the movement of the earthkeeping Spirit, who aims at healing the land by clothing the earth once again with life-restoring vegetation (*kufukidza nyika*, to clothe the earth). This battle takes the form of prophets diagnosing the illness of mother earth in terms of human greed and ecological offences, and prescribing a therapy of Christian renewal and commitment, manifested in earth-keeping action. As this ecological side of the healer and protector Spirit emerges, the wider cosmic dimensions of salvation also gain prominence. This inevitably adds a new perspective to the AIC understanding of the good news of Christ's Saviourhood, so ardently proclaimed during evangelistic and missionary campaigns. For it is in Spirit-led tree-planting activities that the churches are announcing the reign of Christ, to whom belongs 'all authority in heaven and on earth' (Mt. 28.18), a reign which liberates and heals not only human beings but all of creation.

Thirdly, attempts are made to develop, for and with the AICs, a written theology of the environment. Their characteristic theology enacted in dance, song and prophetic revelations is being comple-mented by a somewhat more organized, reflective and written record. In this field the Revd Ruben Marinda and the Revd Solomon Zvanaka, both of them Zionist leaders holding advanced theological qualifica-tions and key positions in ZIRRCON and the AAEC, are assisting me with the drafting of conscientization courses for training programmes in religion and ecology.

Fourthly, Western and AIC theological insights blend in the context of course development and teaching. At this level new trinitarian per-spectives are being worked out and incorporated into training materials. Thus Jürgen Moltmann's emphasis on God's immanence in creation provides an important guideline for a new theology of ecology. He says:

> God is not merely the Creator of the world. He is also the Spirit of the universe. Through the powers and potentialities of the Spirit, the Creator indwells the creatures He has made, animates them, holds them in life, and leads them into the future of His kingdom.[1]

Moltmann's views correlate closely with the convictions of the late Bishop Samuel Mutendi, who preached about the biblical Mwari as a creator truly present and totally involved in all of creation. Through ZCC rituals to bless the seed to be sown and the implements to be used in the fields, Mutendi managed to bring the remote oracular deity

---

1. J. Moltmann, *God in Creation: An Ecological Doctrine of Creation* (London: SCM Press, 1985), p. 14.

(Mwari of the Matopo hills), traditionally approachable only to a few select cultic officials, into daily peasant life. His was already a theology of ecology, albeit focused on seasonal cattle and crop farming. By combining Moltmann's ideas with some of Mutendi's rituals we relate the pervading presence of Mwari, the immanent creator, to a long-term ecological strategy. At this point the message is: Indeed, recognize Mwari as the one who blesses and germinates the seeds for the coming season! But let him also be the God of the seedlings nurtured in church nurseries and the God of tree crops in plantations which will not only provide the building materials and firewood for coming generations, but will also clothe the earth for its own sake.

In the fifth and last place, an attempt is made to reflect on AIC pneumatology and to draw the consequences for church praxis. Special attention is given to the Spirit's ecological healing activity in relation to the sacraments. Here, too, the centrality of the Spirit in prophetic earthkeeping corresponds with current theological notions in the Western world. In his trinitarian interpretation of creation Moltmann deliberately chooses to concentrate on the third person. He argues that all divine activity is pneumatic in its manifestation. It is always the Spirit who brings the activity of the Son to its goal. The cosmic Spirit he refers to has no relation to Stoic pantheism. It remains God's Spirit acting in this world in the differential modes of creating, preserving, renewing and consummating life. Thus he comes to his basic assertion:

> Creation in the Spirit is the theological concept which corresponds best to the ecological doctrine of creation we are looking for and need today. With this concept we are cutting loose the theological doctrine of creation from the age of subjectivity and the mechanistic domination of the world, and are leading it in the direction in which we have to look for the future of an ecological world-community.[1]

> Through the Spirit we are bound together with the natural environment. This association is a system comprising human beings and nature. We might describe it as a spiritual ecosystem. Through the Spirit, human societies as part systems are bound up with the ecosystem 'earth' (*Gaia*). So human beings are participants and subsystems of the cosmic life-system, and the divine Spirit that lives in it.[2]

1. Moltmann, *God in Creation*, p. 112.
2. Moltmann, *God in Creation*, p. 18.

Moltmann's views are entirely relevant to current ecological concerns of the prophetic AICs. His idiom may be alien and the context of his appeal may be mainly the academic West and the threat of modern industrialization to our planet. Yet the AIC prophets of Africa will agree with his emphasis on the need to establish an ecological world community and in their own way express the conviction that only through the indwelling of the Spirit can such a goal be realized. In some respects the AIC prophets probably understand and experience the life-giving power of the outpoured and ever present Spirit better than Moltmann and other Western-oriented theologians like myself. Their intuition was shaped by their forefathers who sensed as well as any Old Testament sage that the spirit (*mweya*) imparted by God the creator (*musiki*) was the source of all life. This intuition ultimately blossomed in an all-absorbing and most persuasive testimony to the life-giving power of the Holy Spirit (*Mweya Mutsvene*) in the Spirit-type churches, especially in their healing colonies. And now the extension in prophetic praxis of the healing power of the Spirit from the specifically human condition to the entire 'cosmic life-system' (to use Moltmann's words) is becoming manifest in the AIC sacraments.

Conversion and sin are being ritually reinterpreted in the sacramental context of baptism and the eucharist. It is in preparation for baptism that the prophetic leader emphasizes the need for radical public rejection of sin under the guidance of the Spirit. Ecologically conscientized prophets now reveal that the Spirit expects novices not only to confess their moral sins in disturbed interpersonal relations, but also their ecological sins: chopping down of trees without planting any in return, overgrazing and neglecting to make contour ridges, thereby causing soil erosion, etc.—in other words admitting to human greed and exploitation of the good earth, taking it for granted without nurturing it or reverencing it in return. At 'Jordan' (any river, called Jordan for the duration of the baptismal ceremony) it makes sense to the newly converted to confess ecological guilt, where the barren treeless plains, the ever deepening erosion gulleys, the denuded river banks and the clouds of dust testifying to wind erosion are clearly in evidence. Here the prophet has a unique opportunity to instruct converts that crossing the river Jordan into a new life implies more than individual incorporation into the body of Christ and the prospect of salvation in heaven. It also requires the new convert's commitment to help restore creation and to engage in ecological stewardship, in recognition of God's grace and in selfless service to the generations yet to come.

To many Independents baptism is also a healing ceremony, in which the life-giving water of 'Jordan', filled by the Spirit, is drunk by baptizands for individual cleansing and curative purposes. In this respect the ceremony offers a unique opportunity for interpreting the Spirit as healer both of the people and of the land. In that case the drinking of Jordan water symbolizes not just the baptizands' healing or salvation, but their identification with desecrated mother earth and their participation in cosmic healing. The focus then shifts from private, personal benefit by the Holy Spirit's healing powers to a statement of solidarity with all creation and an affirmation of new commitment, through individual conversion, to the healing and restoration of nature.

In most of the Spirit-type churches the eucharist is preceded by an even more dramatic public confession of sin than happens at baptism. Johane Maranke's vaPostori spend an entire night performing a preparatory cleansing ritual. Thousands of participants run around huge fires shouting their offences out loud. Then they pass the symbolic gates of heaven, each consisting of twelve prophets standing in pairs. All sins must be confessed at the gates, as the Holy Spirit, through the prophets, detects all hidden sins, from adultery to wizardry. The unrepentant are disqualified from participating in the sacrament. Some of the prophets involved in the AAEC tree-planting programme have started to combat ecological sins. Offences which lead to a shortage of firewood, soil erosion and poor crops are increasingly branded as a form of *uroyi* (wizardry)—the most serious of all sins, as it threatens human existence and life itself. I anticipate that unrepentant ecological wizards will in years to come find themselves debarred at the Zionist and Apostolic gates from participation in the eucharist. Through the earthkeeping Spirit the AAEC prophets already know who such *varoyi* are: the ones in the resettlement schemes who prejudice the common good by chopping down as many trees as they can for a quick profit from selling firewood, those who refuse to accept the principle that firewood can only be used by those who plant the trees that supply it; the resisters of government conservationist measures and of the chiefs' prohibition of chopping down trees in the holy groves of the ancestors, and the destroyers of river banks.

In addition to such reinterpretation of conversion and sin in the sacramental context, our theologizing in the earthkeeping churches includes a strong plea that in an ecologically ravaged environment each church should conduct at least one tree-planting eucharist annually. This would be one of the most relevant and convincing ways of publicly witnessing to Christ's reign over all creation and ritually acknowledging human involvement in its realization. It would be another way of agreeing with Granberg-Michaelson that God's gift of grace received through the bread and wine cannot be treasured and held within our own selves.[1] Instead, we are liberated to pour out our lives for the sake of Christ's reign over all creation, incorporating into our concern for internal, individual spirituality the ministry of global sanctification.

A tree-planting eucharist is one of the most powerful ways of saying that Christ's good news not only liberates and saves human beings, but also heals and protects nature where it agonizingly awaits redemption. Thus the missionary task acquires a wider dimension and sacramental empowerment. For mission, seen in this perspective, entails both evangelistic outreach and environmental restoration.

In the AAEC churches where the eucharist is already linked with tree planting, the realization is dawning that sacramental participation in the body of Christ inspires both spiritual growth and ecological responsibility. Under the guidance of the earthkeeping Spirit the cosmological inferences of Colossians 1.15-20—'in Christ all things hold together'—are being drawn in a profound manner.

Such sacramental activity excludes the pretense that we, the earth-keepers, are the saviours of creation, for that we can never be. But, as believers we are erecting not only symbolic but concrete signposts of life-giving hope in a creation suffering while it awaits redemption. For, as Duchrow and Liedke correctly state:

> Spirit-endowed beings do not save creation, but creation looks to us. The way that we cope with its suffering shows how much hope there is for creation. When we increase the suffering of creation its hope sinks. When we sharpen the conflict between human beings and nature, and also the

1.   W. Granberg-Michaelson, *A Worldly Spirituality—The Call to Redeem Life on Earth* (San Francisco: Harper & Row, 1984), p. 136.

conflict between humans, then creation lapses into resignation. When, instead, in solidarity with nature and our fellow human beings, we reduce suffering, then the hope of creation awakes into new life.[1]

5. *Conclusion*

We have now traced some of the major characteristics of AIC pneumatology as it emerged in response to distinct historical phases and ecclesiastical developments in Zimbabwe. In the process we have gained an impression of how a section of the world church has interpreted and experienced the movement and guidance of God's Spirit in its midst. We have also noted different emphases in the related concepts of salvation.

Of great significance is the fact that the richness of the Spirit's involvement and presence in the movements concerned was never obscured by prophetic preoccupation with historically and contextually determined issues at a given time. As mentioned, the prophets' involvement in the political liberation struggle and the concomitant image of the Holy Spirit as liberator of the oppressed—in spite of a temporarily weakened Christology—in no way quenched their missionary spirit or zeal for individual conversions and the propagation of eternal salvation in the present, yet still coming, kingdom of God. Likewise, the current response of the AICs to the Spirit as Earthkeeper and the resultant widening perspective on salvation as extending to all creation, instead of overriding evangelistic outreach in the traditional sense, is incorporated into and enriches the individual conversion experience. It enhances the hope in the future fulfilment of salvation.

In a sense the earthkeeping venture is part of an ongoing and comprehensive conversion process of the entire church. Thus engaged the church is actually carrying out an expanded missionary mandate: proclaiming through its Spirit-led life and work that the good news of salvation, of God's grace, extends to all of creation. Salvation here and now, manifest in the Black Jerusalems and Holy Cities in this existence—in terms of healing, liberation and earthkeeping—in no way 'snatches the future' but meaningfully concretizes the dominion of Christ over heaven and earth and maintains the eschatological

---

1. U. Duchrow and G. Liedke, *Shalom: Biblical Perspectives on Creation, Justice and Peace* (Geneva: WCC Publications, 1989), p. 64.

tension between the 'already' and 'not yet' of God's kingdom.

In this respect the prophetic movements are enacting their own unique liberation theologies, without falling into the pitfall of reducing the message of salvation exclusively to a this-worldly programme of liberation from socio-political oppression or poverty. They also avoid the pitfall of reducing the good news to one-sided future salvation of souls through their holistic interpretation of the Holy Spirit's comprehensive involvement in all of life. Thereby they escape the Western classifications of 'liberationist', 'evangelical', 'charismatic' or 'ecumenical'. Instead, they encompass all these distinctions and many more, as they uninhibitedly read the Scriptures and intuitively feel for the Holy Spirit's guidance in Africa. Herein lies their challenge to the world church as it ponders both vision and strategy for a renewed evangelistic thrust.

Together with them we pray:

> Come Holy Spirit, come Holy Spirit, come Holy Spirit
> Bless us, your servants.

A RESPONSE TO M.L. DANEEL

Derek B. Mutungu

I am an offspring of mission founded churches in Zambia, trained in western academies. But I applaud Professor Daneel's years of empathetic listening to a despised group in the body of Christ on our continent. Several features strike me from his account of African Independent Churches (AICs): (1) their working world view, (2) their epistemology or framework of knowledge and (3) their practice of ministry. Hearing about AICs makes one wonder: Could this be Africa's jubilee, the *kairos* moment of God's favour to us?

1. *An Alternative World View*

At one level, the failure of love, that is, a rift in relationships, triggered defections from missionary Christianity and led to the rise of AICs. At a deeper level, however, lay a clash between African and western cosmologies or worldviews.[1] Professor Daneel's sample of AICs indicates that the encounter between the African and the New Testament cosmologies propelled the movement forward.[2]

The African and NT worldviews see spiritual and physical beings as real entities which interact with each other in time and space. But the biblical world view rigidly separates divine powers, God and his angels, from fallen principalities and powers, Satan and his hierarchy of demons. In short, the cosmic transfer Christ initiated (Gal. 1.4; Col. 1.13) awakens us to a four-fold cosmology.

---

1. See C. Olowola, 'An Introduction to African Independent Churches', *East African Journal of Evangelical Theology* 3 (1984), pp. 21ff., and Z. Nthamburi, 'Toward Indigenization of Christianity in Africa: A Missiological Task', *International Bulletin of Missionary Research* 13 (1989), pp. 115ff.

2. See M.L. Daneel, 'The Missionary Outreach of African Independent Churches', *Missionalia* 8 (1980), pp. 105ff. and paper as above.

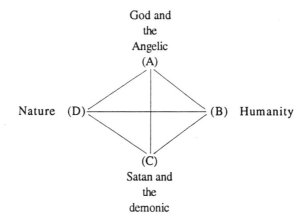

Independent churches retained Africa's lofty regard for *Mwari* (God). But they equated spirits, including ancestral ones, with demons and rejected their control over personal lives and traditional society.[1] These saints garnered the superior power of the Holy Spirit in order to 'decolonize' their societies from the *archai kai exousiai*, (principalities and powers, the B–C axis), and to place it under Christ (the A–B axis).[2] The success at prophetic healing in AICs must be seen as vindication of their polemic against ancestral spirits. In this they were not unlike the East African revival. From Professor Daneel's paper, one wonders whether alliance between Zimbabwean Zion churches and traditional religionists in environmental issues means loss of their original cutting edge.

Nevertheless, AICs implicitly rejected the secularist world view associated with the colonial experience. They also loathed mission Christianity, which syncretized itself to western cosmologies and

1. See J.S. Mbiti, *African Religions and Philosophy* (Nairobi: Heinemann, 1969), pp. 100ff.

2. Students of African theology disagree on the identity of ancestral spirits. The more rationalistic deny spirits ontological reality. So they are inclined to brand apostolic healing as escape from the rigours of modern science (G.C. Oosthuizen, 'Interpretations of Demonic Powers in African Independent Churches', *Missiology* 1 (1988), pp. 3-21) or acquiescence in oppressive socio-political systems (M. Schofeleers, 'Ritual Healing and Political Acquiescence: The case of the Zionist Churches in Southern Africa'. *Africa Review* 60 (1991), pp. 1ff.). Africanists, on the other hand, tend to equate ancestral spirits with departed saints and try to legitimize them on biblical grounds (J.S. Mbiti, *African Religions*, and K. Bediako, 'The Roots of African Theology', *International Bulletin of Missionary Research* 13 (1989), pp. 58-64).

consequently said, 'yes but' to the Spirit's visible activity. Thus AICs have embraced the kind of world view Larry Christenson calls for in *Welcome Holy Spirit*.[1] With the rising tide of neo-paganism in western society, their experience may offer a useful model.

2. *An Integrated Epistemology*

These believers at the same time spurned the 'orthodoxy' they inherited which left serious gaps between beliefs sincerely held and their practical results. This epistemological crisis still exists in the global church. In Africa many praise God effusively on Sundays but demand bribes Monday to Friday. Bishop David Gitari of Kenya once lamented this fact. 'History has shown us that for the government to be run by the church does not necessarily guarantee democracy or justice'.[2] All of us have failed the faith in some way.

AICs forged an alternative epistemology. Max Stackhouse's typology, traced from Greek thought, helps us to see this.[3] Its three aspects included *theoria, poesis* and *praxis*. *Theoria* employs observation, analysis and critical judgment. *Poesis* is imaginative knowing and works with evocative images, metaphors or symbols and the mystical. Lastly *praxis* involves 'intentional, practical engagement'.[4] We may depict this with a triangle.

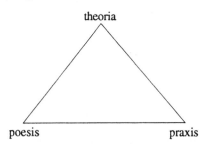

1. L. Christenson (ed.), *Welcome Holy Spirit: A Study of Charismatic Renewal in the Church* (Minneapolis: Augsburg, 1987), pp. 150ff.

2. D. Gitari, 'The Churches' Witness to the Living God: Seeking Just Political, Social and Economic Structures', *Transformation* 5 (1988), pp. 13-20.

3. See M. Stackhouse, *Apologia: Contextualization, Globalization and Mission in Theological Education* (Grand Rapids: Eerdmans, 1988), pp. 84-85.

4. At the expense of oversimplification, systematic or dogmatic theology employs *theoria* and is abetted by grammatical–historical hermeneutical tools. Spiritual and mystical theology comes under the category of *poesis*, while *praxis* describes everything the people of God do in the world.

Professor Daneel cites attempts made by some AICs to integrate right belief with right action.[1] They have restated classical Christian *theoria* or doctrine in African motifs, a *poesis*, immersed in the symbolic.[2] The appeal of preaching by AICs may well lie in their innovative and anointed use of symbols. Thus images like *Dura* (granary) or Zion not only convey rich theological content, but captivate these Christians to indwell and, in so doing, manifest the truth. Michael Polanyi, the philosopher of science, has argued that ideas rarely transform a culture without first becoming personal enough to translate into acts.[3] To the degree the epistemology of AICs does this, they will prove a vital catalyst to a healing praxis on our continent, and a basis for a dynamic theology for Africa.[4]

3. *A Restorative Praxis*

The African Independents Professor Daneel recounts exhibit sharp insight into the Scriptures. First, they rightly adopted the Holy Spirit's charter, making the Spirit's presence the supreme *nota ecclesiae* (Jn 15.5-8).[5] In Christ's new age, the *paracletos* or advocate, like a prosecutor at law, convinces (*elenko*) rebellious humanity. And like a tourist guide, He leads (*hodogeo*) all the laity (*laos*) of God into life of the future. Where the Holy Spirit is not, the Church is not.

Secondly, they have gradually translated the great Zion promise (Isa. 2.1-4; Mic. 4.1-5; Lk. 11.20, 21; Heb. 12.22-24) into mission along the contours of the world view of NT penultimate eschatology.

---

1.   See J.B. Kailing, 'Inside, Outside, Upside Down: In Relation with African Independent Churches', *International Review of Mission* 77, 305 (1988), pp. 42ff. for an AIC typology.

2.   Those of us trained in *theoria* orientated rationalistic hermeneutics sometimes find this hard, e.g. B.H. Kato, *Theological Pitfalls in Africa* (Kisumu; Evangel Publishing House, 1975), pp. 77-128, 172-84.

3.   Cited by W.R. Thorson, 'The Biblical Insights of Michael Polanyi', *Journal of the American Scientific Affiliation* 33 (1981), pp. 129ff. For example, the persuasiveness of science comes not from theories themselves, but from the capacity of some to grasp and indwell abstract concepts enough to translate them into high-tech processes and products.

4.   See T. Tienou, 'The Right to Difference: The Common Roots of African Theology and Philosophy', *African Journal of Evangelical Theology* 9 (1990), pp. 24ff.

5.   See Z. Nthamburi, 'Toward Indigenization', p. 115.

To begin with, they fervently challenge unbelievers to *pindukai*, that is, to turn and posit faith in Israel's God and his Christ. And they nurture believers in exuberant worship.[1] Thirdly, they invite people to become whole in their spirits, bodies, hearts and minds. They have worked for communities of greater justice and mercy.[2] Of late, they are participating in healing to their ecological systems, which are often unpredictable. Fourthly, their *praxis* continues to confront spiritual strongholds of evil (Jn 1.5; Gal. 4.3; Col. 2.8, 20).

In brief, these Africans want their Zions to be cities of refuge. They desire Christ, in kingly power, to chart new paths by His (re)creative word, *dabar*, and normative word, *torah*. It is surprising, however, that despite its Spirit-centredness, social and ecological involvement appear from Professor Daneel more as a reaction and less as an initiative from within.[3] In this they are certainly not unique. But must the Church wait to jump on bandwagons in matters clearly demanded by the Lord?

Professor Daneel's research reveals a dynamic eschatologically-rooted base movement of the Spirit with a well-rounded world view and epistemology. These African charismatics have struggled to overturn centuries of tyranny under spiritual, political and economic manipulation, ecological disasters and epidemics. They have gradually converted biblical ideas by innovative appeal to the African instinct for symbolic language. Theirs is a truth that seeks to heal people, society and ecological environments. Africa has ached for God's jubilee for a very long time. AICs appear to exhibit the Lord's thumbprint sealing our year of liberty. Praise God!

Festo Kivengere, the late East African revivalist bishop, once said 'preaching is a feast of explaining what God is doing'. Similarly, theology must not be a wearisome burden of writing puzzling treatises. Rather it ought to be a feast of clarifying what God is already doing by his Holy Spirit so that all may see, hear, receive and be healed.

1. See Daneel, 'Missionary Outreach', pp. 110ff.
2. See Schofeleers, 'Ritual Healing', pp. 1-25, for a contrary view.
3. See Schofeleers, 'Ritual Healing'.

Part II

EVANGELIZATION AND THE HOLY SPIRIT IN AN URBAN AND MULTICULTURAL SOCIETY: THE EXPERIENCE OF THE PRO-HUMAN RIGHTS ECUMENICAL COMMITTEE

Luis Segreda

1. *Evangelization as an Ethical and Social Alternative: The Experience of Original Pentecostalism*

The North American context at the beginning of this century parallels that of England in the Eighteenth Century. The United States is in its full industrial expansion. Forty years had gone by since the War of Secession (1865) and the industrial revolution of the North had been imposed on the farming exportation projects of the South in such a way that these years solidified the United States as a World power.[1] 'The Civil War is interpreted by many as a type of apocalyptic trial in which American Christians were able to overcome victoriously...'[2] Keeping in mind a prophetic pre- and post-millennial milieu, this victory was identified as the 'national fate', but for Latin America it became simply the displacement of other powers in favor of the influence of the United States. An unbridled Monroe Doctrine gave birth to three concrete developments: the United States exerted its power during the 1895 battle between Great Britain and Venezuela; the war against Spain in 1898, resulting in the imposition of the Platt

---

1.   'In the last years of the 19th century... the country went through a period of political transition, which in result gave an active participation in the affairs of the world and the elevation to the status super power', says G. Pope Atkins (*América latina en el sistema politico internacional* [Spanish edn trans. [from English] M.E. Moreno Canalejas; Madrid: Gernika, 1980], p. 110 [pt. 463]). Cf. A. Birnie, *Historia económica de Europa 1760–1939* (trans. [from English] E.S. Santos; Barcelona: Miracle Editor, 2nd edn, 1957), pp. 14, 15, 17 (pt. 335).

2.   C. Añeque, *Dios en América: Una aproximación al conservadurismo político-religioso en los estados unidos* (Barcelona: Ediciones Península, 1988), p. 30 (pt. 156).

Amendment of Cuba (1902) and the colonial status of Puerto Rico; the political design of 'the Great Garrotte' enunciated by Theodore Roosevelt in his 1904 address to Congress.[1] Without doubt, it was a moment of power, great commercial development, receiving of immigrants, and aggressive international politics. It was also a time of great social ferment for North American society:

> From 1873 to 1893 the North American economy lives through another critical period. The great strikes of 1877 brought a period of intense social struggle, which extends itself until the decade of the '90s. In 1893, more than 600 banks went bankrupt. In 1894, 194 railroad companies went bankrupt. From 1893 to 1898 almost one third of the railroads were suspended. In 1893 there were one to four million workers unemployed. 1895 was the 'culminating point of the depression'.[2]

This is the context for the emergence of the Classical Pentecostal Movement in North America. According to Hollenweger, the Baptism of the Holy Spirit with the gift of speaking in tongues is first identified in a Bible school in Topeka, Kansas directed by Charles Parham. Next comes the black preacher William J. Seymour and an abandoned African Methodist Episcopal church building at 312 Azusa St., which is 'considered by Pentecostal publicists as the starting point of the Pentecostal movement'.[3]

A significant percentage of the earliest Pentecostals were black and usually from the lower classes of society. Moreover, there were greater numbers of black women than black men.[4] Emphasis of the first Pentecostals on the Baptism of the Holy Spirit deserves a more

---

1. Atkins, *América latina en el sistema político internacional*, p. 111.

2. E. Enspes (ed.), *Historia contemporánea de los estados unidos* (Vedado: MEC, 1981), I, pp. 11, 12.

3. W.J. Hollenweger, *El pentecostalismo: Historia y doctrinas* (Buenos Aires: La Aurora, 1976), p. 9 (pt. 527). Note also S.J. Land's perspective:

> Pentecostalism was born in the fires of the millennial expectation in the late nineteenth century. Pentecostal-like revivals, with attendant tongues-speech occurred throughout the 1800s in several places, including England (the Irvingites), Germany, Wales, India, Russia (Armenians, who later showed up in Los Angeles at the Azusa St. Revival), during several holiness revivals (Finney, Moody, etc.) and finally in Topeka, Kansas (1901) and Los Angeles, California (1906–1909).

('Pentecostal Spirituality: Living in the Spirit', in *Christian Spirituality*, III [World Spirituality, New York: Crossroads, 1989], p. 480).

4. Hollenweger, *El pentecostalismo*, p. 12.

in-depth study, but it is needful to affirm, for now, that it carries a two-sided protest: first as a communicative phenomenon, then as a social protest. Religious faith expresses a manner in which we can come in contact with what some philosophers call 'the numinous', impacting affectively a human who suffers such an encounter with an existential or physical scar that leaves a permanent mark. Rational thinking in this instance is limited, or diminished by the vividness of the 'moment' as Kierkegaard would say, by a unique event having marked the individual outside of time and space. Further study is required to determine whether these marginal sectors of the population (blacks, the poor, women) found by way of the Baptism of the Holy Spirit a manner by which to express their discontent and frustration, their praise and thankfulness, or simply a repressed longing for God (restrained by the historical churches). We should study the Baptism of the Holy Spirit as social protest against an adverse world, which coincides without doubt with the anti-world attitude of Pentecostalism:

> The World encloses men and women in a socio-physical structure that denies and opposes that existence of the spirit. The world gains its power through the lust of the eyes, the lust of the flesh, and the ostentation of life... the carnal mind does not submit itself to the disposition of the work of righteousness and to the word of the Spirit (Kingdom of God); in other words, it is enmity against God.[1]

If this is so, it is obvious that there is a social protest against structures of 'perverse' dominion, and it is possible to overcome them only by virtue of a particular seal. The seal of the Baptism of the Holy Spirit, being manifest by those who have experienced and have witnessed the gift of tongues. The Baptism of the Holy Spirit gives us spiritual and moral strength, perhaps because, as Paul says, 'In my weakness is my strength', giving us the capacity therefore to resist evil. A hedonistic world emerged from the industrial revolution which since World War II has been known as a 'consumer society'. This causes a certain fascination in humans with accommodating every desire, many of which are legitimate, but most of which have been created artificially. The Baptism of the Holy Spirit annihilates us, releasing us from all 'rationalization', thus leaving us naked before God. Then, in the most intimate part of our being, God by way of His Spirit ministers to us,

---

1.   Land, 'Pentecostal Spirituality', p. 491.

healing our wounds, and destroying our worldly conception of pleasure and introducing us to a life of freedom, sweetness, and a frankness which enables one to confront powers and principalities present not only in people, but in social and political structures as well. The Baptism of the Holy Spirit gives a special power that allows us to become one with the mind of Christ, resisting all evil.

How then do we understand evangelism in this context? Primarily as recruiting disciples who are willing to be molded and led by the person of the Holy Spirit and at the same time willing to 'resist all evil'. Involves the creation of alternative structures where one is able to live a life that is not otherwise possible—what Frank Hinkelmart would call the utopia of 'building a heaven on earth', even though it may be accomplished in the name of heaven, eschatologically.[1] The Baptism of the Holy Spirit would be ethical, political and social in its resistance against this malignant and perverse world (see Jn 12), and at the same time, having strength and power to fight against evil:

> When Pentecostals are 'praying through' to the baptism in the Spirit, they are struggling with their own selfish desires and motives, their own unavailability for mission and service, against their own fear.[2]

Without a doubt, our acceptance of this mission signals a rejection of a world whose logic is death. So, the Pentecostal movement seems to be saying, 'the world cannot be transformed by following its own logical system'. It is necessary to create an alternative community where we can express our own personal experience of our Christian faith. The future impact of this movement could be momentous:

> Just as Peter, full of the Holy Spirit, was challenged to extend his Christian message to the Gentiles and for their complete acceptance by the

1. J. Míguez Bonino in his book *Espacio para ser hombres*, states that this language, apparently transcendent, has very concrete implications in its surrounding reality.

> It is amazing how the Bible speaks so little about another life. We make it so speak, because we are convinced that it should. However, the expressions which we generally refer to of life after death, such as: 'eternal life' or 'the life in Christ' even 'heavenly life' is referring first of all to this life. 'This is everlasting life', says Jesus: 'that they may know thee, the only true God, and Jesus Christ, whom thou hast sent'. And that happened, just as the gospel declared it *here* and *now*.

Espacio para ser hombres (Buenos Aires: Tierra Nueva, 1975), p. 54 (pt. 89).

2. Land, 'Pentecostal Spirituality', p. 492.

church, likewise the Pentecostals of today must accept the relationship between an authentic personal encounter with God and an authentic liberation.[1]

This Baptism of the Spirit brings authority (*exousia*) and real power (*dunamis*) against oppression and against evil. Perhaps the original Pentecostal experience did not include in its richness the implications of the evil incarnate in social, economic, and political structures. Should this not be our task as we strive for a complete evangelistic endeavor?

'Popular education', as it is called in Latin America, is the 'living dynamic process which develops in the interaction between persons, in their shared reflection of their doing, their seeking, their aspirations, and desires'.[2]

> In the place of super-humans that dominate and threaten minors and proceed over the heads of others making very evident their 'theological apportations', 'the children of God propose a different greatness: in simplicity and humility, serve the people of God'.[3]

It is in the walking together, in the friendship which comes from the encounter between God and humanity, that we find clarity and the discerning of that community called church.

This consciousness emerges on the way to Emmaus. There we find the pedagogy of brotherhood—in our conversations with God, in our relations with his salvific word. We question and we are questioned, then suddenly 'we learn'; that is, when we say, 'Did not our hearts warm within us while we walked with him in the way?' Here it is; this is the presence of the Holy Spirit revealing and persuading us in the depth of our hearts. These disciples discovered in Jesus a traveling companion. We encounter not only the presence—sometimes gratifying and other times bothersome—of a God who permanently persuades us to stand up, to be authentic men and women, to obtain the fullness of liberty and independence, being no longer humiliated and exploited; it is there where we discover the shared bread, the supper that emerges from the people, the call to build the kingdom of God.

1. 'Pentecostal Spirituality', p. 492.
2. R. Leis, *El arco y la flecha. Apuntes sobre metodologia practica transformadora* (Panamá: Instituto Cooperaativo Interamericano, 1987), p. 120 (pc. 35).
3. D.L. Fernandes, *Como se hace una comunidad eclesial de base* (Colombia: Indo-American Press service-editores, 1986), p. 59 (pc. 37).

Luke 24 is the key to this evangelization that could be called 'companionship'. In this passage we see how God draws near, taking the initiative in conversing to persuade in the way of Jesus.[1] God the companion, the fellow-traveller who goes with us, also demands that his power be demonstrated through the giving of oneself. To be a companion is to serve others. Since God always begins where people exist, evangelization can never overlook this profound fact.

2. *A Case Study of the Pro-Human Rights Ecumenical Committee: An Evangelistic Experience by the Power of the Holy Spirit in an Urban and Multicultural World*

1. *The Realities of Central American Refugees*

In its colonial era, Central America was a part of the military government of Guatemala. A Central American Confederacy was formed in the first years of independence (1820s). Even though it failed, there have been more than eighteen attempts towards its reformation. The 1856 intrusion of the William Walker filibuster, designed to make us a part of the United States, helped to consolidate our national awareness when we were forced to unite with all the countries of the Central American Isthmus. The five Central American countries (today seven) have much in common despite many differences. The construction of a canal through Nicaragua first and then Panama has been one of the causes for our separation into small republics.

The multicultural phenomenon known around the world is no stranger to Latin America. Before 1402, more than 70 million native 'Indians' lived in all of America. This multicultural and multireligious phenomenon had three great cultures, namely the Inca, Maya and Aztec civilizations. With the conquest and colonization came a massive immigration of Spaniards and Portuguese. Black slaves came in different epochs, especially during the seventeenth and eighteenth centuries. Black descendants are predominant throughout all of the Caribbean, Brazil, Panama, and the Atlantic coast of Central America. According to Darcy Robeiro, four countries have significant Indian populations: Bolivia, Peru, Ecuador and Guatemala. Guatemala alone has more than 40 different tongues. After independence many Europeans came, especially to Argentina, Brazil, Chile, Costa Rica

---

1.   G. Vahanian, *Ningun otro dios* (Madrid: Ediciones Marova, 1972), p. 32, pt. 179.

and Venezuela. In this century, immigrants have primarily been Asians, Europeans, (East) Indians and even Arabs. All of this forms a 'sunbeam of races and cultures' as German Arciniegas called it. In my own country, there are blacks in the Atlantic zone and in the center of the country, Indians in different rural regions (particularly on the border with Panama); while Jews, Italians and Germans have settled in different periods.

At the beginning of 1970, a civil war raged in Nicaragua and at the same time civil wars emerged in El Salvador and Guatemala. Vicious arms trading brought grave economic, social, political and human consequences throughout the entire region. Serious attempts for peaceful restoration of the democratic governments led to reformation. 'This process intensified itself during the decade of the '70s, as a consequence of the appearance and establishment of political organizations that opposed the system and accumulated political and military strength within society.'[1] Because of the wars in Central America, Costa Rica received a huge influx of refugees; Nicaraguans, Salvadorians and, in a smaller measure, refugees from Guatemala and Panama, which represent Indians, blacks, mestizos, zambos and whites, who bring with them a multiplicity of cultures and religions.

Before the fall of the Berlin Wall, authorities forced Central America into a conflict of West versus East, even though the fundamental causes of the social crises of the '70s were products, on the one hand, of the dependency of our towns upon developed countries, particularly the United States, and on the other hand, of the presence of powerful groups within our countries that have avoided structural transformation for the improvement of the socio-economic situation of its inhabitants. During the '50s there were democratic attempts in several of our countries which failed because of internal groups who opposed changes (e.g. Arbenz in Guatemala). Panama (until December 20, 1989) and Costa Rica alone have been able to achieve progressive reformation.

Central American countries have survived dictatorships that have slowly but surely deteriorated social standards. Statistics show that fundamental causes for the struggle of our people is due to the great poverty of the poorest sections of our population, this being a result of internal as well as external factors. A glance at selected landmarks will give a glimpse into our situation. 1978 reports on Nicaragua

1. *Revista polémica*, la época. No. 21, p. 60.

reveal a general illiteracy level of 71%, with 100% in places such as Matagalpa, Jinotepe and Madeiz. The average caloric intake was 1843 (when the United States established an average of 2500) and 50% of the death rate affected those under the age of 14. There were only 1500 physicians (1 for every 10,000 inhabitants). Only 30% of the population had drinkable water and 47% of the homes in Nicaragua lacked electricity. The disparity between this reality and the economic, social and cultural rights guaranteed by Pacts, registries, agreements and declarations is clear.

Honduras faces a 60% level of illiteracy. In 1971 there were only 12 hospitals operating in Honduras and 362 health centers, and of these only 18 clinics belonged to the state, therefore benefiting only 1.5% of the population. Hospitals operate privately for the service of small minorities. More than 500,000 children suffer high risk malnutrition, with more children dying each passing year. In the year 2000 there will be 5,000,000 suffering from malnutrition and 200,000 of these will be under the age of five. Close to one million homes lack sanitary services. The life expectancy of a Honduran scarcely reaches 55 years of age and 43 out of every 100 children are born abnormal. The income per capita is calculated at $27 monthly. 279 landowners have control of 20% of the fertile lands and more than 185,000 peasant families have never had access to any kind of land ownership.

In Guatemala 41.7% of the population is unemployed and survivors have marginal jobs. The level of illiteracy is 63%. Land is owned by only a small percentage of people; 62% of rural ownership is in the possession of only 2.1% of the entire population. Because of electoral fraud, boycotting in Guatemala went from 55% in 1958 to 63.5% in 1978. In El Salvador illiteracy reaches 37.9% in the urban setting and 53% in the rural zones. The daily caloric intake is 1345 in the rural zones and 1682 in the urban zones. 45% of the children die under the age of four. In El Salvador only 0.0028% of the families hold owner-ship of 43% of the lands and 33% of national territory. In 1969, El Salvador had a shortage of 502,555 houses.[1] We shall see how the socio-economic and political causes determined the massive mobiliza-tion of people throughout the entire area, some as internal refugees and others as political exiles.

1. These data were drawn from M.E. Gallardo and J.R. López (eds.), *Centroamérica en cifras* (San José, Costa Rica: IICA-FLACSO, 1986), p. 260.

2. *Pivotal Characteristics Evident during this Period that Deserve Some Review*

a.   The two largest cities of the world in the year 2000 will be Mexico City and São Paulo with 20 to 25 million people strolling through their streets. In our little country, Costa Rica, the urban process will unite four central cities, forming a megalopolis of more than 2 million people. This urbanization of Central America has to do with immigration from the countryside to the cities, a trend on the rise since the 1960s with the creation of Central America's Common Market and industrialization. Meanwhile, cities envelope the unsuspecting in a world contaminated by smoke, oils, garbage and waste, which contrasts with the luxury and order of the 'other face' of the city. In order to save the illusion of utopia, the city dweller is forced to rejoice at the good side of the city, hiding personal epidemic conditions. However, the good side is most strange to the urbanite who looks up at the skyscrapers and steps into lobbies and halls decked with gold and silver. Brightly lit billboards trumpet companies that are foreign in every sense of the word.

b.   Indigenous sectors became more visible, especially in Guatemala (indigenous maya-quiches), Nicaragua (sambos, ramas and mezquitos) and in Panama (guaymies and kunas).

c.   The religious sectors, Protestants and especially Roman Catholics, began to engage many social issues favoring the marginal sectors.

d.   Transition from the farming industry to the importation industry caused the immigration of farmers to the city. This resulted in a great increase in delinquency, prostitution, unemployment and other social evils; thus worsening the poverty scale in the rural as much as in the urban areas. It is vitally important to see evangelization from the perspective of the victims produced by the cities, those whom Fung declares to be 'victims of the sins of others'. With the ascendance of importation and restoration of the Common Market of Central America, a new social class has emerged whose powers and interests depend upon power held over traditional sectors. This new group are managers of industries born under the sanction of the Common Market.

e.   Economic, social and political crises have had grave reper-
       cussions for greatly populated sectors. The impact of this
       reality in relation to a new interpretation of faith led many
       Christians to new pastoral models. The choices exercised by
       these churches have much in common with the new wave
       declared by Vatican II and Medellin, which opened a door
       for participation in the economic, social and political issues.

f.   At the onslaught of armed conflicts on the Central American
       scene, a great movement of refugees began to take place: El
       Salvadorians fled to Honduras and Guatemala; peasants from
       Guatemala and El Salvador were displaced within their own
       territory; indigenous groups and peasants from Guatemala
       were displaced in Chiapas and Yucatan in Mexico; peasants
       from Nicaragua escaping the war fled towards Costa Rica and
       Honduras; middle sectors of Guatemala and El Salvador
       migrated toward Costa Rica or Mexico City.[1]

Information given by the office of the public security of Costa Rica
mentioned that in August of 1979, 217,000 people came into Costa
Rica from Nicaragua. To this must be added 20,000 refugees from El
Salvador, and another 3000 from Guatemala, plus 10 to 20% of the
entire population of aliens who entered the country. This refugee
population of more than 250,000 people came to be situated mainly in
the prominent cities of the country. September 1978 saw the greatest
increase in refugees fleeing Nicaragua owing to indiscriminate
bombardments on the part of the Somoza dictatorship. In July 1979,
after the fall of the regime, a great percentage of these refugees
returned to their own country. Refugees entered Costa Rica by any
means possible; they would come by foot and enter through the
northern frontier. Various airplanes brought many who were situated
in the airport of Nicaragua named 'Las Mercedes'. They came by
buses, private cars and ships that left from the port of Nicaragua in
Bluefields, and even canoes escaped through the San Juan river. They
arrived precariously, without personal belongings, money, clothes;
they had no place to sleep, no food, no friends or acquaintances in
Costa Rica. Those of peasant stock incorporated suddenly into an
urban context were largely women and children; all were frightened,
with the shock of war on their faces. Most were illiterate and

1.   M.E. Gallardo and J.R. López in *Centroamérica in cifras*, p. 240.

therefore lacking an opportunity to study or work in Costa Rica. The strain in this alien culture was such that many were hesitant to admit they were Nicaraguan, sometimes feeling betrayed by their accent and darker skin.

Confronted with this dilemma, various churches and Christian groups, without previous experience, gathered in September, 1978, for the express purpose of organizing aid. It must be emphasized that from the outset this was the primary concern of the Episcopal Church of Costa Rica (the great majority of whom are blacks from the Atlantic zone). Participating also were about fifteen churches and Christian groups, albeit with great differences in theological, ideological and denominational orientations. There were Roman Catholic organizations such as Caritas, and Protestant ones such as the Salvation Army, who started immediately. The majority of evangelical churches did not participate. However, a social branch of the Evangelical Church of Costa Rica, Carabanas de Buenos Voluntad, collaborated to a great extent even though it remained on the fringes of this ecumenical effort. Pentecostal churches remained on the margins, but several individual Pentecostals cooperated fully.

Without fanfare, a committee void of title commenced work in an Episcopal church, situated on the outskirts of the city. With the Nicaraguan crisis of September, 1978 at hand, the need emerged to form a 'National Committee of Aid to the Nicaraguan Refugee'. After joining this committee, I was given the task of coordinating the main project in the central offices of Costa Rica's Red Cross. These offices opened on the 28th of February, 1979 and closed September 15 of the same year, all this time under my direct supervision.

During this period, we fed more than 10,000 people who came monthly to receive goods acquired from fellow Christians, friends and institutions worldwide. Each refugee was dealt with individually. In addition to 10,000 refugees, we processed 2000 to 3000 people who sought pastoral counselling. Our committee was charged with the work of refugees in the urban areas. Others such as the Salvation Army, Christian Association of Youth and the parish Fatima de Herdeia with Fr Higinio Alas, took on the task of reaching refugees in the rural areas of Liberia, La Cruz and Alajuela. Not all the refugees of the urban areas used our offices. Their fear created distrust towards a committee with which they were not familiar. Living conditions among the refugees in urban areas at times became desperate.

In June of 1979, newspapers publicized conditions of those who slept in parks, plazas and doorsteps of churches, most of whom were adolescents, women and children. It was obvious that we did not have the capacity to confront such an immense task. Nevertheless, the committee was able creatively to overcome each problem encountered. A system was developed with different performance levels, thereby permitting us to serve with greater efficiency. On the second level, our objectives were to give food, legal advice and medical assistance.

On the third level, objectives were designed with a clearer pastoral option. This led to the formation of a self-supported educational enterprise directed at maintaining the hope of their Christian faith, strengthening the love of their country, and building a just and democratic society. Significantly, this cooperative project was a creation of the refugees themselves. We served only as facilitators, assisting the formation of different groups according to occupations and professions.

Many goals were met, not least of all through the able assistance of the Vice-president of the Republic, the commissioner of the United Nations, the director of the Red Cross, the office of National Aid for Production, the Association of Nicaragua in Costa Rica, the Bureau of Labor, the Bureau of Health, the Social Security office of Costa Rica, the Bureau of Public Defense, the International Red Cross, several churches and communities, the Baptist Convention, Salvation Army, Caravans of Good Will, the Caritas, and the legal council of the University of Costa Rica.

With much volunteer assistance and studiously avoiding duplication of tasks, the committee achieved the results of a staff greater than fourteen. The team was composed of people of diverse nationalities, professions (secretaries, nurses, social workers, priests, pastors, lawyers and office workers) and religious faiths (catholics, protestants, evangelicals and even non-believers). An editorial in the committee's first bulletin resolved:

> As Christians, we are convinced that the situation of institutionalized violence against the civic public of Nicaragua is against the will of God since he created all people equal. He gave us the riches of the earth for our joy and benefit (Gen. 1.28-30). He made us according to his image (Gen. 1.26) and promised us a new heaven and a new earth... God's

desire is for all his children to realize a fullness as human beings and he desires that they would enjoy life to its fullest and be content.[1]

Their reservations removed, the refugees not only made use of all existing services, but showed the way as pressing needs arose. We routinely met with the refugees in order to discuss problems and design new policies. Included among the services provided were the following:

Acquisition of permits for employment
Medical aid for emergencies
Blood and lung medical exams
References for hospitals, clinics and health centers
Vaccinations for all infants
Food and other provisions monthly to all families
Housing for all refugees
Legal pressure brought to bear on organizations
    discriminating against the refugees
Legal suits against mistreatment, sexual abuse and
    psychological abuse of the refugees
Pastoral counseling to those who were emotionally
    disturbed because of the war
Distribution of clothing, mattresses, blankets
References for dental care
Facilitated employment in farming, construction,
    transportation, commerce, industries and the like
Revision of passports and legal papers for residency

In 1980, the committee left the Red Cross facility and formed what today is referred to as The Pro-Human Rights Ecumenical Committee (CEPRODHU). Since that time, the committee has made valuable contributions all across Central America. At present, the committee continues to work with the formation of 'animadores eclesiales', which directs special attention to evangelical churches. Recently, the committee has aided the general public affected by natural disasters, such as Hurricane Juana and the earthquakes of December 22, 1990 and April 22, 1991. We have engaged evangelical churches in a protest seeking the first law which would grant greater freedom for such churches in our country.

CEPRODHU was not only the first Christian organization for human rights, it was the first organization for human rights to emerge

1. CEPRODHU, 'Editorial comité ecuménico pro-derechos humanos', *Boletin CEPRODHU* 1.1 (San José), p. 2.

in Costa Rica. It contributed to the formation of several organizations for human rights, national and international, such as the Commission for the Defense of Human Rights in Central America (CODEHUCA). This organization was founded by members of our original committee who wanted to continue in service. Founding this organization required rising above great opposition. Today, CODEHUCA is a solid organization which represents human rights of all Central America and many groups outside Central America as well. CODEHUCA has been recognized by the United Nations as a non-governmental social organization for the defense and protection of human rights.

Some final reflections on the formation of The Pro-Human Rights Ecumenical Committee:

a.   Work among the refugees was motivated by a Christian commitment to aid an unprotected sector abandoned by its own governments. We were not motivated by a political or ideological objective, because no one had previous political involvement. The preoccupation of Jesus for the weakest of people (Lk. 4.18, 19; Mt. 25.40) began to take hold in our collective conscience. A new perspective for pastoral care celebrated the canonical accounts of his protection for peripheral people abandoned by society. The call to realize his kingdom filled with justice and peace swirled around our lives. Stirred by God's love for the refugees, he placed us as servants to their needs. Sacrifice was no stranger to any of us. At times wanting to run, God placed an ardor in our souls giving strength to complete the task.

b.   This was an evangelistic experience led by the Holy Spirit. It was evangelistic because we were evangelized. Contact with refugees, their pain, suffering, anguish, problems, needs and their attitude towards life marked us for life. I remember a certain sixteen year old young girl who had both hands amputated by a bomb when helping a neighbor escape. She helped around the office for several days. In spite of her physical handicap, she was always happy and alert. One day I told her that it was pleasing to see she had no inferiority complex about lacking hands. She replied, 'Brother Luis, so many in my country have given their entire lives, why should I not give my hands?' 'Why should I feel such a complex? I feel proud'. I wondered how many Christians would be willing to suffer in the same way. The gospel cause is not only personal, it is also social. Authentic evangelization must start by identifying with a given social segment. Known in Latin American as a 'theology of accompaniment', one cannot simply record the suffering of a refugee at a distance.

c.   It was an evangelistic experience for the refugees, understanding evangelization as spreading the good news of salvation. Many of us came with the thought of proselytizing, and many of us attempted to proselytize. But in concert we came to realize this was wrongheaded, causing division and straying off course. The committee—made up of Roman Catholics, Episcopalians, Baptists and Pentecostals—agreed that we needed to be evangelistic but not sectarian. We decided to give pastoral counseling based on fundamentals and our own testimonies. We proclaimed a God present in this hurting world who walks beside those who are suffering. Our main focus was to maintain in the refugees hope of their liberation and to make them aware that God shared in their anguish and pain. This was exceedingly difficult because there were many who had lost all hope. They had lived from war to war and could see no end in sight. Our labor became evangelistic because we were able to offer the hope of the good news of salvation. Even though we were not able to measure the impact of this evangelistic labor with statistics, we saw transformed lives.

May the Lord Jesus Christ allow that seed which was sown to grow and may he allow the narration of this experience to serve as a challenge to the faith of many, as he did with us. If we are correct, may God reaffirm it, if not, may the Lord show us the right path.

POVERTY, PERSECUTION AND DEPRIVATION IN THE LIGHT OF JESUS' CROSS AND RESURRECTION*

1. *Ioan Sauca*

Fr Sauca began by stressing the importance of the cross for the Orthodox faith. After enumerating specific occasions for signing the cross, he spoke of a heavy cross put on the shoulders of Orthodox churches. Sauca had reference to 400 years of Islamic domination replaced by a twin evil—communism with its atheistic dictatorship. Under such a regime, one spoke only of survival, not of progress.

Reflecting the ravages of persecution, Sauca turned to 2 Timothy 3.12, exclaiming that the absence of a thorn is cause for intense introspection. Pointing to paradoxes of resurrection and the grave, eternal life and death, Sauca argued that joy cannot be experienced separate from an internal crucifixion that actuates union with Christ.

The world's eyes were on Eastern Europe in 1989 as 'the wall' crumbled. Yet a cross remains on the shoulders of Romanian Christians because secularization is worse than atheistic communism. Government prohibitions regarding religion were routinely defied by even leading communists who would secretly frequent churches. Freedom decreases spirituality as packed churches are drained by enticements to leap out of the economic doldrums and follow any pied piper. A previously sheltered people now without covering are excessively vulnerable to alien philosophies and ideologies.

Freedom now sparks an internal conflict among Christians, as evangelistic maps color Romania 'untouched' by the gospel. This means that rather than outsiders from the West searching for former communists who do not know the Bible, a great deal of energy is spent trying to convert Orthodox members. Having been trained theologically in the West, Sauca chides these ecclesiastical warmongers for

* Space limitations permit only summaries featuring highlights from the following papers.

leaving behind empty churches and dividing Romanian believers.

A nominal component in the Orthodox church does not justify breaking the bond of peace forged under Islamic domination. If moral and biblical appeals fail to slow these intruders, then they must consider the cost of the onslaught of Western secularization and Muslim aggression. The exportation of Western schisms must give way to creative celebrations of a common spirituality among Christians.

2. *Anthony Lim*

Lim lifted up the word 'encounter' to describe the way of a Roman Catholic charismatic community of lay people who practice evangelization while alleviating suffering of those boxed in by severe poverty. Their target terrain is the jungle north of Baling. Deprived in every sense of the word, the village dwellers know neither hygiene, money nor agriculture. Rather, they struggle in an environment dominated by deadly snakes, infectious insects and rampant diseases. Starvation or disease end the life of most children before they can reach the age of 10.

The community deliberately places proclamation of the gospel as their priority. They are met with refrains like: Can Jesus Christ deliver me from poverty? Can he rid me of diseases? The response rests on the mandate to put first the kingdom of God. Having done so, the believer can take comfort in the assurance of Jesus not to worry about food and clothing (Mt. 6.25-34).

Stressing the Lordship of Jesus is not the end of ministry, but rather its proper context. These poverty stricken people are weighed down by an oppressive government as well as by the endemic practice of black magic. Their hearts laid bare by the probing Holy Spirit make clear the need for radical conversion. Human emotions overwhelm the person who walks into these villages because no one can tolerate such a plummeting scale of misery. The core problem is not solved by alleviating our sense of guilt by heaping crops on the villagers. The story too often repeated is that those who receive do not share but hoard.

This proves a clear study in contrasts, as authentic conversion came to an entire village where the community established a mission station. Medical care and agricultural development went hand in hand with gospel proclamation. In short order it was reported that disease disorders dropped by 90%. Past rivalries that bred violence now gave way to relationships based on trust. Other villages were astounded as they saw the same goods perish in their possession while this Christian village had an abundant harvest.

No more poignant tale could be told about the need for grafting in branches to the vine (see Jn 15.5) than another village that had welcomed missionaries for twenty years. Although achieving agricultural self-sufficiency, the people remained distressingly poor. These missionaries despaired of the endless cycle in which money fed intoxication and violence. Mr Lim's community was encouraged to introduce its concept of comprehensive transformation. Stunned observers saw the village turn around in two months, thus illustrating that the cross and resurrection of Jesus is truly hope for the poor.

3. *Ronald Sider*

Sider drew heavily from his seminal *Rich Christians in an Age of Hunger* to make a pointed jab at the misdirection of pentecostals and charismatics in the West. Exuberant claims of biblical elitism are erased by tragically low scores on awareness of God's special concern for the poor.

'Imagine what would happen if all our charismatic institutions would dare to undertake a comprehensive two-year examination of their total program and activity to answer the question: Is there the same balance and emphasis on justice for the poor and oppressed in our programs as there is in Scripture? I am willing to predict that if we did that with an unconditional readiness to change whatever did not correspond with the scriptural revelation of God's special concern for the poor and oppressed we would unleash a new movement of biblical evangelism and social concern that would change the course of modern history.

'I am afraid evangelicals and charismatics have fallen into theological liberalism...the essence of [which] is allowing our thinking and living to be shaped by surrounding society's views and values rather than by biblical revelation. We have allowed the values of our affluent materialistic society to shape our thinking and acting toward the poor.

'We urgently need three streams of contemporary church life to flow together, renewing and empowering each other. Social activists, evangelists and charismatics all need each other—in order both to be biblical and to be effective. Evangelism among the poor has integrity and is most effective when it is linked to self-help projects that empower the poor to earn their own way. And both interrelated tasks need the daily presence, power and gifts of the Holy Spirit.'

PENTECOSTAL SPIRITUALITY AND THE
CONSCIENTIZATION OF WOMEN

Cheryl Bridges Johns

As an expression of human sinfulness, the oppression of women is a cultural universal. Such oppression can be seen in societies which rejoice at the birth of sons and regret the birth of daughters. It is reflected in cultures that deny women the dignity of being fully adult—forbidding them such basic rights as ownership of property, public employment, political participation and choices in education, marriage and divorce. Such oppression of women manifests itself when they are forced to be covered in public and made to walk behind men. Within the painful reality of human sinfulness women are beaten, raped, set on fire and sold for profit. They often bear the burden of poverty and are at best second class citizens.

While it is true that Christianity has done more for the cause of women than any other movement in history, it may be argued that the results are merely a more comfortable form of oppression. Within the modern church women are often denied the dignity of being fully Christian. They are forbidden such basic participation as a voice in church government, public ministry, and choices in theological education. The church forces women to be covered both literally and symbolically. Seldom allowed to participate fully in the mainstream of church life, they are relegated to the 'court of women'. Women are abused through overwork, often bearing the financial burden of parishes while being treated as second class believers.

Alongside such oppression there is deep within the human experience of being female the desire to be fully human. To be fully human means both freedom of personal choice and the responsibilities of interdependent relationships.[1] The conflict between freedom and

1. While on one hand there is a strong longing for freedom within women, the experience of being female in a male dominated world strongly counters this desire.

relationship has led the modern woman to choose between being either 'pro-liberation' or 'pro-family'. She must deny either her longings for relationship or her desire for freedom.

Many who desire freedom from oppression view bitter warfare against those who would enslave them as the only alternative. So-called 'radical feminism' is a modern response to centuries of exploitation and domination. The fight against injustice is a normal response. As a result, men become (or remain) enemies who are to be conquered, and true humanization and partnership are denied both men and women. Those who desire relationship may suppress their own oppression.[1] They internalize the images offered them by their oppressors.

In stark contrast to bitter warfare is God's freedom and his shalom in Christ. The redemption of Christ restored women to their created vocation of ruling the earth jointly with men as their friends and equals. That God intended men and women to share tasks and to share authority in order to reflect God's full image and reach his goals is a basic presupposition of this paper.[2] One aspect of the redemptive

While male identity is defined in separateness and individuality, female identity is founded on oneness and connection with the mother. To be female is to be like the mother. Traversing the generations, from mother to daughter, the art of survival in a patriarchal culture has been handed down. This shared gender identity creates an ethos in which deference, submission and passivity are standards of behavior. To desire to be independent, therefore, is to be 'unfeminine' and 'subversive'. Consequently, women often repress such feelings and are openly hostile to those who challenge the status quo. For more information regarding the issues of female versus male identity and development, see C. Gilligan, *In a Different Voice* (Cambridge, MA: Harvard University Press, 1982); see also A. Wilson Schaef, *Women's Reality* (San Francisco: Harper & Row, 1985).

1.   This desire for relationship has been exploited by those who would lord it over women (Gen. 3.16). Many Christians have chosen to perpetuate sinful oppression rather than partnership, as numerous conservative Christians understand 'the created order' to be that of male domination. Such a view comes from an interpretation of Gen. 2 which characterizes the creation of Adam and Eve in a hierarchical relationship. Eve was made auxiliary to Adam, serving as a 'help-meet'. Women, therefore, are to be under the authority of men, existing as somewhat lower created things. Such a view has ramifications for the redemption of women, which is never as 'complete' as the redemption of men. Therefore, in the church, women are unfit for 'higher' offices which would indicate authority and holiness.

2.   A. Besancon Spencer, *Beyond the Curse* (New York: T. Nelson, 1985). Spencer's exegesis of Gen. 1 indicates that both Adam and Eve were created in

mission of Christ included liberation of women from entrenched male domination caused by the fall. This redemption is a present reality manifest by tangible signs of shalom.

However, women's redemption has not fully arrived; there is the 'not yetness' of the kingdom marked by the groaning of the whole unredeemed world. Women and men today live between the cross and the parousia, holding up hope for God's coming in the painful realities of this world.[1] The reality of the present is that women are oppressed. The reality of the present which is the reality of our future breaking in upon our present, is that Christ has liberated and reconciled us. This future has announced itself in our past and is making itself known in our present. We as Christians, therefore, are, in Moltmann's words, 'asked to see human dignity and existence from the viewpoint of the future announced by God'.[2]

How can we live out our eschatological–ontological vocation in a world which so strongly seeks to deny us freedom and shalom? We are empowered to live from the viewpoint of God's future by the Holy Spirit who is at work on the earth waging his own holy war against the powers of darkness. This war, as Paul Valliere has pointed out, is the 'quarrel of Pentecost',[3] which actualizes God's future in the historical present. Therefore, the liberation of women paid for at Calvary can only be fully achieved in the charismatic community of the Spirit. The liberating work of the Holy Spirit provides the necessary

God's image and were commanded to rule over the earth (Gen. 1.28). She offers a literal reading of 2.18 as, 'And the Lord God thought it was not good for the Adam to be by himself; I will make for him a helper as if in front of him'. The phrase 'in front of him' utilizes the word *kᵉnegdô* which is made up of three thought units: the prefix *k*, the preposition *neged* and the suffix *ô*. The prefix *k* indicates comparison, similarity, while the suffix *ô* signifies 'him'. The preposition *neged* which lies between the prefix and the suffix literally describes physical relationships as being to 'the front' or 'the visible'. God therefore made Adam a helper 'as in front of him'. Had Eve been created in an inferior position, the writer should have used a term to mean 'after' or 'behind'. Further, the word helper (*ēzer*) does not imply inherent subordination. The term most frequently refers to God (thirteen times). Clearly, Adam and Eve were created as mutual partners.

1.   J. Moltmann, *The Future of Hope* (New York: Herder & Herder, 1970), p. 8.

2.   J. Moltmann, *The Experiment Hope* (Philadelphia: Fortress Press, 1975), p. 39.

3.   P. Valliere, *Holy War and Pentecostal Peace* (New York: The Seabury Press, 1983).

context for the conscientization of women as to their eschatological-ontological vocation as subjects of history.[1]

This paper attempts briefly to describe the aspects of such a community of the Spirit which would have implications for the conscientization of women. I wish to offer symbols of hope which allow us to 'live already here out of the promised future of our true home'.[2] My approach will be to analyze dimensions of the eschatological vision of reality inherent in pentecostalism which announce, in the present, God's future for women and men. I envision this task as an attempt to ignite what Walter Brueggemann has labeled as the 'prophetic imagination'. The objective is 'to move back into the deepest memories of... community and activate those very symbols that have always been the basis for contradicting the regnant consciousness'.[3] It is important, therefore, that the symbols utilized in conscientization not be 'general and universal... but those that have been known concretely in this particular history'.[4] Thus, conscientization would not involve the tacking on of a new ideology (e.g. secular feminism) to serve a crisis, but would involve what Brueggemann has called 'the primal dimension of every memory' of the pentecostal community. This 'primal dimension' includes the biblical witness as well as the story of those of us who claim the fullness of the Spirit. The structure of this paper will therefore involve a consideration of biblical precedents and historical antecedents which will be brought into dialogue with the mythologized reality of contemporary pentecostalism.[5]

---

1. The term 'conscientization' was coined by the Brazilian educator Paulo Freire, who defines its meaning as the means in which women and men become aware of their sociocultural reality and take action as subjects of their historical future. For Freire, conscientization is 'more than a simple *prise de conscience*, ...it...implies the insertion of the conscientized person into a demythologized reality. It also involves 'a radical denunciation of dehumanizing structures accompanied by the proclamation of a new reality'. See *Pedagogy of the Oppressed* (trans. M. Bergman Ramos; New York: Seabury Press, 1970), p. 46.

2. J. Moltmann, 'Theology as Eschatology', in F. Herzog (ed.), *The Future of Hope* (New York: Herder & Herder), p. 38.

3. Brueggemann, *The Prophetic Imagination* (Philadelphia: Fortress Press, 1978), p. 66.

4. Brueggemann, *The Prophetic Imagination*.

5. For this paper pentecostalism will be defined as a worldwide movement which has as its common denominator the baptism of the Spirit following what is known as the re-birth or salvation experience. This definition is based upon an

Biblical Precedents

The Bible tells a story of hope inasmuch as it reveals God's future. Therefore, 'the writings in the Old and New Testaments comprise the history book of God's promises'.[1] These promises are given and actualized by the Holy Spirit who is at work today calling us into remembrance of 'these dangerous and liberating memories which crowd in upon our present and place it in question by warning us of our unattained future'.[2] The Bible is God's hope for women. It contains God's promises to us. It points to our future which the Holy Spirit is now actualizing.

Old Testament

In the Old Testament the Spirit is *rûaḥ* God's breath which fills ultimate void and creates life. Such a power unleashed is creative and life-giving, bringing nomos (order) out of chaos. This Spirit is ultimate power—power which cannot be tamed or domesticated. It is the wind that dried up the flood waters that covered the earth. It is the power which held back the waters of the Sea. The Spirit's power is liberating. It frees the world from chaos and people from oppression.

The power of the Spirit also impinged upon individuals and allowed them to see an alternative reading of reality that is the revelation of God's purpose and intent for the world. These prophets were often uncredentialed by the world's standards, but were nonetheless subjects of a divine historical process. God's word was the power of conscientization which 'included both insight into underlying reality and action based on that insight'.[3] The combination of insight and action created events which shaped the flow of history. God's word carried forth his intentions, despite human efforts to counter his will.

Isaiah 11 indicates the agenda of the Spirit through the one who would have the Spirit's anointing:

---

understanding of pentecostalism as a movement with certain characteristics which can be isolated as common among many groups.

1. Moltmann, *The Experiment Hope*. p. 45.
2. Moltmann, *The Experiment Hope*. p. 45.
3. R. Tholin, 'The Holy Spirit and Liberation Movements: The Response of the Church', in D. Kirkpatrick (ed.), *The Holy Spirit* (Nashville: Tidings, 1974), p. 43.

He shall not judge by what his eyes see,
or decide by what his ears hear;

but with righteousness he shall judge the poor,
and decide with equity for the meek of the earth;
he shall strike the earth with the rod of his mouth,
      And with the breath of his lip he shall kill the wicked.

Righteousness shall be the belt around his waist,
And faithfulness the belt around his loins (11.4-5 NRSV).

While the human agenda is to exercise power and control, the Spirit's agenda is the actualizing of justice and righteousness via the Anointed One.

Prophetic voices also spoke of a time in the future in which all people would know about God's alternative reality:

And it shall come to pass afterward, that I will pout out my *rûah* upon all
      flesh;
Your sons and your daughters shall prophesy, your old men shall dream
      dreams, and your young men shall see visions.
Even upon the menservants and maidservants in those days I will pour out
      my *rûah* (Joel 2.28-29).

Such a time would involve the *rûah* of God indwelling both male and female, who would 'bring into public expression those very hopes and yearnings that have been denied so long and suppressed so deeply that we no longer know they are there'.[1] Within the human heart there is hope and longing for the restoration of the created order in which women are equal partners in working and ruling. The prophets dared to speak this hope.

The Example of Christ

In the New Testament the Spirit's activity is renewed and fully actualized in the messianic mission of Jesus. The gospel of Luke gives clearest witness to this mission. Luke's account describes the energizing and creative power of the Spirit in ushering in the fulfillment of that

---

1.   Brueggemann, *The Prophetic Imagination*, p. 67. Brueggemann's thesis is that the prophetic function involves the expression of hope, which is 'the refusal to accept the reading of reality which is the majority opinion; and one does that only at great political and existential risk'. Such hope is grounded in the 'promising speech of God' which is 'true even in a world where kings have tried to banish all speech but their own'.

which was begun at creation. This powerfully 'new' outpouring of the Holy Spirit is proclaimed through the prophetic speech of people such as Mary, Zechariah, Simeon and John the Baptist.

Jesus himself announced his mission in terms of the Spirit's anointing:

> The Spirit of the Lord is upon me, because he has anointed me to preach good news to the poor. He has sent me to proclaim release to the captives and recovery of sight to the blind, to let the oppressed go free, to proclaim the year of the Lord's favor (Luke 4.18-19 NRSV).

Christ's mission clearly was directed by the Holy Spirit and involved liberation for the oppressed. Through Christ God was at work establishing a 'new Israel' which Gerhard Lohfink describes as a contrast society whose people in their conduct 'correspond to the liberating action of God who chose Israel from all nations and saved it from Egypt'.[1] Jesus' establishment of a new order involved the dismantling of Israel's social barriers by the Spirit. His new community welcomed those who were formerly denied community: the poor, women, Gentiles, children, Samaritans. This re-drawing of the lines of Israel was revolutionary; it was welcomed by some and disdained by others.

Jesus' solidarity with the marginalized is characterized by compassion. This compassion constitutes a radical form of criticism, because it announces that hurt is to be taken seriously, that pain and grief are not normal.[2] Specifically, Jesus' compassion for women (e.g. the Samaritan woman, Mary Magdalene, the grieving widow) is not to be understood simply as 'personal emotion but as public criticism in which he dares to act upon his concern against the entire numbness of his social context'.[3] He reconciled women unto himself, and in order to do this marvelous action he dared to enter their world of alienation and pain.

Therefore, Jesus' compassion involved the embracing of the hurt in such a manner as to enter into the pain and embody it. Jesus did this to

---

1. Lohfink proposes that Jesus' gathering of disciples must be understood in light of the eschatological vision of re-establishing God's people in order to carry out irrevocably his plan of having a holy people in the midst of the nations. Such a vision aimed for the social order in which the reign of God would be lived. This social order was to exist in stark contrast to the rest of society (G. Lohfink, *Jesus and Community* [London: SPCK, 1984]).

2. Brueggemann, *The Prophetic Imagination*, p. 85.

3. Brueggemann, *The Prophetic Imagination*.

the degree that the pain of the marginalized became his pain and his own history. Women, who were viewed as ritually unclean, spiritually inferior and socially outcast were invited by Christ to partake of his 'living water' and to proclaim his gospel (Jn 4). Their redemption was not secondary to the redemption of the 'sons of Abraham'. Abraham *also* had daughters (Lk. 13.10-13). Through faith in Christ women were brought into the direct inheritance of the covenant.

The Early Church

The apostle Paul describes in Galatians this direct inheritance as being actualized in a community of the Spirit characterized by freedom from the bondage of the law, justification and the right to rule over Christ's estate.[1] Both women and men are now 'joint heirs with Christ Jesus'. Herein is the presence of shalom. Where there was once fractured relationship now there is unity with the Creator and unity between male and female.

The New Testament communities understood that their adoption as daughters and sons was being actualized through the Holy Spirit, who reconciles humanity to Christ and bears witness that we are indeed the children of God. The seal of the Holy Spirit is a 'guarantee' of our inheritance. Pentecost, therefore, signifies the fullest expression of this adoption. It brought the power to actualize God's intentions for humanity, as partners with Jesus in manifesting the kingdom of God.[2] The purpose of being filled with the Spirit, therefore, is for the accomplishing of mission. It is the equipping for continuing the ministry which Jesus inaugurated. This purpose includes the ministry of reconciliation—entering into worlds marked by pain and alienation and announcing the good news of shalom.

The mission of Pentecost involves both men and women as co-laborers and joint heirs as members of God's new *ekklēsia* (1 Cor. 15.9; Gal. 1.13). The New Testament communities exhibited a conscious awareness of their role in continuing the mission of Christ. Lohfink sees this continuation in the presence of miracles, the elimination of

1. Spencer parallels this inheritance with the original occupations of humanity found in Gen. 1–2. Once again humans have been given the world and are called to oversee their inheritance. See *Beyond the Curse*, pp. 65-71.
2. R. Stronstad, *The Charismatic Theology of St Luke* (Peabody, MA: Hendrickson, 1984), p. 51.

social barriers,[1] the praxis of togetherness, brotherly love, and the renunciation of domination. Such communities existed as radical contrast societies to the dominant order. There was the experience of conscientization—a reading of reality as subjects of a divine historical process. God's people were empowered to live out in their present God's promised future.

Clearly, there is abundant biblical evidence that the Holy Spirit serves as actualizer of the liberating presence of God. There is the freeing from the bondage of sin in all of its ugliness. Women are freed at the cross and empowered by the Holy Spirit to go beyond the curse to their eschatological ontological vocation as subjects of God's holy history.

Historical Antecedents

As Christians, not only is our present praxis to be informed by *The Story* of Scripture, but we are also to interpret critically our present reality in light of the story of our historical past. Within the corporate story of contemporary pentecostalism there exists the witness of the liberating power of the Holy Spirit. Specifically, the pentecostal story contains the story of the conscientization of women.[2] It is a story of

1.   Lohfink argues that while Jesus called no women into the circle of the Twelve, this action does not depreciate the role of women in the reign of God. Lohfink sees the constitution of the Twelve as a symbolic prophetic act representing Jesus' claim on the twelve-tribe people. This new Israel could not be symbolized by women—at least not in a patriarchal milieu. Lohfink sees the incorporation of women in the ranks of disciples as a clear indication of their inclusion in the eschatological people of God. He further acknowledges that 'Only in the Spirit is it possible to dismantle national and social barriers, group interests, caste systems, and domination of one sex over the other' (*Jesus and Community*, p. 93).

2.   The field of women's studies in religion has largely overlooked the pentecostal movement and its contribution to the liberation of women. David Roebuck, in a recent review of the research on women in pentecostalism, found very few references to Pentecostal women in bibliographies concerning women in religion. Likewise, bibliographies written specifically about the pentecostal movement or about the Holy Spirit often fail to give attention to women. Most of these works deal with the theology of the Holy Spirit or the phenomenon of glossolalia. Roebuck's research found two bibliographies to be helpful for research concerning women in the pentecostal movement: D.W. Faupel's *The American Pentecostal Movement: A Bibliographic Essay* (Wilmore, KY: B.L. Fisher Library, Asbury Theological Seminary, 1972), and C.E. Jones's *Guide to the Study of the Pentecostal Movement*

people who violated that which was considered to be the will of God in order to do the will of God. It is a story rich with symbols of freedom, partnership and hope.

With the inception of modern day pentecostalism, women, as recipients of the gift of the Holy Spirit, found themselves experiencing a new dimension of freedom. They found themselves preaching, speaking in tongues and giving interpretations, laying hands on the sick for healing. Women became writers, defending their new found liberty. Many left for the mission field, in spite of the fact that there was little institutional support for their venture.

Ordination by an organized church was irrelevant because Spirit baptism was the only credential necessary for ministry. The 'call' was enough for both women and men. God was sovereign, choosing whom he willed. For the end time harvest of souls men were compelled to leave fields and factories and women were called from their kitchens.

Such a compulsion to 'go and tell' pre-empted social norms and accepted patterns of ministry. Women were liberated for public ministry. Blacks and whites worshipped together. The rich and the poor danced together in the Spirit. The fuel for these manifestations was an eschatological urgency and equality in which the Spirit enlisted everyone for the mission at hand. These were the days of the 'latter rain' (Joel 2.28).[1] God's promised future was again breaking into human history.

These early days, which have been characterized as the era of

(2 vols., Metuchen, NJ: Scarecrow/American Theological Library Association, 1983). See D.G. Roebuck, 'Pentecostal Women in Ministry: A Review of Selected Documents', *Perspectives in Religious Studies* 16.1 (Spring, 1989), pp. 29-44.

    More attention has been given to women in Pentecostalism from a sociological perspective. E. Lawless's *Handmaidens of the Lord* (Philadelphia: University of Pennsylvania Press, 1988) gives an in depth field study of women ministers in the state of Missouri, USA. See also C. Barfoot and G. Sheppard, 'Prophetic vs. Priestly Religion: The Changing Role of Women Clergy in Classical Pentecostal Churches', *Review of Religious Research* 22.1 (September, 1980), pp. 2-17.

    1.   For an excellent treatment of Pentecostal spirituality, especially regarding its eschatological vision, see S.J. Land, *Pentecostal Spirituality: A Passion for the Kingdom* (JPTS, 1; Sheffield: Sheffield Academic Press, forthcoming). See also D.W. Faupel's comprehensive and insightful 'The Everlasting Gospel: The Significance of Eschatology in the Development of Pentecostal Thought' (PhD Dissertation, University of Birmingham, England, 1989).

'prophetic pentecostalism',[1] were highlighted by strong female imagery. The Church of the last days was the 'Bride' being prepared for the Bridegroom. Such feminization of the church was an affront to society and to traditional churches. In addition, the high percentage of women within the movement and the large number of females in leadership positions were scandalous marks of a 'devilish cult'.

Along with the recognition of the charism of the Spirit upon women there existed within pentecostalism a critical-reflective reinterpretation of Scriptures concerning the 'silence' of women. This reinterpretation, which had already begun in the holiness movement of the 19th century, was now given new impetus and meaning.[2] Scripture was to be interpreted within its teleological framework for the effecting of God's salvation history. The Bible was a closed canon and as such was normative for faith and practice, but God was continuing to speak and to act in ways that brought fulfillment to the purposes of Scripture. In gist, it was expected that the church of God's latter rain would more completely fulfill the character of kingdom of God as revealed in Scripture than did its first century counterpart (the early rain). Problems confronting the early church were to be overcome. Galatians 2.28 was to be actualized. Women silenced by custom or creed were now by the Spirit free to speak.

In summary, as Walter Hollenweger has observed, manifestations

1. Building upon Max Weber's insight that 'the religion of the disprivileged classes is characterized by a tendency to allot equality to women, but that after the first stage of a religious movement there is reaction against pneumatic manifestations of charisma among women', Charles Barfoot and Gerald Sheppard have labeled the period from the turn of the century until the mid 1920's as 'prophetic Pentecostalism'. This period is characterized by an abundance of female mystical imagery and by equality for women, but quickly gave way to 'priestly Pentecostalism', which came as a result of institutionalization. Consequently, there was a marked shift in the symbolic function of Pentecostal leadership from 'prophet' to 'priest'. Reactions against the manifestations of charisma among women occurred and the number of women in leadership positions rapidly declined. Barfoot and Sheppard tested their thesis by examining the decline in the number of women ministers in several traditional pentecostal denominations. See their 'Prophetic vs. Priestly Religion'.

2. The Holiness movement, with its emphasis on the 'latter rain', presents a strong historical witness to the equality of women and men. For an excellent treatment of the movement's radical stance toward women, see L.S. Dayton and D. Dayton, 'Your Daughters Shall Prophesy: Feminism in the Holiness Movement', *Methodist History* 14 (July, 1976), pp. 67-92.

of the Spirit such as speaking in tongues, visions, dreams, and the like, have historically served to liberate the people from dehumanizing cultural, economic and social forces.[1] They have provided a voice to people who have been reduced to silence by cultural prejudices.[2] They have announced the presence of God's promising future. Such manifestations have provided hope for the hopeless. This power of the Spirit is dangerous, for it makes people aware of their dignity and significance. When they experience such conscientization there is freedom to reflect and to act as historical subjects of God's inbreaking future.

The Spirit's power is also relational. Pentecostals had a vision which included both liberation and reconciliation. In regard to this vision Hollenweger has observed that:

> the time before the birth of the pentecostal movement is accordingly painted in dark and hopeless colors and in fact as 'a Babylonian captivity of the church'. Then came the miraculous liberation movement, the pentecostal communities, to put an end to all strife within Christendom... Prior to the return of Jesus on the clouds of heaven there was only one legitimate goal: the sanctification and unification of the children of God and the evangelization of the world within a generation.[3]

Contemporary Implications: Where are we Now?

Since World War II much of the prophetic, counter–cultural zeal of pentecostals has waned. The exception to this is within parts of the so-called Third World. Many of us have been co-opted out of our

1.　W.J. Hollenweger, 'Creator Spiritus', *Theology* 81 (1978), pp. 32–40. See also his 'The Social and Ecumenical Significance of Pentecostal Liturgy', *Studia Liturgica* 8 (November 4, 1971–72), pp. 207-15. Also his 'Flowers and Songs: A Mexican Contribution to Theological Hermeneutics', *International Review of Mission* 60 (1971), pp. 232-44 (238). Hollenweger's work on the revolutionary nature of Pentecostalism has been ground breaking and insightful. He has challenged those of us within the tradition to theologize out of our distinctive ethos rather than 'adding to' the standard theological fare the doctrine of the baptism of the Holy Spirit as if such a doctrine had no hermeneutical, epistemological or social distinctive.

2.　W.J. Hollenweger, 'Pentecostalism and Black Power', *Theology Today* 30 (October, 1973), pp. 228-38.

3.　Hollenweger, 'Charismatic and Pentecostal Movements: A Challenge to the Churches', in D. Kirkpatrick (ed.), *The Holy Spirit* (Nashville: Tidings, 1974), pp. 210-11.

revolutionary mission and accommodated to culture. In many instances the pentecostal movement has failed to address social evil, at times choosing to perpetuate cultural oppression, especially in regard to gender, race and caste. We have chosen to live as if the imposed reality of the present was our reality.

Currently, we have an abundance of 'priestly pentecostalism' which is characterized by a hierarchial male clergy and a high degree of institutionalism. In such an ethos, it is not enough that women have the charism of the Holy Spirit. They have the wrong chromosomal structure to enter the priesthood. Those groups that do allow women ordination have found that fewer women are seeking to enter the ranks of ministry due to lack of encouragement and institutional support.

The difference in the 'place' for women in pentecostalism, when we were the 'orphan daughter' of the religious world, and women's 'place' as we are becoming a 'mighty man' can be seen in the relegation of women to auxiliary ministries. Such relegation follows the pattern of mainstream churches in which women are free to perform service projects, do fund raising and hold prayer meetings. But it must be understood that their 'place' is in the court of women. Moves toward integrating women into the mainstream of church life have been met with accusations of radical, secular feminism.

In spite of these changes within the movement, there exists within pentecostalism a dangerous corporate memory of its revolutionary roots. Concurrently, there is also the presence of the Holy Spirit who is manifesting himself today in powerful ways in the lives of many women.

It is the task of pentecostals to interpret our present in light of God's future which is now present and revealed through the written word and our own story. Such a task will require that we seek to be filled with the Spirit, not only in worship, but in lifestyle.

As we drink from our own wells of spirituality we will find a corporate confessional identity which includes the symbols of revolution and shalom. We then should confessionally offer these symbols as a basis for confronting a world full of pain and oppression.

In conclusion, pentecostal spirituality offers an alternative reading of reality, a reading marked by an eschatological vision of God's new order. Ours is a spirituality of hope, hope for the conscientization of all God's children.

PENTECOSTAL ORIGINS FROM A GLOBAL PERSPECTIVE

Cecil M. Robeck, Jr

The subject of Pentecostal origins is a multi-faceted one which is very much on the agenda of modern Pentecostal historiography. There are those who desire to connect the origins of the modern Pentecostal movement with the work of Charles F. Parham who proclaimed himself to be the founder and projector of the movement.[1] There are those who desire to connect the origins of Pentecostalism to the work of Pastor William Joseph Seymour and the Apostolic Faith Mission which arose in Los Angeles, California in April 1906.[2] There are

1.   It is clear that the Azusa Street Mission readily acknowledged the formative role of Charles F. Parham in the founding of the Apostolic Faith Mission in Kansas in 1901. Cf. 'Letter from Bro Parham', *The Apostolic Faith* [Los Angeles] 1.1 (September, 1906), 1.1; 'The Old Time Pentecost', *The Apostolic Faith* [Los Angeles] 1.1 (September, 1906), 1.2; 'The Pentecostal Baptism Restored', *The Apostolic Faith* [Los Angeles] 1.2 (October, 1906), 1.1. By late November, 1906, however, Parham and Seymour had sundered any further association with one another. Parham, however, continued to claim leadership in the origins of the Apostolic Faith Movement, as for instance in his article 'Leadership', *The Apostolic Faith* [Baxter Springs, KS] 1.4 (June, 1912), pp. 7-9. The term 'Projector' of the Movement is applied to Parham in Houston as early as August, 1906. Cf. 'Dr Parham Arrives', *Houston Daily Post*, August 10, 1906, p. 4. Parham's original biography, by Sarah F. Parham, was entitled *The Life of Charles F. Parham: Founder of the Apostolic Faith Movement* (Joplin, MO: Hunter Printing Company, 1930, rpt. 1969 and rpt. New York: Garland Publishing, 1985).

2.   Following the rupture in the relationship between Parham and Seymour in late November and early December, 1906, the Azusa Street newspaper published an article entitled 'Pentecost with Signs Following', *The Apostolic Faith* [Los Angeles] 1.4 (December, 1906), 1.1-2. This article noted that 'Some are asking if Dr Chas. F. Parham is the leader of this movement. We can answer, no he is not the leader of this movement of Azusa Mission'. The article affirmed, however, that 'The Lord was the founder and He is the Projector of this movement'. Later historians of the Movement such as James Tinney (William J. Seymour [1855?–1920?]; Father

those who see themselves as constituting the earliest Pentecostal denomination, thereby claiming to be the original Pentecostals by noting that some of their leaders or members spoke in tongues prior to either Parham or Seymour.[1] There are those who view the origins of Pentecostalism as a sovereign work of God which can be traced to no single leader or group, but rather to a spontaneous and simultaneous outpouring of the Holy Spirit around the world.[2]

The subject of Pentecostal origins is made more complex when the question of what defines or constitutes a Pentecostal is raised. In North America, and especially among white North America, the definition of a Pentecostal is usually related to the doctrine that the initial evidence or the initial *physical* evidence of the baptism in the Holy Spirit is an ability to speak in tongues.[3] Sometimes this has been labeled 'the Pentecostal distinctive'.[4] Others, such as Professor

of Modern Day Pentecostalism', *The Journal of the Interdenominational Theological Center* 4 [Fall, 1976], pp. 33-34, also published under the same title in *The Journal of Religious Thought* 4.1 [1976], pp. 33-34, and rpt. in James S. Tinney and Stephen N. Short, *In the Tradition of William J. Seymour: Essays Commemorating the Dedication of Seymour House at Howard University* [Washington, DC: Spirit Press, 1978], pp. 10-20), Douglas J. Nelson ('For Such a Time as This: The Story of Bishop William J. Seymour and the Azusa Street Revival: A Search for Pentecostal Roots' [PhD dissertation, University of Birmingham, England, 1981]) and Iain MacRobert (*The Black Roots and White Racism of Early Pentecostalism in the USA* [New York: St Martin's Press, 1988]), all tend to view Seymour as the real founder of the Movement.

1.   See, for example, the claim of C.W. Conn (*Like a Mighty Army: Moves the Church of God, 1896–1955* [Cleveland, TN: Church of God Publishing House, 1955], p. 25), that 'Spirit baptism... with the accompanying manifestation of speaking in tongues', 'happened in 1896—ten years before the outpouring of the Holy Ghost in California' among the earliest pioneers of the Church of God.

2.   This position was popularized in part by Donald Gee (*Wind and Flame* [Croydon, England: Heath Press, 1967], pp. 29-30) and championed by Carl Brumback (*Suddenly... From Heaven* [Springfield, MO: Gospel Publishing House, 1961], pp. 48-63), who calls the Pentecostal Movement a 'child of the Holy Ghost'.

3.   On the importance of this idea for North American Pentecostals, see G.B. McGee (ed.), *Initial Evidence: Historical and Biblical Perspectives on the Pentecostal Doctrine of Spirit Baptism* (Peabody, MA: Hendrickson Publishers, 1991).

4.   In 1918 the issue of the relationship between speaking in tongues and the baptism was raised within the General Council of the Assemblies of God. It was described as 'what has always been considered the distinctive testimony of the Pentecostal people'. A resolution declaring it to be the 'distinctive testimony' of the

Donald Dayton have urged Pentecostals to understand themselves
through a paradigm involving several theological factors.[1] The four
he identifies were present in a slightly different form in the American
Wesleyan/Holiness Movement of the 19th century, but they were
reconfigured in Pentecostal thinking and used quite forcefully and
effectively in the form which Aimee Semple McPherson popularized.
'Sister' McPherson taught that Jesus Christ, who was 'the same
yesterday, today, and forever' (Heb. 13.8), was to be understood as
Savior, Baptizer in the Holy Spirit, Divine Healer and Coming King.[2]
Still others, such as Professor Walter J. Hollenweger, have argued
that the paradigm must be understood more broadly yet. He argues
that one must also include a variety of cultural, sociological and
psychological factors within the Pentecostal self-understanding. He
makes room for narrative theology, oral liturgical practice through
song and testimony, appeal to dreams and visions, understandings of
the interrelatedness between body and mind, and participation in
prayer and the processes of decision making by members of the whole
community.[3] In still other definitions, the role of speaking in tongues
might be diminished, and set alongside other charisms such as
prophecy or healing.[4]

Assemblies of God was adopted. See *Minutes of the General Council of the
Assemblies of God*, September 4–11, 1918, especially Saturday Afternoon,
September 7, 1918, pp. 7-8.

1.   D.W. Dayton, *Theological Roots of Pentecostalism* (Grand Rapids:
Zondervan Publishing Company, 1987; Meteuchen, NJ: The Scarecrow Press,
1987).

2.   Dayton, *Theological Roots*, p. 21. See Aimee Semple McPherson, with
Georgia Stiffler, collaborator, *The Foursquare Gospel* (Los Angeles: Echo Park
Evangelistic Association, 1946), pp. 13-14.

3.   See, for example, W.J. Hollenweger, 'After Twenty Years' Research on
Pentecostalism', *International Review of Mission* 85 No. 297 (January, 1986),
pp. 3-12; *idem*, 'Pentecostal Research in Europe: Problems, Promises, and People',
EPTA Bulletin 4.4 (1985), pp. 124-53; 'Priorities in Pentecostal Research: Historio-
graphy, Missiology, Hermeneutics and Pneumatology', in J.A.B. Jongeneel (ed.),
*Experiences of the Spirit: Conference on Pentecostal and Charismatic Research in
Europe at Utrecht University, 1989* (Studies in the Intercultural History of
Christianity, 68; Frankfurt am Main: Peter Lang, 1991), pp. 7-22.

4.   J. Sepulveda, 'Pentecostal Theology in the Context of the Struggle for Life',
in D. Kirkpatrick (ed.), *Faith Born in the Struggle for Life: A Re-Reading of
Protestant Faith in Latin America Today* (trans. L. McCo; Grand Rapids: Eerdmans,
1988), pp. 298-318, esp. pp. 317-18.

The issue of Pentecostal identity is an important one which, in recent years, has been the subject of considerable discussion.[1] Whoever determines that identity for the Pentecostal movement is placed in a unique and privileged role. In this definitional act, there is power. The movement may be variously understood as white in its origins, thereby favoring members of certain North American churches,[2] or having black origins, thereby providing a source of pride and inspiration to African-American Pentecostals and other people of color.[3] It may be held up as spontaneously originating *'Suddenly...from Heaven'*,[4] as one historian of the movement noted, thereby avoiding either the historical question or any clear dependence on a single, and presumably problematic individual,[5] or any clear dependence upon a discordant 'Pentecostal' work elsewhere in the world.[6] Attempts have also been made to understand Pentecostals as having either a Wesleyan–Holiness heritage[7] or a Reformed

1. This is especially true in Latin America. Cf. Sepulveda, 'Pentecostal Theology', pp. 298-318, and G.O. Vaccaro, *Identidad pentecostal* (Quito, Ecuador: Editorial del Consejo Latinoamericano de Iglesias, 1990).

2. Those who favor the priority of Parham, especially those of Parham's own Apostolic Faith movement (Baxter Springs, KS) may be motivated in this way. It is evident that Parham's rejection of Seymour was at least partially based on racial bias. See C.F. Parham, *New Years Greeting* (Baxter Springs, KS) (January, 1912), p. 6.

3. . See above, n. 2, and J.S. Tinney, 'The Blackness of Pentecostalism', *Spirit: A Journal of Issues Incident to Black Pentecostalism* 3.2 (1979), pp. 27-36. Other Pentecostals of color who look fondly at the heritage they see in the Black origins on Azusa Street are writers of the *Relevant Pentecostal Witness* ([Catsglen, RSA: no publisher, no date], pp. 3-4), an important statement on social justice within the South African context.

4. Brumback, *Suddenly...From Heaven*, p. 48.

5. C. Parham, for instance, proved to be a problematic leader of the movement once he had been arrested on charges of homosexuality. See on this J.R. Goff, Jr, *Fields White unto Harvest: Charles F. Parham and the Missionary Origins of Pentecostalism* (Fayetteville, AR: The University of Arkansas Press, 1988), pp. 136-41.

6. Criticism of certain Latin American autochthonous works by North American Pentecostals as well as criticism of certain North American Pentecostal denominations and their missionary churches by certain Latin American autochthonous church leaders seem to contribute to this idea.

7. Dayton, *Theological Roots of Pentecostalism*, pp. 35-84; V. Synan, *The Holiness-Pentecostal Movement in the United States* (Grand Rapids: Eerdmans, 1971), pp. 217-18; R.M. Anderson, *Vision of the Disinherited: The Making of*

heritage,[1] each with its corresponding implications.

In an attempt to come to terms with whether there is a single location for Pentecostal origins we must first set to rest the theory of multiple origins in the form of spontaneous and simultaneous outpourings of the Spirit around the world. To date this has not been fully accomplished, although as new sources have emerged, they have revealed a great deal about the nature of Pentecostal origins in a variety of locations. The tendency on the whole is not to take the spontaneous outpouring theory as a serious contender for explaining Pentecostal origins. There are two very significant factors which make this so. First, there is a great deal of interconnectedness between what appears to be the source of Pentecostal origins and the places where it was previously thought that independent spontaneity had been the key factor. Secondly, without wishing to be triumphalistic, the evidence gathered in all serious quests for the origins of the modern Pentecostal movement appears inevitably to point to North America.[2]

To say all of this is not to deny that spiritual ground was being turned in other places around the world where people were said to be seeking God. The famous Welsh revival was in full force in 1904–1905, the 1905–1907 revival among Pandita Ramabai's girls in Mukti, India was very significant, and the famous Korean 'Pentecost' came in 1907.[3] Yet none of these revivals came to be identified with

American Pentecostalism (New York: Oxford University Press, 1979), p. 28.

1.   E.L. Waldvogel, 'The "Overcoming Life": A Study in the Reformed Evangelical Origins of Pentecostalism' (PhD thesis, Cambridge, MA: Harvard University, 1977.

2.   The role of personal correspondence and publications such as Azusa Street's *The Apostolic Faith* are not to be underestimated (see, for example, T.B. Barratt's inquiries into the subject: *When the Fire Fell and an Outline of My Life* [Oslo, Norway: T.B. Barratt, 1927), pp. 103-109, 123-27). The role of missionaries sent from Azusa Street must also be taken seriously at this point.

3.   On Wales see S.B. Shaw, *The Great Revival in Wales* (Chicago, IL: S.B. Shaw, 1905). The revival among Pandita Ramabai's girls is described in M.F. Abrams, *The Baptism of the Holy Ghost and Fire (Matt. 3.11)* (Kedgaon, India: 'Mukti Mission' Press, 1906), and in tract form by R. Nalder, 'Pandita Ramabai and the Child Widows of India' (Evangel Tracts, 6; Chicago, IL: The Evangel Publishing House, 1908, 32 pages). The story of the revival in Korea is told in W.N. Blair, *The Korean Pentecost and the Sufferings Which Followed* (Edinburgh: The Banner of Truth Trust, 1909, rpt. 1977).

the Pentecostal movement until quite recently, and then only apart from self-definition.[1]

The claim made by one or more denominations that they had members who spoke in tongues prior to the Topeka, Kansas outburst on December 31, 1900 among the students of Charles Parham and the establishment of Seymour's Apostolic Faith Mission at 312 Azusa Street in Los Angeles, California is not a serious contender either. The expectation that people might receive the 'gift of tongues' at the end of the 19th Century and the beginning of the 20th Century was a common one, especially among members of the Wesleyan Holiness movement.[2] The claim that certain persons spoke in tongues only served to raise that expectation. It was not until well after the establishment of the mission on Azusa Street that Pentacostals began to claim, at least in writing, that such activity had taken place in earlier years.[3] Only then could they argue that they had been 'baptized in the Spirit' in the 1890s or earlier, but they had had to wait until 1906 or 1907 for a full understanding consistent with emerging Pentecostal theology in order to interpret their experience in these terms.[4] But to

1. See, for instance, Boo-Woong Yoo, *Korean Pentecostalism: Its History and Theology* (Studies in the Intercultural History of Christianity, 52, Frankfurt am Main: Peter Lang, 1988).

2. W.B. Godbey (*Spiritual Gifts and Graces* [Cincinnati, OH: God's Revivalist Office, 1895], p. 43) maintained that the gift of tongues 'is destined to play a conspicuous part in the evangelization of the heathen world, amid the glorious prophetical fulfillment of the latter days. All missionaries in heathen lands should seek and expect this Gift to enable them to preach fluently in the vernacular tongue at the same time not depreciating their own efforts'. This work has been reprinted in *Six Tracts by W.B. Godbey* (New York: Garland Publishing, 1985). In Los Angeles, Joseph Smale had encouraged his congregation at First New Testament Church to pray in 1905 for the restoration of all the gifts. Cf. 'Queer "Gift" Given Many', *Los Angeles Daily Times*, July 23, 1906, I.5.

3. See, for instance, B.F. Lawrence, *The Apostolic Faith Restored* (St Louis, MO: The Gospel Publishing House, 1916), pp. 44-51 rpt. in *Three Early Pentecostal Tracts* (New York: Garland Publishing, 1985), and 'History of Pentecost', *The Faithful Standard* 1.6 (September, 1922), pp. 5-6, pp. 20-21.

4. A prime example is A.J. Tomlinson, General Overseer of the Church of God (Cleveland, TN). It was in January, 1907 after G.B. Cashwell had visited Azusa Street and taken the message to North Carolina and elsewhere in the South that Tomlinson began to preach baptism in the Spirit. It was not until a year later (January, 1908), that at Tomlinson's request Cashwell visited Cleveland, Tennessee and Tomlinson spoke in tongues. A.J. Tomlinson, *Answering the Call of God*

acknowledge this fact is to speak against any understanding of self-consciously Pentecostal origins as dating from the time their members began to speak in tongues.

In a sense, the real issue of Pentecostal origins is planted firmly at the feet of Charles F. Parham and William J. Seymour. What remains is to establish their connection, to evaluate their relationship and to determine what, if anything, these men might have shared which was and is uniquely formative for Pentecostalism. To do this, we must begin with Charles F. Parham, for he is clearly the earlier of the two, and he alone claims to be founder and projector of the Apostolic Faith movement.

That Parham and Seymour had worked together in the Houston, Texas area in early 1906 is a documentable fact. Seymour was enrolled in one of Parham's short-term Bible schools in January and February, and the two held meetings together in the black area of Houston.[1] By the time February of 1906 was into full swing, however, Seymour had determined that he would leave Houston to take an offer to serve as pastor in a small Holiness church in Los Angeles. Traveling from Houston to Los Angeles by way of Denver, where he visited Alma White and the Pillar of Fire, Seymour arrived in Los Angeles on February 22, 1906.[2]

Los Angeles was a thriving city of 230,000, of whom about 5000 were black. It was growing at a rate of 100 persons each day, and in 1906 became the nation's 17th largest city. Each arriving train brought more immigrants to the city, and travel baggage began to collect in ever larger piles on the railroad docks.[3]

The African-American population of Los Angeles was served by roughly 10 historic black churches. First African Methodist Episcopal was the largest, with 900 members. Formerly known as Steven's AME

(Cleveland, TN: The White Wing Publishing House, no date), pp. 10-12. See also D.D. Preston, *The Era of A.J. Tomlinson* (Cleveland, TN: White Wing Publishing House and Press, 1984), pp. 50-51.

1. Nelson, 'For Such a Time as This', p. 167.

2. Alma White describes Seymour's visit to Denver in *Demons and Tongues* (Zaraphath, NJ: Pillar of Fire, 1936), pp. 67-68. The date of Seymour's arrival in Los Angeles is given in W.J. Seymour, *The Doctrines and Discipline of the Azusa Street Apostolic Faith Mission of Los Angeles, Cal.* (Los Angeles, CA: W.J. Seymour, 1915), p. 12.

3. 'Colonist Baggage Congestion on the Banner Day of Season Test of Nerves and Capacity', *Los Angeles Express*, November 4, 1907, p. 1.

Church, it had property at 312 Azusa Street which was gathering dust. The lower floor was used for storage, and as a stable, while a number of rooms on the second floor served briefly as a series of apartments.[1]

There was no *official* policy of racial segregation in the city at that time, but the lines were nonetheless quite clear. Most of the black population could be found near the railroad tracks just east of downtown. There were, however, more or less isolated racial incidents which erupted from time to time.[2] There were a number of lower to lower-middle class blacks who made Los Angeles their home, but there was also a substantial middle to upper-middle class including some professional people in the African-American community.[3]

Seymour began his work in Los Angeles, bringing what he had to bear on the small black Holiness Church on Santa Fe Street, which was being led by Mrs Julia W. Hutchins. What he brought included a teaching he had received from Charles F. Parham, a doctrine in which the ability to speak in tongues was understood to be the 'Bible evidence' of baptism in the Spirit in keeping with the apostolic experience described in Acts 2.4.

Exactly what transpired at the first meeting at which Seymour preached at the Santa Fe Street mission may be more complex than the simple explanation that Seymour was rejected by Mrs Hutchins for preaching Parham's theory. Regardless of the reason, Seymour was locked out of the church and soon turned his attention to a home Bible study group which met on North Bonnie Brae Street. There, Seymour was free to explain Parham's theory, and the group began to pray for revival.

When in April, 1906, people from the group began to speak in tongues, the word spread quickly and the group was forced to move outside to accommodate the crowds. A search for space was conducted

1. Revd G.W. Bryant, 'Religious Life of Los Angeles Negroes', *Los Angeles Daily Times*, February 12, 1909, III.7; C.M. Robeck, Jr, 'The Earliest Pentecostal Missions of Los Angeles', *Heritage* 3.3 (Fall, 1983), p. 3.

2. 'Police Hold Mob at Bay', *Los Angeles Herald*, April 7, 1906, p. 7; 'Try to Mob Negro Preacher', *Los Angeles Daily Times*, June 7, 1906, II.10; 'Puts Ban on Anti-Negro Signs', *Los Angeles Herald*, May 7, 1907, p. 12; 'Edendale Indignant over Negro Neighbors', *Los Angeles Express*, October 2, 1907, II.11; 'Police Aid Negroes to Occupy House', *Los Angeles Herald*, October 8, 1907, p. 6.

3. Dr A.C. Garrot, 'Negro Professional Men in the City', *Los Angeles Daily Times*, February 12, 1909, III.2; K. Bradley Stovall, 'Both Refined and Cultured in Life', *Los Angeles Daily Times*, February 12, 1909, III.4.

and by April 15, the group had located and renovated the old building
on Azusa Street which would become known as the Apostolic Faith
Mission.[1]

Word spread quickly through the entire city as the *Los Angeles
Times* announced that a 'Weird Babble of Tongues' had hit the city.
To Los Angeles, already known for its eclectic and entrepreneurial
spirit, this was a totally new experience. 'Another new religion had
been started—in Los Angeles, of course', observed one perceptive
skeptic. 'The intention seems to be to keep on inventing new religions
until every man has his own. Then maybe we'll have peace.'[2]

Seymour brought more than Parham's theory on the 'Bible
evidence' when he went to Los Angeles. He was open to the new.
From the first, he led a racially integrated Bible study on Bonnie
Brae,[3] then a racially integrated mission on Azusa Street. It was not
the only racially integrated church in town,[4] but it was probably the
only such church whose pastor was an African-American.
Furthermore, while it began as a predominantly black church, the
number of whites who visited Azusa Street grew rapidly so that the
congregation was not only larger, with attendance reaching as high as
700, but the racial makeup of the congregation was more evenly
divided. While newspapers called it a 'negro' church, they were scan-
dalized by the way whites and blacks worshipped so freely together,
often praying with one another, touching and embracing one another,
even kissing across racial lines. 'Women with Men Embrace', head-
lines blared. 'Whites and Blacks Mix in a Religious Frenzy', they

1.   C.M. Robeck, Jr, 'William J. Seymour and "The Bible Evidence"', in
McGee, *Initial Evidence*, pp. 72-95.

2.   'Weird Babel of Tongues', *Los Angeles Daily Times*, April 18, 1906, II.1;
'Pen Points', *Los Angeles Daily Times*, April 19, 1906, II.4.

3.   While it was a largely Black gathering, several whites, including
Frank Bartleman, attended these meetings. So Frank Bartleman, *How Pentecost
Came to Los Angeles* (Los Angeles: F. Bartleman, 1925), pp. 43-44. This work is
reprinted in *Witness to Pentecost: The Life of Frank Bartleman* (New York: Garland
Publishing, 1985).

4.   First New Testament Church had both Black and White members. The
Holiness Church of Southern California was also often an integrated church. See on
this Josephine M. Washburn, *History and Reminiscences of the Holiness Church
Work in Southern California and Arizona* (South Pasadena, CA: Record Press,
1912; rpt. New York: Garland Publishing, 1985).

proclaimed self-righteously.[1] This fact, along with the Pentecostal acrobatics including jumping, shouting, rolling, diving, swooning and dancing, all of which joined speaking in tongues on a more or less regular basis at Azusa Street, led one local Baptist pastor to caricature the place as a 'disgusting amalgamation of African voodoo superstition and Caucasian insanity', which he predicted would disappear just as quickly as it had appeared.[2]

Seymour's services were innovative in that the people were just as welcome to speak—or testify, or read Scripture, or sing, or manifest some charism—as he was. Women and men, old and young, white and black, poor and rich were all treated equally. Everyone waited before God, and when someone believed that he or she had something to share they did it. It was a community which took very seriously the concept of a 'priesthood of all believers'.[3]

Foremost among Seymour's concerns was not merely a doctrine of baptism in the Spirit, but a concern to steer people toward the giver of the gifts rather than the gifts themselves,[4] and a serious regard for a genuine priesthood of all believers. High in priority was the enlistment of people for evangelistic and missionary activities. Seymour established Monday morning 'leaders' meetings which enabled the Mission to undertake coordinated evangelistic efforts in local and outlying areas.[5] Wherever the various streetcar lines went, a tent meeting, street meeting, storefront church or rented hall meeting was set up. When workers were arrested in Whittier, other workers were recruited and sent on the next street car to take their place.[6] Evangelism placed high on the mission's agenda.

Within three months, evangelists who had been commissioned by the mission were traversing the western US. Within four months they

1. 'Women with Men Embrace', *Los Angeles Daily Times*, September 3, 1906, p. 11.
2. 'New Religions Come, Then Go', *Los Angeles Herald*, September 24, 1906, p. 7.
3. 'How Holy Roller Gets Religion', *Los Angeles Herald*, September 10, 1906, p. 7.
4. 'The Baptism with the Holy Spirit', *The Apostolic Faith* [Los Angeles] 1.11 (October–January, 1908), 4.1.
5. 'Beginning of World Wide Revival', *The Apostolic Faith* [Los Angeles] 1.5 (January, 1907), 1.2.
6. 'Unusual Noise', *The Apostolic Faith* [Los Angeles] 1.3 (November, 1906), 1.4.

were moving into the southern and eastern US, and the message was reaching into Canada. Within five months the Mission had commissioned missionaries to Africa, notably Liberia and Egypt as well as the Middle East. By the end of the year it had missionaries in each of those places as well as Angola and Scandinavia, and more were preparing to go to the Far East, notably the Philippines, Japan, Hong Kong, Malaysia, China and India.[1]

The mission's newspaper, *The Apostolic Faith*, issued thirteen times between September 1906 and 1908, played a significant missionary role as well. It carried news, testimonies, sermons, exhortations and reports from around the world to as many as 50,000 subscribers. Thomas Ball Barratt, a Methodist minister from Norway, began corresponding with people at the mission as a result of reports he read in *The Apostolic Faith*. While he was in New York on a fund-raising tour he connected with missionaries from Azusa Street who were going to Africa and the Middle East. He prayed with them, received his 'baptism in the Spirit', and left on the same ship with them for Liverpool, England. Within a week he was holding meetings in Norway and telling of his experience.[2] Later he was called by Alexander Boddy to England to tell of the Pentecostal experience and he was widely used on the continent to do the same.[3]

M.L. Ryan of Spokane, Washington heard evangelists from the mission who made their way to the Northwest. He subsequently traveled to Los Angeles to see for himself what was taking place on Azusa Street. Inspired by what he saw there he returned to the Spokane area where he recruited a number of followers who traveled

1.   Untitled article, *The Apostolic Faith* [Los Angeles] 1.1 (September, 1906), 1.4; 'Good News from Danville, VA', *The Apostolic Faith* [Los Angeles] 1.1 (September, 1906), 4.2; 'Testimonies of Outgoing Missionaries', *The Apostolic Faith* [Los Angeles] 1.2 (October, 1906), 1.4; 'The Work in Virginia', *The Apostolic Faith* [Los Angeles] 1.2 (October, 1906), 3.2; 'Spreading the Full Gospel', *The Apostolic Faith* 1.3 (November, 1906), 1.4; 'Pentecost in Seattle', *The Apostolic Faith* 1.4 (December, 1906), 1.2; 'From Los Angeles to Home and Foreign Fields', *The Apostolic Faith* 1.4 (December, 1906), 4.1; 'En Route to Africa', *The Apostolic Faith* 1.4 (December, 1906), 4.1; etc.

2.   Barratt, *When the Fire Fell*, pp. 108-9, 123-24, 128; T.B. Barratt, 'The Seal of My Pentecost', *Living Truths* 6.12 (December, 1906), pp. 736-38; 'Baptized in New York', *The Apostolic Faith* 1.4 (December, 1906), 3.2; 'Speeding to Foreign Lands', *The Apostolic Faith* [Los Angeles] 1.5 (January, 1907), 3.1.

3.   Barratt, *When the Fire Fell*, p. 143.

with him to the Philippines, Japan and China in 1907.[1]

Latin America, too, was touched by the revival at Azusa Street, though generally by a more indirect means. To be sure, a number of Hispanic workers went from Azusa Street to Mexico.[2] William H. Durham, a Chicago pastor, came to Azusa Street in 1906 where he received the Pentecostal experience. Returning to Chicago with his testimony of what God was doing in Los Angeles, his ministry became a Pentecostal one.[3] Two Swedes, Gunnar Vingren and Daniel Berg, who came into contact with Durham's ministry, established the Pentecostal work in Brazil.[4] In Chile, Reverend Willis C. Hoover was touched by the reports he heard coming from Azusa Street through correspondence with Minnie Abrams who had received her Pentecost at Azusa Street.[5] The later immigrant- and missionary-established churches in Latin America clearly had direct influence from Azusa Street, while the early autochthonous churches such as Hoover's work in Chile were more indirectly touched and were much less influenced in later years by external forces.

Seymour's work at Azusa Street, however, was not embraced by Parham as Seymour had hoped it might be. Parham visited the mission

1. 'Editors Receive the Pentecost', *The Apostolic Faith* [Los Angeles] 1.3 (November, 1906), 3.4; 'In Spokane', *The Apostolic Faith* [Los Angeles] 1.6 (February–March, 1907), 3.1; M.L. Ryan, 'Pentecost in Spokane, Wash.', *The Apostolic Faith* [Los Angeles] 1.7 (April, 1907), 4.3; 'Missionaries Depart in a Tearful Mood', *Seattle Post–Intelligencer*, August 29, 1907, p. 6; 'Ryan Leader of a Peculiar Sect', *Seattle Post–Intelligencer*, September 3, 1907, p. 4. The personal correspondence of one young woman who travelled from Spokane to China with Ryan has been compiled by Homer and Alice Fritsch, *Letters from Cora* (no city, privately published, 1987).

2. See M. Gaxiola-Gaxiola, 'Latin American Pentecostalism: A Mosaic within a Mosaic', *Pneuma: The Journal of the Society for Pentecostal Studies* 13.2 (Fall, 1991), pp. 115 and 121.

3. W.H. Durham, 'A Chicago Evangelist's Pentecost', *The Apostolic Faith* [Los Angeles] 1.6 (February–March, 1907), 4.2-3.

4. 'Secrets of the Remarkable Pentecostal Revival in Brazil', *Pentecost* 77 (September–November, 1966), p. 2; W.J. Hollenweger, *The Pentecostals: The Charismatic Movement in the Churches* (Minneapolis, MN: Augsburg Publishing House, 1972; rpt. Peabody, MA: Hendrickson Publishers, 1988), pp. 75-77.

5. M.C. Hoover, 'Willis Hoover Took a Stand', *Heritage* 8.3 (Fall, 1988), p. 5. See also Hoover's own 1909 account reprinted in *Historia del Avivamiento Origin y Desarrollo de la Iglesia Evangelica Pentecostal* (Santiago, Chile: Eben-Ezer, 1978), p. 28.

in December, 1906 and rejected Seymour's work and was himself ejected from the mission. His assistant W.R. Quinton announced to one local paper,

> We conduct dignified religious services, and have no connection with the sort which is characterized by trances, fits and spasms, jerks, shakes and contortions. We are wholly foreign to the religious anarchy which marks the Los Angeles Azusa street meetings, and expect to do good... along proper and profound Christian lines.[1]

Parham went on to hold meetings at the location of what would soon become the white Pentecostal mission which drew from Azusa Street and First New Testament Church. That mission became known as the Upper Room Mission.[2]

Parham's rejection of what was happening at Azusa Street, coupled by his arrest in San Antonio, Texas in 1907, and persistent rumors over his lifestyle, ultimately led to rejection of his continuing leadership in the movement.[3]

Seymour's rejection of Parham, and ultimately his rejection of Parham's teaching that speaking in tongues was the 'Bible evidence' of baptism in the Holy Spirit, did not endear him to all Pentecostals either. Seymour went on to argue profoundly that the fruits of the Spirit were essentially evidential of Spirit baptism as well, and that the evidence of the Spirit's work had to be measured with an ethical component in combination with or even in lieu of any charismatic manifestation.[4] The Upper Room Mission strongly disagreed.[5] Ultimately, too, Seymour's leadership was rejected by white Pentecostals who migrated from Azusa Street to the Upper Room Mission.[6]

On the whole, then, white Pentecostals in North America and those churches which they have most directly influenced continue to embrace Parham's teaching that tongues were the Bible evidence,

1. 'Apostolic Faith People Here Again', *Whittier Daily News*, December 13, 1906, p. 1.

2. The article 'Hold Meetings Daily', *Los Angeles Herald*, November 7, 1906, p. 7) lists Parham's noon meetings as being conducted at Metropolitan Hall, 327-1/2 South Spring Street. That was also the address of the Upper Room Mission.

3. 'Evangelist is Arrested', *San Antonio Light*, July 21, 1907, p. 2.

4. Robeck, 'William J. Seymour and "the Bible Evidence"', esp. pp. 82-89.

5. E.K. Fisher, 'Stand for the Bible Evidence', *The Upper Room* 1.1 (June, 1909), 3.3.

6. Bartleman, *How Pentecost Came to Los Angeles*, p. 84.

though they tend to disassociate themselves from Parham. That teaching, first pioneered by Parham, was later modified to become the 'initial evidence' or the 'initial *physical* evidence.' On the whole, black Pentecostals in North America and those churches which were most directly influenced by William Seymour and Azusa Street have tended to look at the ethical dimension and, while remaining open to tongues as a charism or as a 'sign which follows' the baptism in the Spirit, have been more reticent to accept a hard-line doctrinal commitment to any initial evidence doctrine.[1]

While Parham may have contributed one or two items of significance to early Pentecostal self-understanding, such as (1) his doctrine of the 'Bible evidence', (2) his hope that tongues would further the missionary and evangelistic efforts of the Church, and (3) his vision that the Pentecostal movement would provide a great ecumenical experience which would ultimately bring all Christians together, it is clearly the thinking of William J. Seymour and the experience of Azusa Street which has played the more significant role in Pentecostal *and* Charismatic self-definition.

It should come as no surprise that Latin American Pentecostals meeting in an *encuentro* in Santiago Chile in December, 1990 have proposed an agenda for further study, the first point of which is 'to study and delve into the historical origins of Pentecostal faith, with the goal of characterizing the particular Pentecostal identity as a catalyzing agent for social change'.[2]

Nor should it come as a surprise to find black Pentecostals in South Africa writing,

> In the Azusa Street Revival we find the legitimacy to continue our witness as Pentecostals. It was here that God called to himself a prophetic movement in an oppressive society that belied the dignity of black people. It was here [sic] that powerless people were baptized in the Holy Spirit and endued with power to preach the good news of Jesus Christ with 'signs following'. It is in this tradition that we come bearing a Relevant Pentecostal Witness.[3]

1.   Robeck, 'William J. Seymour and "the Bible Evidence"', pp. 88-89.
2.   R. Cabezas, 'The Experience of the Latin American Pentecostal *Encuentro*', *Pneuma: The Journal of the Society for Pentecostal Studies* 13.2 (Fall, 1991), p. 184.
3.   *Relevant Pentecostal Witness*, p. 3.

The Azusa Street Mission needs to be studied in order to rid us of our less than pristine mythologies regarding Pentecostal origins. We need not fear what we might find, but rather, we need to open ourselves once again to what God's Holy Spirit might be saying to us through the Azusa Street experience. To be sure it was charismatic. To be sure, it hoped to bring an end to racism in the Church. To be sure, it was committed to the idea that every member was in ministry. To be sure it was ecumenical in its character. To be sure it was evangelistic and missionary minded. To be sure it was deeply concerned with personal and social ethics. To be sure, it may still hold the seeds to the continued success of the Pentecostal and Charismatic movements as they look to the ways in which God would have them proceed into the 21st Century.

A RESPONSE TO CECIL M. ROBECK

Japie J. Lapoorta

I want to congratulate Dr Robeck on his well documented and stimulating presentation. He more than adequately highlights significant aspects of Pentecostal beginnings. Being in basic harmony with this version, there remain various facets which merit closer inspection in an effort to evaluate properly the African contribution.

1. Robeck correctly traces roots of the North American Pentecostal Movement from the 18th century Wesleyanism via the 19th century Holiness Movement to the Azusa Street Revival.

2. Robeck identified two main actors in the early days, viz. Charles F. Parham and William J. Seymour. By doing this, he refutes the myth that the Pentecostal Movement had no human leader(s). This argument is especially popular among white Pentecostals who do not want to name Parham because of the homosexual allegation, or Seymour because of his blackness.

3. Robeck correctly holds also that Parham gave the Movement the doctrine of 'biblical or initial evidence', that is, speaking in tongues as sign that one has been baptized in the Spirit. This doctrine was passed on to Seymour while a student at Parham's school in Houston. Seymour publicly advocated such a teaching during campaigns in Los Angeles that preceded his own experience of Spirit baptism.

3.1. Seymour's contribution to the Pentecostal Movement, according to Robeck, was more than just propagating the 'initial evidence' dogma. In this regard, Robeck refers to the *racial equality* evident when the Spirit was poured out in Bonnie Brae then Azusa Street under the leadership of Seymour, who probably was the only

African-American pastor of an integrated church in Los Angeles.

Integration, equality and black leadership owe something to the Holy Spirit and Seymour's African world-view. The Holy Spirit dealt with the breaking down of sinful barriers which separated Spirit-filled children of God. The African world-view is a holistic perspective where there is no dichotomy of spiritual and material, secular or sacred. Humankind are seen first as individuals in Western thinking, while the communal takes precedence over the individual in the common African perspective.[1]

3.2. Flowing from this African impetus is the situation of black suffering and oppression. Leonard Lovett says in this regard '...that black pentecostalism emerged out of the context of the brokenness of black existence'.[2] It is precisely for this reason that it is difficult for serious, black pentecostals to close their eyes to stifling oppression. Speaking in the early 1970's, Lovett laments, 'Previous studies on pentecostalism have not viewed black pentecostals in proper historical context because of a failure to appreciate the full spectrum of the heritage of blacks who were numbered among the pentecostals'.[3] Lovett further explained that black pentecostalism affirms:

> Authentic liberation can never occur apart from genuine pentecostal encounter (i.e. the presence of the Spirit and likewise, authentic pentecostal encounter does not occur without liberation. No man can genuinely experience the fullness of the Spirit and remain a bona fide racist.[4]

3.3. Racial and gender equality were further evident in the board of the first elders in the Apostolic Faith Mission at Azusa, where seven of its members were women with five men, three black and nine white.[5] Such action crushed the walls of racism and sexism both in the pulpit and the pews. The Azusa Street Revival exemplified Acts 2, where the Spirit fell and shattered barriers of race, gender and class delineated in Gal. 3.28.

---

1. I. MacRobert, *The Black Roots and White Racism of Early Pentecostalism in the USA* (New York: St Martin's Press, 1988), p. 101.
2. L. Lovett, 'Black Origins of the Pentecostal Movement', *Aspects of Pentecostal-Charismatic Origins* (ed. V. Synan; Plainfield, NJ: Logos, 1975), p. 138.
3. Lovett, 'Black Origins of the Pentecostal Movement', p. 127.
4. Lovett, 'Black Origins of the Pentecostal Movement', p. 140.
5. R.M. Anderson, *Vision of the Disinherited* (Oxford: Oxford University Press, 1979), p. 56.

3.4. The aforementioned events at Azusa constitute a relevant prophetic witness, because they defied structures of society designed with the intent of keeping blacks in subjection. The Azusa Street Mission did not simply reflect the face of society—segregated and unjust—but it endeavored to express characteristics of the kingdom of God where justice reigns. In this regard, Azusa provides us as pentecostals, confronting racial oppression, economic injustice and severe discrimination against our sisters simply on the basis of their womanhood, an excellent hermeneutical key.[1]

4. It is important to note that the newly emerged Pentecostal Movement quickly suffered three secessions. This in turn resulted in the rebuilding of the broken walls.

4.1. The first break, as is acknowledged by Robeck, revolved around Parham in 1906. According to historian Douglas Nelson, Parham heard rumors about the behavior of the Azusa Street Mission. These rumors alleged that whites and blacks were intermingling, kissing one another with the holy kiss across the racial line and that whites were imitating blacks in their 'jumping, shouting, rolling, diving, swooning and dancing'.[2] Parham came to Azusa at the invitation of Seymour, but was greatly agitated by what he saw because it was against every acceptable custom in mainstream American society. Parham's rebuke for such ghastly behavior led to the irreconcilable rift between Seymour and himself. Parham then briefly led a break-away group with about 200 to 300 people from Azusa.[3]

4.2. The second fracture occurred in 1908 when Seymour married Jenny Evans Moore. A small, influential group under Sisters Lum and Crawford moved to Portland, Oregon and started a new mission.

---

1. *Relevant Pentecostal Witness in South Africa* (Durban, R.S.A.: Relevant Pentecostal Witness Press, 1988), pp. 3-4.
2. *Los Angeles Herald*, September 24, 1906, p. 7, as quoted by Robeck, p. 174.
3. D. Nelson, 'For Such a Time as This: The Story of Bishop William Joseph Seymour and the Azusa Street Revival' (PhD dissertation, University of Birmingham [England], 1981), p. 203.

Clara Lum, secretary, took the mailing list of Seymour's *Apostolic Faith* newspaper with them.[1]

4.3. The third incident developed while Seymour was busy with a campaign in New York. In the absence of Seymour, Durham confused Azusa congregants with his teaching about the 'finished work of Calvary'. Nelson calculates the inevitable rupture as the start of a new movement.[2]

MacRobert has this to say about the schisms:

> All of the white Pentecostal leaders sooner or later separated themselves from Seymour and Azusa. Their rationalisations for doing so varied as did their time of leaving, but ultimately the whites split away from Seymour and their black religious origins, and Seymour's dream of equality and interracial fellowship was left in tatters.[3]

This fragmentation led to more schisms and ultimately culminated in segregation marking the movement world-wide. Typically, predominantly white Pentecostal churches who have links with blacks want to control and keep black churches in subjection through financial means.

5. I plead for a return to our roots. Twentieth century Pentecostalism has become a radical contradiction of the original divine intervention. God desires that the church, which is his body, should be one so that the world may believe. John 17 depicts an inseparable link between unity and evangelization. It is not an either–or thing. Going back to our roots implies that we are challenged to remove walls of racism, classism and sexism erected after Azusa.

The problem in Pentecostalism for blacks is not 'initial evidence' but racism. Blacks are trying to get back to the holistic approach by examining the black roots. Blacks are acutely aware of the fact that this is the only way of dealing adequately with sins like structural racism and economic exploitation. For this reason, they want to proclaim the Lordship of Christ over everything that exists. They are not looking for ways and means to run away from the world, because God died for this world. Jesus prayed to the Father (John 17.15) to keep

1.   Nelson, 'For Such a Time as This', pp. 246-48.

2.   Nelson, 'For Such a Time as This, pp. 246-48.

3.   MacRobert, *Black Roots and White Racism*, p. 64.

them in the world. Blacks are not searching for a utopia that escapes the realities of life here on earth.

Let us not evaluate the Pentecostal Movement on the basis of its present divisions, which cast a shameful shadow over the divine intention. The words of Jesus as recorded in Mk 10.6 seem applicable to our discussion. When asked about the letter of divorce which Moses permitted due to the hardness of hearts, Jesus replied, 'It was not like this in the beginning'.

CHARLES PARHAM AND THE PROBLEM OF HISTORY IN THE PENTECOSTAL MOVEMENT

James R. Goff, Jr

Pentecostals have been less than candid about their past. A lack of historical perspective has created the tendency, shared by many religious movements, to glorify the past and seek support for a theological interpretation of the present. When that happens, history becomes at best a back-slapping affirmation of a spiritual agenda and, at worst, a series of white-washes. The objective observer knows that neither is prudent—from an institutional standpoint, both cause credibility problems in the long run, and, from a theological standpoint, a divine Creator would not be in need of such help.

The problem becomes particularly acute with respect to the origins of the movement. Early Pentecostals saw no need to record history; like most millennial groups, and early Christianity in general, they focused on the primary task of spreading what they felt was an inspired word for their generation. Nevertheless, a few wrote memoirs or journalistic accounts.[1] By the time the second generation got around to interpreting and writing history, the process of institutionalization was in full swing. The parousia would surely take place, but in the meantime, it may pay to write the human story down. The history the second generation wrote was not always objective, but it did serve the purpose of listing names, dates and signal events.[2] Most

---

1. The best in this category are F. Bartlemann's *How Pentecost Came to Los Angeles* (Los Angeles: By the Author, 1925); T.B. Barratt's *When the Fire Fell and An Outline of my Life* (Larvik, Norway: Alfons Hansen and Soner, 1927); and B.F. Lawrence's *The Apostolic Faith Restored* (St Louis: Gospel Publishing House, 1916). For an analysis of the merits and pitfalls of these early accounts, see G. Wacker, 'Are the Golden Oldies Still Worth Playing? Reflections on History Writing among Early Pentecostals' *Pneuma* 8 (Fall, 1986): 81-100.

2. In this category, consult J.E. Campbell, *The Pentecostal Holiness Church,*

non-Pentecostals took scant note of their brethren on the other side of the tracks, and when they did, their accounts were usually not very informed.[1]

Conspicuously absent in the notes of the first generation of Pentecostal historians was the work of the single most significant figure in its origins. Charles Fox Parham was not the most likeable figure in the movement's history; nevertheless, no one was more important in shaping its thought and directing its future. Born in the American Midwest in 1873, Parham came into contact with the wide variety of religious ideas which ultimately forged early Pentecostalism. Personal conversion, holiness or sanctification, divine healing and premillennialism were not innovations of Charles Parham; nevertheless, he encountered and adopted them all, becoming a part of the developing theological fringe that would provide Pentecostalism with its initial generation of prophets and proponents.[2]

What Parham did that others did not do (or at least he seems to have done it first) was to draw a clear connection between belief in a new spiritual experience sent from heaven specifically for humanity's final generation and the tangible sign of glossolalia. For Parham, and other Pentecostals during the pivotal first decade of the movement's existence, the significance of tongues lay in its promise as a missionary tool. Glossolalia was assumed to be xenoglossia, actual foreign languages. Though the promise of such a miracle faded after the first decade, Pentecostals retained an important part of its message and implication.[3] Their movement had emerged as a signal of the endtime

1898–1948 (Franklin Springs, GA: Pentecostal Holiness Church Press, 1951), F.J. Ewart, *The Phenomenon of Pentecost* (St Louis: Pentecostal Publishing House, 1947); S.H. Frodsham, *With Signs Following* (Springfield, MO: Gospel Publishing House, 1926; rev. edn, 1946), and E.E. Goss, *The Winds of God: The Story of the Early Pentecostal Days (1901–1914) in the Life of Howard A. Goss* (New York: Comet Press, 1958).

1.   The best early study by a non-Pentecostal is C.W. Shumway, 'A Critical History of Glossolalia' (PhD dissertation, Boston University, 1919). For a less credible example, see H.J. Stolee, *Pentecostalism: The Problem of the Modern Tongues Movement* (Minneapolis: Augsburg Publishing House, 1936).

2.   For an extensive treatment of the theological development of Pentecostalism, see D. Dayton, *Theological Roots of Pentecostalism* (Metuchen, NJ: Scarecrow Press, 1987).

3.   While this is generally true throughout the movement, Parham himself continued not only to espouse its feasibility but also to claim positive proof of success.

and would ultimately spark the worldwide revival destined to prepare the globe for the miraculous reappearing of Jesus Christ. That vision has been the one true constant in the Pentecostal movement; more than anything else, it has prompted the movement to be missions-oriented and has resulted in an impressive showing of success.

Much of the problem with historical analysis of the movement flows from the fact that Pentecostalism grew without benefit of great organization; in fact, the movement's success seems traced, in large part, to a lack of organization. The vision spread with almost limitless zeal, but still managed to allow sufficient room for local innovation. Thus, each continent could seemingly claim credit for its own Pentecost with only mild credit passed along to the pioneers of the American Midwest. The phenomenon, however, has led to much ahistorical interpretation, including the fabled 'no founder' school, content to acknowledge only divine intervention, and the 'we prayed down our own Pentecost' school, which argued similarly that the movement emerged simultaneously in various parts of the world. Arguments in this vein were prevalent as early as Parham's falling-out with William Seymour and the Azusa Street Mission in the fall of 1906.[1] Subsequent to Parham's visit to the Azusa Street Mission in October, 1906, the Azusa-based periodical *Apostolic Faith* noted with more than a touch of pride that only 'the Lord was the founder...of this movement'.[2]

Finally there are those who have assumed that glossolalia equals Pentecostalism and, as a result, make claims for the origins of the movement on that basis alone. The result is a study focusing on the

---

Apostolic Faith (Baxter Springs, KS) 2 (November 1913), p. 14 and 2 (August 1926): 15-16. Also C.F. Parham, *The Everlasting Gospel* (n.p., [1919–20]), pp. 66-69.

1.   For examples of the 'no founder' school, see D. Gee, 'Movement without a Man', *Christian Life* 28 (July 1966), pp. 27-29; C. Brumback, *A Sound from Heaven* (Springfield, MO: Gospel Publishing House, 1977), pp. 55-61; and H.N. Kenyon, 'An Analysis of Racial Separation within the Early Pentecostal Movement' (MA thesis, Baylor University, 1978), p. 8. For examples of works which argue for the simultaneous global eruption of the Pentecostal experience, see J.L. Sherrill, *They Speak with Other Tongues* (New York: Pillar Books, 1964), pp. 44-46; W.H. Turner, *Pentecost and Tongues* (Franklin Springs, GA: Advocate Press, 2nd edn, 1968), pp. 97-115; and *Historical Account of the Apostolic Faith* (Portland, OR: Apostolic Faith Publishing House, 1965), p. 19.

2.   *Apostolic Faith* (Los Angeles) 1 (December 1906), p. 1.

phenomenon of glossolalia; it tells us quite a bit about the sociological and psychological development of humankind, but nothing about the origins of the modern Pentecostal movement.[1]

The real problem, of course, is one of definition. How should historians define this amorphous animal called Pentecostalism?—the question is made all the more difficult by its somewhat distant cousin, the Charismatic movement. The answer lies in the movement's uniqueness. What was new about its message? What became its identifying badge? What served as its chief point of departure from 19th–20th century orthodoxy? Clearly the answer to each is glossolalia interpreted as initial evidence and as an endtime sign. Some will argue that it should not have been; however, that is a theological problem, not a historical observation. Others will say that it should have been but with a slightly different interpretation. Again, it does not matter. 'Shoulds' work well in ethics class; they fall miserably short in objectively trying to understand our past. As a result, we are left with the theological demarcation in the Midwestern American movement under Charles Parham. That movement spread to Azusa Street where it took on its own character—as it would do time and again throughout America and throughout the world.

Parham was clearly recognized by the earliest Pentecostals as the most important leader in their midst.[2] He was the first to piece together Pentecostal theology and clearly inaugurated the vision which has become the movement's unifying theme. Though less successful, he also provided the movement with its first official organizational

1.   For examples of works which make such an assumption, see W.S. Merricks, *Edward Irving: The Forgotten Giant* (East Peoria, IL: Scribe's Chamber Publications, 1983), pp. 179-262; J.E. Orr, *The Flaming Tongue* (Chicago: Moody Press, 1975), pp. 178-85; L. Christenson, 'Pentecostalism's Forgotten Forerunner', in V. Synan (ed.), *Aspects of Pentecostal-Charismatic Origins* (Plainfield, NJ: Logos International, 1975), pp. 15-37; C.W. Conn, *Like a Mighty Army* (Cleveland, TN: Church of God Publishing House, 1955), pp. 3-55; and M. Crews, *The Church of God: A Social History* (Knoxville: University of Tennessee Press, 1990), pp. 10-19.

2.   This is crucial to my analysis of Pentecostalism, discussed in detail in *Fields White unto Harvest: Charles F. Parham and the Missionary Origins of Pentecostalism* (Fayetteville: University of Arkansas Press, 1988). See especially pp. 106-27 and 163-66. For an analysis which downplays Parham's contribution, cf. Douglas J. Nelson, 'For Such a Time as This: The Story of Bishop William J. Seymour and the Azusa Street Revival' (PhD dissertation, University of Birmingham, England, 1981).

structure, created its first educational institutions, published its first apologetic works, first promoted its message, and garnered its first widespread publicity. However, he suffered a quick demise, and as a result made a quick exit from most Pentecostal memoirs. Perhaps as early as 1906, rumors regarding his character began to circulate within the burgeoning Pentecostal community. At the time, Parham was engaged in a struggle for control of the movement with other prospective leaders, most notably William Seymour and W. Faye Carothers, an official of Parham's growing work in Houston, Texas. In addition, he was the focus of much publicity with respect to his plan to usurp the local religious authority of Wilbur Glenn Voliva, the leading contender for the throne of John Alexander Dowie in Zion City, Illinois. By the summer of 1907, Parham's bid to control the movement he had founded came to a startling halt. Accused and imprisoned on a charge of sodomy in San Antonio, Texas, his leadership role ended—save a small following which remained loyal in the Midwestern United States.[1] Though the charges were dropped and the accusations were never conclusively proven, Parham continued to suffer the indignity such charges brought. The episode, more than anything else, resulted in the first unofficial coverup in Pentecostal history. Parham's contribution to the origins of the movement remained obscured for decades.

By the 1960s, Parham's name had once again been firmly linked with the movement he helped to organize.[2] Historians were quick to

1.   The story was originally reported in the *San Antonio Light*, 19 July, 1907, p. 1 and appeared the following day in the *San Antonio Daily Express*, 20 July, 1907, p. 12. A much more damaging account appeared two days later in the *Houston Chronicle*, 21 July, 1907, p. 14. The *Chronicle* account included references to 'eye witnesses' and a 'written confession', intriguing bits of information never reported by the San Antonio press. The *Chronicle* account appears to be related to subsequent releases which, gaining wide circulation in the areas where Parham's following was strongest, proved to damage permanently Parham's reputation. Cf. *Waukegan* [IL] *Daily Sun*, 27 July, 1907, pp. 1, 5; *Supplement to the Zion* [IL] *Herald*, 26 July, 1907; and *Burning Bush* [Waukesha, WS] 6 (19 September, 1907), pp. 6-7.

2.   Though Parham was prominently portrayed in Shumway's initial investigation in 1914, the first Pentecostal writer to give him central stage in the story of the movement's origins was Frank Ewart. Cf. C.W. Shumway, 'A Study of "The Gift of Tongues"' (AB thesis, University of Southern California, Los Angeles, 1914), pp. 164-71 and Ewart, *The Phenomenon of Pentecost*, pp. 30-45. Following

recognize him as a pioneer, though in part his place continued to be obscured by the volatile nature of the movement itself. With the dawn of the Charismatic revival, theologians and historians alike have sought a reinterpretation of the movement's essence. As a result, Parham sometimes emerges as an anachronism, clearly out of place with the modern re-evaluation. Some of his ideas, most notably his preference for triune immersion, his espousal of the racist Anglo–Israeli theory, his belief in the utter destruction of the wicked, and his insistence that all tongues were actual foreign languages, place him outside of what many interpret as the orthodox Pentecostal package. And with the emergence of the Charismatic movement, he seems even more remote—a religious zealot convinced that the mainline denominations were evil institutions abandoned by God as a result of their own corruption. Yet historians know that Parham's place cannot be easily submerged again. It is the historical nature of movements to change and, in time, to evolve into new things. That the Pentecostal movement has done that does not erase the contributions of those who formed its initial character.

K. Kendrick's *The Promise Fulfilled: A History of the Modern Pentecostal Movement* (Springfield, MO: Gospel Publishing House, 1961), most Pentecostal writers gave Parham's contribution more press.

THIS-WORLDLY REALITIES AND PROGRESS IN THE LIGHT OF THE ESCHATOLOGICAL KINGDOM

Tormod Engelsviken

In this short paper I would like to present a model for understanding this topic that at first glance may seem somewhat traditional, but nonetheless, I believe that with certain adjustments it may answer some of the questions posed by what is frequently called 'kingdom theology'.

In recent years a consensus has developed concerning the importance of the concept of the 'kingdom of God' in the ministry of Jesus, and in the Church and its mission today. The kingdom is seen as the main paradigm to solve the tension between the vertical and the horizontal, the personal and the collective, the strictly religious and the socio-political in the ministry of the Church.

The term *holistic* is also frequently used in contrast to the traditional distinctions of much Western theology. However, the term *holistic*, though emphasizing a legitimate concern, should not be used to put all truths on the same level, or to negate the important distinctions that must be made to avoid fuzzy thinking or the blurring of truth, as for example the distinctions between Creator and creation, humanity and nature, Church and world, this age and the coming age. Distinction is not the same as separation; a balanced holistic position may be reached through a dialectical approach.

There is still a need for more thorough exegetical work on the notion of the kingdom of God in the New Testament; and the New Testament concept must be normative for the Church's use of the term today. Let me make two critical comments on the prevailing 'consensus'.

First, I would maintain the 'kingdom of God' should not only be understood as the 'rule' or 'reign' of God, but also—and more importantly—as the 'realm' of salvation, as the totality of salvation.

The term 'enter' (e.g. Mk. 10.15) and the distinction between being 'inside' and 'outside' the future kingdom (e.g. Mt. 8.11-12) suggest that the kingdom is not an all-embracing reality such as the 'rule' of God must be. How could anybody be 'outside' the 'rule of God'? If the kingdom, however, is identical with God's future salvation, which is also affecting the present reality, then those who are not saved may be outside the kingdom, but still under the rule of God or Christ as supreme Lord and king. This can also be seen from the way the terms 'kingdom of God', 'salvation' and 'eternal life' are used almost interchangeably, as for example in Lk. 18.18-30.

Secondly, it follows that the kingdom of God is first and foremost a soteriological concept—the gospel of the kingdom is 'good news' to lost sinners—and only secondly an ethical concept—the area where God's will is realized on earth. The kingdom ethic of the Sermon on the Mount is preceded by the Beatitudes where the kingdom is given to the 'poor in spirit' (Mt. 5.3).

I can illustrate the importance of this distinction and the difficulties created by placing the soteriological and the ethical on the same level by comparing the two societies where I have had the privilege of living and serving. Note that I do not identify the soteriological with the 'spiritual' and the ethical with the socio-political. The comparison of these two societies and their respective Churches will show that people's relationship to God in Christ is primary, and that the social effects of the kingdom of God in terms of 'this worldly-progress' in society are secondary, and always ambiguous.

Initially I pose the general and very simple question: Is progress in terms of peace, justice, equality, welfare and environmental protection also a progress in terms of the kingdom of God?

The first society is the Scandinavian welfare state. I believe that in Scandinavia we have created one of the most egalitarian, just, peaceful and prosperous welfare societies in the history of the world. This can be documented statistically. As Christians we are grateful for this. At the same time, however, we see an alarming increase in divorce, abortions, drug abuse, violent crime, suicide, loneliness, and so on. Secularization has also advanced further than almost anywhere else in the world. There is only a small minority of active confessing Christians. Only 3–5% of the population attend church regularly. There are relatively few conversions, although there is much gospel proclamation, relatively few signs of the power of the Spirit, and almost no suffering for the sake of the gospel. The question is: Are we closer to the kingdom in Scandinavia? Has the kingdom come more fully in our countries than in other parts of the world?

I have been a missionary in Ethiopia and have visited the country several times over the last 20 years. During those years the country has been plagued by extreme poverty, starvation, illiteracy, injustice, oppression, war, famine, division and persecution. Still Churches of all denominations are growing, people in the thousands fill the churches. The signs of the kingdom are there: conversions, healings, exorcisms, Church growth, suffering for the sake of the gospel. My conviction is this: The kingdom of God is more powerfully present and advancing in Ethiopia than it is in Norway. I believe that the sign that people enter into the kingdom or the 'poor having the gospel preached to them' (Lk. 7.22) is much more significant than the political, social and economic 'signs' in Norway. Or, to put it even more strongly: I do not think the Scandinavian welfare state is a sign of the kingdom of God at all.

I do not want to deny the influence of Christianity on Western thought and culture and, in this instance, on Scandinavian culture. Rather than interpreting the good and beneficial traits of our civilization in terms of the kingdom of God, I see it primarily as a result of God's law as revealed in general revelation and of Christian influence on society at large. All human beings are created in the image of God and have what the law requires written on their hearts (cf. Rom. 2.14-15). This distinction between law and gospel (distinction, not separation) corresponds largely to the distinction between creation and redemption. The Scandinavian welfare state has to be understood in terms of 'law' and 'creation', not in terms of 'gospel' and 'salvation', that is the kingdom of God.

The Lutheran theological tradition has used the phraseology of the 'two kingdoms', the secular and the spiritual. This terminology, especially in its English translation, has been quite unfortunate and has led to much misunderstanding. It seems to separate the one kingdom of God spoken of in the Bible into two spheres, each with its own laws and rules. The doctrine has in recent years met with much opposition, and has consequently been discarded by many, even among Lutherans. One reason was its use, or rather abuse, during the Nazi period in Germany by the *Deutsche Christen* as a pretext for preventing the Church from speaking or acting against the evils of Nazism. It has been used in similar ways when political authorities want to silence the Church. Then the argument is always that the Church should concentrate on spiritual matters while leaving the political, social and economic questions to the state.

However, abuse does not abolish proper use. During the Second World War the same doctrine was used in exactly the opposite direction. In its confession 'The basis of the Church' (*Kirkens Grunn*), the Norwegian Lutheran Church openly protested against the totalitarian ideological claims of the Nazi government during the German occupation. Charging that the government had overstepped its bounds, the Church rejected its claims and entered into a period of active civil resistance. Similarly, but under quite different circumstances, the Lutheran Church in Ethiopia has spoken out openly against injustice and oppression, both under the regime of Haile Selassie and the later Marxist regime.

It should be kept in mind that this doctrine—when properly understood and applied—presupposes that God is Lord and King in both 'kingdoms' or 'reigns'. They are kept together as the works of the two hands of God. In his kingdom of the left, the secular kingdom or the reign of the world, God rules by his law. This law is most clearly revealed in the Scriptures, but the same law is also revealed in the hearts of all human beings as a result of natural revelation, or 'common grace', as it is often called in the Reformed tradition. When it is called secular or 'worldly' (*weltlich*), this does not suggest that this area is without God or unrelated to God. What it does mean is that it encompasses all human beings, Christians as well as non-Christians, with a common base in a general ethic that is also the law of God.

One of the great advantages of this view is that it helps cooperation on social and ethical concerns between Christians and non-Christians, between those who have entered the kingdom of God (in its biblical sense), and those who have not done so, without in any way compromising the uniqueness of the gospel and all people's need for salvation in Christ.

In this 'secular'—or universal—kingdom or reign, the law of God has two functions: it promotes good, such as love, justice, peace, fellowship; and it restrains evil. For the latter purpose society at large in keeping with God's will may even have to resort to force against criminals, aggressors, and the like. This means that Christians and non-Christians of 'good will' can work together for a more just and peaceful world. Real progress can be made. There is a realistic hope of change. Christians have a significant task, as individuals, as citizens, and corporately as a Church, to speak and act to further this end. Hence, there is a place, a necessary place, for the Christian social activist. He or she needs the love, the power and the charisms of the Holy Spirit for this ministry in the world.

This world will not, however, be fully changed or wholly redeemed until the return of Christ. Therefore all progress in this world is in a sense preliminary. Lutheran theology has traditionally held a rather pessimistic view of human nature. Its doctrine of 'total depravity' has, however, also been misunderstood. In relation to God, in the vertical dimension, unredeemed human beings are unable to do good, being totally incapable of saving themselves. In the horizontal dimension, in relation to other people and the created world, they both can and should do all kinds of good deeds.

There is, however, a limit. The fall, the consequent sinfulness of human beings and the present state of the world preclude any utopian visions for this world. History has shown how all utopian dreams have failed—and even worse—how they have been used to manipulate and oppress other people. This applies to the capitalist dream, the Nazi dream, the communist dream and all other visions—including various 'Christian' ones—of a perfect society in this world prior to the return of Christ.

As long as we live on earth we will experience sin and the consequences of sin, including death. The only vision of perfection allowed for a Christian is that of the kingdom of God coming in power. That kingdom, however, is wholly God's doing, not that of human beings. It will imply a complete restoration of God's creation and the final consummation of his plan of salvation realized in history. It is the ultimate goal of all God's redemptive activity.

Since victory over death inaugurates the kingdom when it comes in fullness, there will be a radical discontinuity between this world and the coming world. The new world is a new creation. At the same time there will be a continuity, the nature of which can only be hinted at through pictures such as the seed of wheat that is sown and will grow into something wholly new, different but still identical with that which was sown (cf. 1 Cor. 15.37-44).

I would like to challenge the common assumption that those who

hold a rather pessimistic view of human nature and emphasize the discontinuity between this age and the coming one tend to be exclusively
occupied with the 'saving cf souls' or the oral proclamation of the
gospel, and uninterested in serving physical needs and improving
human conditions. It may apply to some groups, but cannot be proven
to be generally true. Lutheran evangelical missions from the Pietistic
movement (early 18th century onwards) have shown the opposite,
although direct political involvement is more recent. In the mission of
the Church, proclamation and social service have always gone together.

Let us return to the kingdom of the right hand, the so-called 'spiritual
kingdom'. The term 'spiritual' is also unfortunate, since this kingdom
is not only concerned with 'spiritual' matters but embraces all aspects
of reality. Characteristically, this kingdom is created by the gospel.
The message of forgiveness of sin and new life in the Spirit is
addressed to all human beings, but only those who receive this
message in personal faith and are baptized enter the kingdom of God.
In this kingdom no force may be used—the gospel appeals to the conscience of each person. There must be a complete liberty of conscience. The Church as a communion of believers in the gospel is an
expression and an instrument of this kingdom. It is the people of the
kingdom on their way towards its consummation.

As Christians we are citizens of two worlds or ages—the present
and the coming, which is also already among us making its influence
known. Both worlds are God's worlds. He is the king and ruler over
all—although in this age always opposed by the kingdom of darkness
with the devil as its prince. This does not create a 'divided' Christian.
In this world, the secular kingdom, the Christian is called to realize
the values of the kingdom of God. God's law is one and applies to
everyone everywhere at all times. In the world the Christian cooperates with all people of good will on the basis of God's law. The goal is
'this-worldly progress', improvement of human conditions and
relations on all levels and the protection of God's creation.

In the kingdom of God, in the Church, the Christian cooperates
with other Christians on the basis of the law and the gospel, sharing
the same salvation, being children of the same father. Here the
gospel—proclaimed and demonstrated—aims at evangelism (*martyria*),
service (*diakonia*) and communion (*koinonia*). Here the Holy Spirit
inspires and empowers Christian ministry. In this realm Christians
experience a foretaste of the consummated kingdom, whose powers

are already at work. Life in the kingdom of God is thus an eschatological existence, between the 'already' and the 'not yet'.

Finally, I will comment on the trinitarian aspect of our theme. Too
often in Protestant theology creation has been associated solely with
the Father (the first article of the Apostles' Creed), redemption with
the Son (the second article) and sanctification with the Holy Spirit (the
third article). All three persons in the Godhead are, however, tied
both to creation and to redemption. The Father is the Creator, but
creation takes place through the Son, the eternal Logos (1 Cor. 8.6; Jn
1.3; Col. 1.16). The Spirit is God's life-giving power, active in the
initial creation and in continually giving life and breath to all living
things (Gen. 1.2; Ps. 104.29-30). It would be possible to develop a
theology (in the narrow sense), a Christology and a pneumatology of
creation, of the world and of nature.

This presence of the triune God in creation is not, however, salvific
or redemptive. It is not an expression or a sign of the kingdom of
God. Salvation is, in the New Testament, exclusively tied to the historical message of Jesus Christ, his incarnation, life, death and
resurrection, and the people who believe in him and serve him in the
Holy Spirit. This redemptive work is the subject of special revelation—in history, in the Scriptures, in the Church—to be proclaimed
in the mission of the Church.

Hence, parallel to the distinction already made between law and
gospel, the world and the Church, there is a distinction to be made
between general history (which also is God's history!) and redemptive
history. It is the latter, and only the latter, that represents the kingdom
of God, although this kingdom has all kinds of influences on the world
and on general history. When Jesus returns in glory and establishes his
kingdom in power, there will only be one world, one history and one
kingdom, where 'God may be all in all' (1 Cor. 15.28).

THE CHURCH, THE WORLD AND PROGRESS IN LATIN AMERICA, IN LIGHT OF THE ESCHATOLOGICAL KINGDOM

Guillermo Cook

Introduction

Briefly I want to present four different ways in which evangelical Protestantism in Latin America approaches the questions of world, progress and the eschatological kingdom. The first two streams of Protestant Christianity that I will sketch appeared fairly early on the scene. The last two have only been around since the late 1970s and, each in its own way, are changing the theology and worldview of their predecessors. This is having a profound effect on the life and mission of the Church in Latin America.

World Affirming Christianity: The Kingdom Now and Not Yet

The first Protestant missionaries arrived in Latin America between a century and a century and a half ago. They preached and taught a Gospel of individual transformation which would naturally produce good works and eventuate in material progress for those who became true disciples of Jesus Christ. The effects of this witness should become noticeable even beyond the boundaries of the Protestant churches. Imbued with a Calvinist ethic and a Wesleyan fervor, they founded churches, hospitals and clinics, orphanages and day-care centres. Some attempted to transform Latin America 'from the top down' by reaching out the liberal elite. They founded excellent schools and initiated English language churches during the period in which the laws of the land outlawed proselytism. Within two or three generations, upward social mobility had initiated a noticeable Protestant presence among the middle classes in Latin America. Although proclaiming the 'Gospel of the Kingdom' had not as yet become theologically fashionable, those who belonged to the mainline denominations in particular were motivated by a desire to manifest (or even bring in) God's Kingdom among the people whom they served. This understanding of 'worldly realities' has continued until today wherever historical churches have maintained their identity and a strong witness. However, beginning in the late 1960s, these churches began to lose large segments of their membership to secularism and also to Pentecostalism, usually by way of the Charismatic Renewal. In this way, their perception of 'this worldly realities' began to change.

World Denying Christianity: The Future Kingdom

Latin American Pentecostalism was born almost immediately after the Azusa Street Revival. Although its founders came from Sweden, via the USA, it was largely a home-grown phenomenon. US denominational Pentecostalism arrived several decades later. In Brazil and Chile it grew quite rapidly. Throughout the rest of Latin America, after years of relatively slow growth, healing evangelists jump-started the movement in the 1950s, even in more conservative societies such as Argentina and Costa Rica. The Pentecostal message brought a sense of worth and identity to the outcasts of society. Barely literate men could become pastors of flocks numbering in the thousands. Voiceless women found a place where they could find release for their longings and anxieties, in songs of praise, in dance and speaking in tongues. Because of this, Pentecostalism became known as 'the haven of the masses'.[1] New believers learned that this world of suffering is inherently evil, that it must be rejected—all of it. To expect anything good to come from the world is a contradiction in terms, because it is ruled by Satan. Informed by Dispensationalism, Pentecostal preachers told their followers that it was wrong to try to change this world, because it would delay our Lord's return. In a similar vein, doctrinaire Marxist-Leninists discouraged small acts of social transformation because it would delay the proletarian uprisings that would bring in the new utopia. Listen to these excerpts from our conversations with dirt-poor Pentecostals in Honduras:

---

1.   The title of an early book on Chilean Pentecostalism by Swiss researcher C. LaLive d'Epinay.

I was selling coffee in the street. The devil attacked me. I fell and broke my arm. He that perseveres to the end will be saved. Sometimes I work in houses. Then I get sick and Jesus heals me. I have epilepsy and three children. My mother lost her sight.

We came a year ago. We have only a *chozita* (a hut), not a house (= wooden frame building). We are rich in Christ. What is most important is to finish the church, make the walls—when it rains or it's cold we suffer. The only thing that is of value in life is to serve the Lord. We work when we can, he gives health...

Brothers, this life is of little value, and it gives us nothing. But since we know Christ Jesus, we must build him a church so we can place our burdens, our lives in his hands. I am poor, but we are rich in the Lord. God is preparing us for that place to which he will rapture us to be with him forever.

Before, we picked coffee. Now there is no more work. Now we sew bits of cloth to make mop rags. Then we walk the streets trying to sell one or two to buy food for the children. Often we can sell none, so we do not eat. What can we do? Only Christ is the way. He will give a better life; we long for it, our eternal home.[1]

Pentecostalism encouraged the natural fatalism of the Catholic poor. But the solution was different than in either Catholicism or Afro and Amerindian spiritism. Instead of lighting votive candles to Mary, the saints and to the voodoo spirits, salvation is God's free gift through Jesus Christ. True liberation, they insist, will come only through the power of the Holy Spirit, and not through the Marxist appeal to the power of the people to change society. In a very real sense, Pentecostals believe that Christ's Kingdom becomes present in their midst when the Holy Spirit rains down his power upon them in signs and wonders. Yet, the present reality of the eschatological kingdom is in conflict with the world. 'This worldly realities' are to be rejected because God's Kingdom, while manifest in this world through the Holy Spirit in the Church, is definitely not of this world. Thus, in seeming contradiction, the upward mobility that was generated by the Protestant ethic brought about an ambivalent attitude toward material progress. Though society is evil, somehow we can manage to avail ourselves of opportunities to become moderately wealthy through a combination of frugality and hard work. We can avail ourselves of

---

1.   G.S. Spykman, G. Cook, *et al.*, *Let My People Live: Faith and Struggle in Central America* (Grand Rapids: Eerdmans, 1989), pp. 78, 219.

modern conveniences, particularly of the television media, as a means to communicate the Gospel, but we must be wary of the messages from the world that will ultimately begin to undermine our fundamental presuppositions.

Despite this 'otherworldly' perspective, Professor David Martin[1] suggests that as Pentecostalism moves up the social scale it will become more aware of its civic responsibilities, and will participate in politics, working toward the greater good of society. Be that as it may, the experience of Pentecostal political participation in recent years, in countries like Brazil and Guatemala, has not been too encouraging in this regard.

World Dominating Christianity: The Now and Future Kingdom

The Charismatic Renewal reached Latin America in the mid 1960s. In its earliest stages there was a healthy interaction between the Protestant and Catholic varieties of the movement. It was also possible to distinguish between Pentecostalism and the Charismatic Renewal because of social class, the depth of the latter's theological reflection, as well as its world affirming approach. Less than a decade later, the Catholic Charismatic renewal had retreated largely into a more traditional and sectarian religiosity to an extent that cooperation with Protestants was no longer possible. A large number of Catholic groups opted out of their Church and gradually were absorbed by Pentecostalism. Indeed, the Protestant Renewal and Pentecostalism became indistinguishable in theology, in practice and in their attitude toward the world. If there was any difference, it was in the mainly middle class aspirations of Charismatic churches, over against the daily struggle for existence of impoverished grass roots Pentecostals.

Enter the Shepherding Movement. There is some evidence that the Kingdom theology which *New Wine Magazine* and various television evangelists have propagated throughout Latin America may have been influenced to some degree by the theocratic political model of Old Testament Reconstructionism.[2] The Holy Spirit calls Christians to

---

1. D. Martin, *Tongues of Fire: The Explosion of Protestantism in Latin America* (Oxford: Blackwell, 1990).

2. The chief proponent of OT Reconstructionism is the Chalcedon Institute, chiefly in the book by R.J. Rushdoony and G. North, *The Institutes of Biblical Law* (Philadelphia: Presbyterian and Reformed Publishing Company, 1973).

exercise their calling to rule the earth in the name of Christ the Lord. While not as harshly levitical as Reconstructionism, Latin American Protestant Charismatics do not hesitate to apply Old Testament laws to people whom they deem to be outside the pale—particularly drug runners and suspected terrorists, 'liberationists' and people who dare to question the status quo.

In 1985 I was part of a team that interviewed General Efrain Rios–Montt, a Charismatic evangelical, and an ex-president of Guatemala. Breaking with traditional Protestant views on political involvement, the general holds that Christians should participate in social change. But his change agents act more like soldiers than self-effacing leaven. 'He views the church as a Guatemalan-style military campaign'.

> As a soldier, the Christian must know how to follow orders. He marches, he salutes, he shoots [all of this punctuated by expressive actions]. Order must be maintained. When there are uprisings, those caught need justice, not mercy. Execute them! That's what God wants, and what the people want. Such exercise of authority destroys communism and brings peace.

Yet, in seeming contradiction, the general believes that the answers to human needs are not found in society. Only Christ is the answer. Despite his militant anticommunism, he considers the United States to be as much of a threat to his nation as the Soviet Union. When we asked him about his program for the future of his country, his response was to 'pray and pray and pray'.[1]

From a purely political standpoint, this can be a very dangerous theology. It may, in fact, be heretical. When, as is happening right now in at least one country that I have visited, prominent politicians are becoming Pentecostals and founding churches with large followings, concerned Christians are beginning to ask whether there might not be a covert political agenda. Discerning Christians become suspicious when a leading Pentecostal pastor announces his intention to throw his hat into a right-wing political ring. Is this just another attempt to dress up military oppression in the garments of the eschatological kingdom?

Closely related to the above is 'Health and Wealth—Name it and Claim it' Pentecostalism. The dwindling middle class that sees itself losing its grip on society are all too easily attracted to this brand of Charismatic Pentecostalism. The followers of this new faith number in

1. Spykman, Cook *et al.*, *Let My People Live*, p. 220.

the tens of thousands. How easily is the Christian's walk in the Spirit confused with material progress! When we make prosperity the touchstone of divine blessing we are saying that the millions of poor Christians are, somehow, second-rate citizens of the Kingdom of God. That the Kingdom is the property of a privileged few. Needless to say, this is a colossal heresy.

World-dominating Christianity is caught between a traditional Pentecostal rejection of the world and the opportunities for political power and material prosperity that are becoming every day more available to charismatic leaders with large followings. The temptation to confuse Christ's eschatological Kingdom with material progress and 'this worldly' power has become very strong in Latin America. The Kingdom theology which is emerging in order to justify this ancient heresy is built upon *Christus Victor*—the post-resurrection Christ, minus the Suffering Servant of Yahweh, the crucified God. While the cross is preached as a means of salvation, it is not proclaimed, and scarcely practiced, as a way of life. Large numbers of our Charismatic sisters and brothers in Latin America have fallen into a trap.

World Transforming Christianity: The Kingdom Now—*and Not Yet*

As the social and economic situation in the 1950s and '60s worsened in Latin America, concerned priests and nuns began working with their dirt-poor parishioners in Northeastern Brazil, in Panama and Nicaragua. Gradually, without any contact with each other at first, small groups of lay people began to meet weekly for prayer, Bible reflection and the Eucharist—and to exchange ideas concerning survival in situations of dire penury. Each group had a name, but they eventually were given the collective name of base (or basic) ecclesial (or Christian) communities (BCC), with the exception of Guatemala, which, to our knowledge, had no contact with the Charismatic renewal. In fact, in both Catholicism and Protestantism the politically radical BCCs and the politically conservative Charismatic movement have viewed each other with considerable suspicion. This is lamentable because it has resulted in harmful polarization.

This is not the place to discuss the BCCs.[1] It is their Protestant

---

1.   I have written about them at length in G. Cook, *The Expectation of the Poor: Latin American Base Ecclesial Communities in Protestant Perspective* (Maryknoll, NY: Orbis Books, 1985).

counterparts that should interest us. In several countries, there is a growing number of small Protestant and ecumenical communities who share a common concern to live and proclaim the Gospel of the Kingdom in their context of extreme poverty and oppression. They represent the bottom rung in virtually every denomination, including Pentecostals. These Christians view the world as evil by definition (have they not felt Satan's whip upon their backs, and the oppressors' chains upon their wrists and ankles?). But it is, to a degree, transformable through the power of God and the concerted actions of his true disciples on earth. In the words of a spokesperson from this movement,

> What God is doing amidst his people really escapes our theological comprehension... especially among the base of the Christian community... This eagerness for liberty, this enthusiasm for building a new society. This revolution, is evangelizing the church... Never before have we seen how evangelical Christians and Catholics can meet together in a village of the highlands to celebrate their faith, because there are no longer ministers or priests in this zone.[1]

Much is being made of the rapid growth of Protestantism in Guatemala, as a sign of Protestant progress. But little mention is made of the large influx of Indians and other peasants into a dissident church. So much so that Protestant and Catholic pastoral training teams have their hands full in coping with this new phenomenon. This is a situation, the above-mentioned spokesperson confesses, which 'for those of us who have worked in the service of the Lord as Protestants is a miracle of God'.[2] This 'this worldly' eschatology has toppled tyrannical regimes in Brazil and the Philippines, and brought more democratic governments to power in Haiti and Chile. Though not all of these Christians are Pentecostals, they have a strong awareness of the presence of the renewing and transforming Spirit in their midst.

According to a recent study in Brazil, large numbers of Catholic BCC members are moving into grassroots pentecostalism, as the pressure from the Vatican to conform becomes more intolerable. This could mean that a more socially militant Protestantism is in the making, with profound implications for mission and evangelization in

1. Cook, *Faith and Struggle*, p. 222. Quoted from 'Religion and Revolution: A Protestant Voice', in J.L. Fried and M. Gettlemen (eds.), *Guatemala in Rebellion: Unfinished History* (New York: Grove Press, 1983), pp. 230-31.
2. Cook, *Faith and Struggle*, p. 222.

Latin America. When Pentecostal fire and radical reformist fervor reach a critical mass, the explosion can have profound social impact. This is the assessment of even a few Marxist-leaning sociologists. It is also suggested by David Stoll in his recent book on the politics of evangelical growth.[1]

Summary: The Eschatological Kingdom in Latin America

Each of the four streams of Protestant Christianity in Latin America holds to a Kingdom that is present today in the power of the Spirit and which will become fully present at the Parousia. But the Pentecostal and Radical Evangelical streams would emphasize, respectively, the *future* and the *present* dimensions of the eschatological kingdom. Through no coincidence, because they are both poor, both movements would reject material progress as a sign of the Kingdom. Their material poverty, and the scant hope of any change for years to come, are opening the way for a greater degree of mutual crossfertilization and enrichment. The historical denominations and the Charismatics draw their followings from the middle classes; together they uphold the 'now' and the 'not yet' of the Kingdom, but with different intents. The first group would avoid political involvement in favor of deploying regenerated Christians as individual change agents, while the latter would work toward political power (even with unregenerate people who shared their temporal goals) and see material wealth as a sign of God's blessing upon their work. The fact that many of our Charismatic sisters and brothers are caught in a 'this-worldly' trap, confusing material progress with Holy Spirit power, should be a matter of active concern to Pentecostals everywhere.

---

1.   D. Stoll, *Is Latin America Turning Protestant?: The Politics of Evangelical Growth* (Berkeley: University of California Press, 1990).

Part III

EVANGELISM AND OTHER LIVING FAITHS: AN EVANGELICAL CHARISMATIC PERSPECTIVE

Clark H. Pinnock

The Second Vatican Council upheld two propositions in several of its documents. It stated that world evangelization is an urgent Christian responsibility and also that God is at work in the life of all peoples.[1] This dialectical pattern of beliefs was reiterated recently by Pope John Paul II in a major encyclical entitled 'Redemptoris Missio' which expresses hope for a new day of missionary activity.[2]

The two commitments are in tension and not easy to reconcile, however. On the one hand, Christians who hold strongly to world evangelization frequently deny a gracious work of God in the world outside the church. Such sentiments are especially prominent in evangelical circles, where it is often maintained that the motivation behind world evangelization rests on a denial of any work of grace outside the church. This was audible in the uncompromising tones of the Berlin statement (1966), the Frankfurt Declaration (1970) and less stridently the Lausanne Covenant (1974).[3]

Those, on the other hand, who acknowledge a gracious work of God among all nations are often critical of world evangelization aimed at conversion. Opposition is strongly expressed not only by pluralists like John Hick and Paul Knitter, but also by inclusivists like Hans Kung and Eugene Hillman, who fear that world evangelization

---

1. The two convictions can be read in the 'Dogmatic Constitution on the Church' (ch. 16), in the 'Decree on the Church's Missionary Activity' and in the 'Declaration on the Relationship of the Church to Non-Christian Religions', as well as other places.

2. The encyclical, possibly the most important so far in his papacy, was published as 'Redemptoris Missio', *Origins: CNS Documentary Service* 20.34 (January 31, 1991).

3. For documentation and discussion, see P. Knitter, *No Other Name?* (Maryknoll, NY: Orbis Books, 1985), ch. 4.

appears to deny divine grace already present among the nations. This kind of cautious attitude may help to account for the decline in evangelistic activity both by Protestant mainline churches and the missionary orders of the Roman Catholic church.

The idea that God is already graciously active in the whole world does create tension for belief in the urgency of world missions. The two beliefs are in dialectical tension. Nevertheless, I commend the Second Vatican Council for affirming both of these propositions and will explore the problem in this essay. After spelling out the Pope's vision of the rationale of world missions in the context of his wider hope, I will offer thoughts of my own about the same issue from the standpoint of evangelical Protestantism and an experience of Pentecost.

In his encyclical of 1991, the present Pope offers a textured rationale for the urgency of world missions, consistent with his belief in a divine and gracious activity in all cultures. Several motivations for world missions can be found scattered throughout the long document. Here are a few of them. First, mission is a sign of a vital church—this is clear in the New Testament. What kind of Christians are we if we refuse to share the good news with other people? Secondly, love for neighbor mandates sharing Christ with all nations. There is much talk today about human rights; the Pope asks, do people not have the right to know of God's love for them and make a decision about it? Thirdly, behind the important commitment to ecumenical unity which we have, there stands a deeper goal, that of world evangelization. This is why the churches are seeking to come together in greater unity, in order that the world might believe. Fourthly, the church is a missionary agency by its very nature, sent forth by Jesus to continue the mission he began. In conclusion, Pope John Paul II holds two propositions: (1) that God is everywhere at work graciously so that everyone has an opportunity to accept salvation, and (2) that world missions are both necessary and urgent.[1]

I stand with the Pope in this matter and appreciate the balance struck between these two ideas. I will now present some thoughts of my own and try to make the balance more intelligible to evangelicals and charismatic Protestants.

1. R.J. Neuhaus examines the Pope's motivations for world mission expressed in the encyclical in *First Things 16* (October, 1991), pp. 61-64.

1. *Belief in the Triune God*

Faith in the triune God gives us the basis for a solution to this problem because it combines the universal and the particular so magnificently. God is both creator and redeemer and is at work in all of history as well as the incarnation. The triune God is present in his love both outside and inside churches. The Logos both upholds creation and is incarnate in Jesus; the Spirit both moves over the face of the deep and is poured out at Pentecost. Belief in the holy trinity is the key to maintaining both universality and particularity.[1]

To be specific, when we confess God the Father almighty, we exalt One who created the world and loves all humanity with an everlasting love. We worship a God whose generosity toward sinners is boundless and whose plans for them involve welfare, not disaster. The Father offers salvation to every person in Jesus Christ and is not willing that any should perish. His goal is to gather all the nations around a banqueting table. Confessing God our Father thus generates hope in us for all people, including believers of other living faiths. God wants them to be saved and come to knowledge of the truth (1 Tim. 2.4; 4.10). We reject Augustine's and Calvin's pessimistic view of humanity as a mass of damnation but entertain an optimism of salvation and a spirit of hopefulness for people based on the gospel. God is seriously seeking to save them all. The experience of Pentecost only deepens our grasp of how profound the Father's love for humanity is. The Spirit helps us to grasp in our hearts the boundless mercy of God our Father and gives us confidence as we approach every person. The secret things belong to God and we certainly do not know all of God's arrangements with the nations (Deut. 29.29). But there can be no doubt that 'abba' Father loves them and from this conviction our attitude of loving inclusivism can grow.

When we confess Jesus Christ, God's only Son our Lord, we lift up One who gave himself up for all humanity. We acknowledge him who loves Samaritans, outcasts, sinners, outsiders, children, sick, women and the oppressed. This is the mediator between God and humanity, the one who made peace by the blood of his cross and created a whole

---

1. G. D'Costa calls our attention to this fact in *Christian Uniqueness Reconsidered: The Myth of a Pluralistic Theology of Religions* (Maryknoll, NY: Orbis Books, 1990), chs. 1–3.

new race. He is the exalted one, who is even now drawing all men and women to himself (Jn 12.32). The Son of God is also the everlasting Word by whom God created the universe and the Logos who is thus not ontologically swallowed up in Jesus of Nazareth but enlightens every human life, even where Jesus is not yet named (Jn 1.9). Believing in God the Son means that the love of God visible in Jesus has always been operating in the world from the beginning of time. God has never left himself without witness (Acts 14.17). The church's high Christology has inclusive not exclusive implications. And the experience of Pentecost, while it lifts Jesus up in his uniqueness, also assures us of the outpouring of his Spirit on all flesh. God's heart desires that all flesh should see the glory of God.

When we confess the Holy Spirit, Lord and Giver of life, we acknowledge a divine breath not limited to our ecclesiastical structures but free to blow where it wills throughout the whole creation. The creator Spirit is everywhere active and at the same time busy creating a profounder grasp of who the God revealed in Jesus Christ is. The Spirit is thus present before any evangelist arrives and prepares the world for Jesus to come. The experience of Pentecost accentuates this confidence in the Spirit's freedom and kindles a desire in us to meet the Spirit wherever it has gone among men and women. We go forth in mission expecting to meet the Spirit who has gone ahead of us to prepare hearts to receive Christ.

Our faith in the triune God is a sound basis for an attitude of faith, hope and love in us. It gives us a solid framework for thinking in terms of both universality and particularity.[1]

2. *Some Other Considerations*

1. If God is graciously at work in the world, is God at work in the sphere of other religions? The Second Vatican Council was right (in my opinion) to say positive things about other faiths. The scriptures themselves identify both negative and positive aspects, not just negative features in them. Karl Barth and the Protestant tradition are onesided when they declare other religions to be little more than unbelief. Certainly there are deceptions and Satanic delusions in the realm of

---

1. R.H. Drummond also points to the trinity as the key to an inclusive spirit of openness and hopefulness: *Toward a New Age in Christian Theology* (Maryknoll, NY: Orbis Books, 1985), ch. 8.

these religions, deceptions which must be confronted by gospel truth in the power of the Spirit. The experience of Pentecost surely reinforces this dark reality. But there are also positive features in living faiths which derive from a genuine, heart response to God and his revelation. This is confirmed in the scriptures that point us to Noah, Enoch, Job, Melchizedek, Abimelech, Jethro, Cornelius and so on—to 'holy pagans' who responded to God as they knew him with true faith. The Bible lifts them up as examples to us, and it does not dismiss them as rejected heathen. The same situation obtains today. Have we not all met our Melchizedeks, pious and godly believers in God, who are ripe for the fuller revelation of grace in Jesus? The experience of Pentecost intensifies our capacity to believe and hope all things for these pagan saints who love God and are loved by him. We must not allow our traditions to silence this aspect of the witness of Scripture.[1]

2. A spirit of openness means that the activities of missions must be expanded to include dialogue. Dialogue is important because we are not called to shout at people but to communicate with them in loving ways. Love in communication means showing respect by taking the beliefs of other people seriously and being open to take account of them. Dialogue opens the way for us to share our faith in Jesus with them and lets them tell us what they have learned about God and about life. Dialogue goes beyond sharing, of course, and includes the posing of probing questions to those of other faiths, questions which aim at truth. The experience of Pentecost encourages dialogue by creating greater love in us for others and quickening faith in us about the possibilities of God's grace at work in their lives.[2]

3. As respects divine judgment, there is so much we do not know, and Scripture says that there will be many surprises. Nevertheless, the faith principle is most important (Heb. 11.6). We all believe and know that Abraham was saved by faith, even though he had a minimum of

1.   K. Cracknell retrieves neglected aspects of the biblical witness along these lines: *Toward a New Relationship: Christians and People of Other Faiths* (London: Epworth Press, 1986), chs. 2-3.
2.   W. Pannenberg understands the role of dialogue in the historical contest of the gods: see *Basic Questions in Theology*, II (Philadelphia: Fortress Press, 1971), pp. 65-118. H. Kung is often skilled at posing these probing questions: see *On Being a Christian* (London: Collins, 1974), pp. 104-109.

redemptive information to go on. Evidently God did not judge him on the basis of later orthodox theology but in relation to the faith direction of his heart. To take another example, Job was a pagan in the Near East, who was saved by faith with even less information than Abraham to go on. The idea that Catholics call 'baptism of desire', which holds that people anywhere can call out to God to save them, even though their intellectual knowledge of theology is slight, has validity. Let us observe an important distinction: Jesus Christ is ontologically but not epistemologically necessary for salvation. Abraham was saved by the work of Jesus Christ, even though he had never heard and did not call on the name of Jesus. In the same way, on the basis of God's loving fairness, we can be certain that no one who desires to know God will fail to be given the opportunity to know him.[1]

4. In a theology with this direction, the motivation for missions cannot be solely construed in terms of deliverance from divine wrath, since according to Scripture not all non-Christians are hell-bound. Missionary commitment must rest on a larger foundation of factors. We would do well to think along the lines suggested by Pope John Paul II in his encyclical and develop a broader and more coherent basis of missionary motivations. Our motivation ought to focus on good news, not bad news: on sharing the unsearchable riches of Christ, which is the news everybody on earth needs to know, whether evangelized or unevangelized. Those who have responded in faith to God before (like Job) need to know about the fulness of God's love for them and experience the fulness of God's love for them and experience the full measure of his grace and power. Those who have not yet responded to God on the basis of available light ought to be given an opportunity to respond to Jesus Christ. The main challenge here is to hold on to the wider hope in such a way as not to reduce the urgency of missions but to increase it.[2]

1. See J. Sanders, *No Other Name! A Biblical, Historical, and Theological Investigation into the Destiny of the Unevangelised* (Grand Rapids: Eerdmans, 1992). This book should do much to ease the minds of conservative Christians in this matter.
2. See W.J. Abraham, *The Logic of Evangelism* (Grand Rapids: Eerdmans, 1989), ch. 10.

Let us continue to labour on a theology in which the urgency of missions and belief in the genuinely universal, salvific will of God are maintained together.

EVANGELIZATION AND OTHER LIVING FAITHS

Anthony O. Gbuji

Introduction

This paper invites us to a critical survey of Christian attitudes towards the other world religions. As the second millennium after Christ's coming draws to an end, the mandate to proclaim the Good News to all creation (Mt. 28.19-20; Mk 16.15) is far from completion. In Acts 4.12 we read about Jesus: 'There is no salvation in anyone else, for there is no other name in the whole world given to men by which we are to be saved'. Thus Christ is to be proclaimed as an ultimate value—a *conditio sine qua non*—for salvation. We ask: Can a person be 'saved', that is, come to live a truly human life, by some other name than that of Jesus Christ?

1. *Statistics of the Five Major Religions*

David B. Barrett and Todd M. Johnson have provided the following figures for the five major religions in 1990 and the projected figures for the year 2000:[1]

Religion	1990	2000	Annual Increase in 2000	Percentage
Buddhists	323,000,000	359,000,000	5,000,000	6.1
Christians	1,758,000,000	2,130,000,000	51,200,000	33.2
Hindus	705,000,000	859,000,000	18,000,000	13.3
Jews	18,000,000	20,000,000	220,000	
Muslims	935,000,000	1,201,000,000	30,000,000	17.7

1. D.B. Barrett and T.M. Johnson, *Our Globe and How to Reach it: Seeing the World Evangelized by AD 2000 and Beyond* (Birmingham, AL: New Hope, 1990).

2. *The Theological Issues*

1. *Evangelization and Religious Freedom*

In its declaration on religious liberty, the Second Vatican Council declared that 'the human person has a right to religious freedom', to be 'immune from coercion' in relation to 'his convictions in religious matters', and that this 'right to religious freedom is based on the very dignity of the human person as known through the revealed word of God and by reason itself' (*Dignitatis Humanae*, 2)

Pope John Paul II has addressed the issue of evangelism in relation to freedom of conscience:

> the call to conversion... is seen as an act of 'proselytizing'; it is claimed that it is enough to help people to become more human or more faithful to their own religion, that it is enough to build communities capable of working for justice, freedom, peace and solidarity. What is overlooked is that every person has the right to hear the Good News (*Redemptoris Missio*, 46).

2. *The Salvation of Those Outside the Church*

The Second Vatican Council makes frequent references to the Church's role in the salvation of humankind. The Catholic Church believes that God has established Christ as the one mediator and that she herself has been established as the universal sacrament of salvation (cf. *Lumen Gentium*, 48). To this Catholic unity of the people of God, therefore, all are called, and they belong to it or are ordered to it in various ways, whether they be Catholic faithful or others who believe in Christ or finally all people everywhere who by the grace of God are called to salvation (cf. *Lumen Gentium*, 13).

The universality of salvation in Christ was spelled out by the Council:

> since salvation is offered to all, it must be made concretely available to all. But it is clear that today, as in the past, many people do not have an opportunity to come to know or accept the Gospel revelation or to enter the Church. The social and cultural conditions in which they live do not permit this, and frequently they have been brought up in other religious traditions. For such people salvation in Christ is accessible by virtue of a grace which, while having a mysterious relationship to the Church, does not make them *formally* part of the Church but enlightens them in a way which is accommodated to their spiritual and material situation. This grace

comes from Christ; it is the result of his sacrifice and is communicated by the Holy Spirit. It enables each person to attain salvation through his or her free cooperation (*Gaudium et Spes*, 22).

3. *Evangelization and Dialogue*

In 1974 Pope Paul VI set up the Council for Inter-Religious dialogue and the Council for dialogue with non-believers. There is need for good relations and collaboration between Christians and adherents of non-Christian religions. Christian and non-Christian dialogues promote mutual understanding, respect and love. Fellow citizens who belong to different religions can learn to know one another, accept and respect one another, and together build up their countries in unity, progress and peace. Where Christians and non-Christians ignore one another and engage in unfriendly and sometimes violent rivalries, they bring doom on themselves from political, economic, racial or cultural factors rather than religious. But we have to ask if these inter-religious dialogues have not replaced evangelistic efforts.

Pope John Paul II has stated that 'Inter-religious dialogue is a part of the Church's evangelizing mission' which 'is addressed to those who do not know Christ and his Gospel, and who belong for the most part to other religions'. In Christ, God calls all peoples to himself and he wishes to share with them the fulness of his revelation and love. He does not fail to make himself present in many ways, not only to individuals but also to entire peoples through their spiritual riches, of which their religions are the main and essential expression, even when they contain 'gaps, insufficiencies and errors'.

> the Church sees no conflict between proclaiming Christ and engaging in inter-religious dialogue. Instead, she feels the need to link the two in the context of her mission *ad gentes*. These two elements must maintain both their intimate connection and their distinctiveness; therefore they should not be confused, manipulated or regarded as identical, as though they were interchangeable (*Redemptoris Missio*, 55).

This dialogue 'is based on hope and love, and will bear fruit in the Spirit' (*Redemptoris Missio*, 56).

Conclusion

With the Apostles we must conclude that 'we cannot but speak' (Acts 4.20). While we respect the beliefs and sensitivities of all, we respond to the great command of Our Lord to direct evangelization: 'Go into the whole world and proclaim the Good News to every creature' (Mk 16.15). With the promise of Christ, 'you will receive power when the Holy Spirit comes down on you', there is strength to face the task of proclaiming the Good news to all non-Christian believers (Acts 1.4, 8). And the hour is *now*. By the year 2000 CE it will be too late!

EVANGELISM AND CHARISMATIC SIGNS

Norbert Baumert

Jesus says: 'If you believe in me, then believe at least because of the works' (Jn 10.38; 3.2; 5.36; 14.11). Let us consider our theme in five steps: 1. the realities, 2. the concepts, 3. the dealing with charismatic signs, 4. proof of their authenticity, and finally 5. our mission.

1. *The Realities*

To the question of John's disciples: 'Are you the one...?' Jesus answers, 'The blind see, the lame walk...' (Mt. 10.5). His listeners know that already Moses and the Prophets were confirmed by signs from God. Paul lays claim to 'signs, wonders and deeds', which confirm him as an apostle (Rom. 15.19; 1 Cor. 2.4; 2 Cor. 12.12).

In the second century Justin emphasizes (*Dial. Tryph.* 82, 87-88) that 'the powers of the Spirit' have now passed from the Jews to Christian 'men and women', and Irenaeus defends the truth of Christian teaching 'against the heretics' by references to prayer in tongues, prophecies, raising of the dead and 'many other gifts which the Church imparts'. And so he says, 'where the gifts of God have been deposited, there one must learn the truth'.[1] The texts of the Greek Fathers are full of references to such signs, especially the accounts concerning the Fathers of the desert and the monks.

In the West we continually find signs and wonders in the case of the great missionaries: among the Celtic monks on the continent, with St Francis Xavier at the beginning of modern times, in the missions of the 19th and 20th centuries, as among those renewers of the Church

---

1. 'Ubi igitur charismata Domini posita sunt, ibi discere oportet veritatem', (*Adv. Haer.* 4.26.5); cf. also 5.6.1; 2.31.2; 32.4; and N. Baumert, 'Zur Semantik von χάρισμα bei den Frühen Vätern', *Theologie und Philosophie* 63 (1988), pp. 60-78 (here pp. 67ff.).

with a missionary vocation such as Francis of Assisi, Catherine of Siena, Don Bosco (reported to have multiplied bread), the saints and staretzes of the Eastern Church, figures like John Wesley, the Curé of Ars, Christof Blumhardt and many others. Here signs and wonders are entrusted to *persons*.

In the Roman and Orthodox traditions some *places* are especially favoured, where prayers are offered in a special way, beginning at the tombs of the apostles down to the places of pilgrimage like Guadalupe, Lourdes and Czestochowa. Some signs are connected with special dates, such as the liquefaction of the blood of St Januarius, and with recurring apparitions of Jesus, Mary or other saints. These always have a strong power to awaken faith.

Church history is full of such events, and teachers like Thomas Aquinas are aware of their missionary significance. They are fundamental to Catholic life and teaching even till today, more often arising from the faith of people than defended by theologians.

2. *Concepts*

Although there is an unbroken tradition of such signs, yet the designations differ. Besides signs and wonders there is both in the early Church and modern times the concept of *'charisma'*. Yet there has been a great change in this concept.[1]

In St Paul *charisma* always has the general meaning of 'a gift or present', never a special meaning. Even in 1 Corinthians 12, *charismata* are not an ability of the persons, but an event, a content, a sign itself: not the ability or endowment to speak in tongues or prophetically, but the single prayer of tongues, the single prophecy itself, the word of knowledge, and so on.

The Greek Fathers of the first millennium signified by *charisma* all types of God's gifts: the creation, the eternal reward in heaven, the eucharist, virtues like the seven gifts in Isa. 11.2, all types of signs and wonders, even the Holy Spirit himself, and above all baptism.

In connection with the concept of *gratia gratis data*, which developed in the middle ages independently of charism, *charisma* gradually became in modern times in the West a technical term

---

1. I have investigated this point in seven articles, summarized in 'Charisma'— Versuch einer Sprachregelung', *Theologie und Philosophie* 66 (1991), pp. 21-48; further references are given there.

meaning an endowment of the Spirit in service to the salvation of others for the building up of the Church. Only since 1900 has there been a distinction between charism and office. Sometimes the concept is limited to miraculous powers or abilities to serve. But today one should extend the concept further, namely: 'Charism is a particular gift for life and service to the Church and the world coming from the grace of God and bestowed individually by God'.[1] Thus charism should be distinguished from other gifts like the virtues, which are common to all the faithful; charisms, however, are given immediately from God to the individual and though everyone has some charisms, nobody has the same charisms.

The adjective 'charismatic' is broader: it can indicate the activity of the Spirit in the charisms as well as in the basic charismatic experience of God. Here one should make a distinction. Just as there are both simpler and more impressive charisms, so there are simpler and more impressive experiences of the Spirit. By the term 'baptism in the Spirit' the early Church means every kind of first reception and vivid experience of the Spirit of God, whereas the 20th century use at first meant only an outstanding experience with the gift of tongues. But this is only one kind of 'experience of the Spirit', and not necessarily the 'first', but a 'new grace' of God, given in our days in a new way. One should not insist that this kind of experience is required in order to be a Christian, because it is a free gift of God. The Spirit imparts freely both the charisms and the varied ways in which God makes the divine presence felt. So one must say that God surely gives to everyone who is open an experience of the Spirit, but not necessarily to everyone a 'baptism in the Spirit' in the narrow sense mentioned above. At least we should not say that as long as someone does not have the prayer of tongues, he or she has not yet received the fullness of the Spirit that God would offer him (1 Cor. 12.30).

And likewise on the broad scale: the Charismatic Renewal is itself a 'charism', as are other contemporary Christian movements inspired by the Spirit. Here there is much confusion as to the thing itself and as

---

1. Quoted from *The Spirit Gives Life: Charismatic Community Renewal in the Catholic Church in the Federal Republic of Germany: A Theologial Guide* (approved by the German Episcopal Conference) (Rome: ICCRO). German original: *Der Geist macht lebendig* (Sekretariat der KCGE, Marienstr. 80, D7500 Karlsruhe 1), cf. §VI.1.

to the terminology.[1] This matter is important, because when we bring someone to the Lord, we are not authorized to say: 'You will receive the Holy Spirit in the way of a peak experience with the gift of tongues', but they surely will receive a vital encounter with God—whether it is called charismatic or not.

The problem returns in the case of the charismatic signs; these too can be great or small, striking or restrained. I distinguish three types of charismatic signs, namely the bodily perceptible, the internal and the ethical signs:

1. Bodily perceptible signs: those like multiplication of bread, or physical healing, praying in tongues or prophecy; there are also many small signs of God's love in daily life, happy events like finding a parking place or help in an emergency. Very often it is only the recipient who knows that it is a gift of God.

2. Internal signs: some internal deliverance, an inner healing, visions, pictures or words, but also impressions, inspirations or simple 'impulses' from the Holy Spirit. Similar to these signs is the event of a felt nearness of God: baptism in the Spirit or simply an enlightenment, being filled with joy or a quiet peace (2 Cor. 12.1-6; Rom. 14.17). This often has the character of a sign for the recipient.

3. Ethical signs: receiving within oneself a power for good and acting accordingly, so that people can perceive that 'it must be God, and not anything in the person, that gives that sovereign power' (cf. 2 Cor. 4.7-11; 6.2-10). All signs have this in common: it can be seen that God is working in them. It does not matter whether the sign is great or small, striking or ordinary; the important thing is that the Spirit of God is perceived as an inner working power.

Thus charismatic signs are something different from charism in the present-day sense of the word; they are rather that which the early

---

1.   When K. McDonnell and G. Montague (*Christian Initiation and Baptism in the Holy Spirit* [Collegeville: The Liturgical Press], p. 191) use the word in the wide biblical and early Church sense, we have to notice what the consequences are for the kind of experiences that one can have today. See *The Spirit gives Life* (§V.1, p. 2 n. 3).

Church meant by *charisma*/gift, whether effected through abilities entrusted to a person or simply as objective events.

3. *Dealing with Charismatic Signs*

From the point of view of the bestower, signs are a type of non-verbal communication of God with people; they require the interpreting word, but are often more immediately intelligible than conceptual speech. In these signs God shares with us from the divine being. In counterdistinction to a sacramental sign, which has one unchangeable meaning, God adapts to the person according to the individual situation. Through this present reality and uniqueness, charismatic signs often possess a living immediacy and freshness. They are a sign of the utterly personal attention of God to the individual. They are deeply personal experiences. They are unforeseeable and beyond our control, so that they make perfectly clear that God's ways are not our ways. We can only pray and receive them with reverence and gratitude.

From the point of view of the receiver, charisms, though not foreseeable, do require a definite predisposition. We can block them through lack of faith or through apathy, as well as through an unhealthy fascination with miracles and feverish piety. If the signs are emphasized in a false manner, that blocks evangelization (Mk 1.43-45) and narrows the true charismatic activity of God. The signs simply lose their signification and the door is opened to self-deception.

From the point of view of the process itself, any unhealthy craze for miracles makes the sign an end in itself, so that ends and means are reversed. Ignatius of Loyola warns strongly against this, namely that the felt effects of grace become more sought after than the bestower of grace. The worship of God must always come first, if we are to enjoy the effects of grace purely and unselfishly. Ignatius says of himself: 'When I had first attended to worshipping God, the consolations came only as consequence, and I came to the insight that the contrary was bad, namely to seek first the consolation and then turn to worship' (*Spiritual Journal*, 16 March).

From the point of view of fellowship, charismatic signs can be misused, if our intention is not purely directed to God, as Paul shows in his symbol of the body. If somebody does not have a certain gift, they must beware of envy and inferiority complexes; if one has such gifts, he or she must beware of arrogance and boasting. That holds true not only for individuals, but also for Christian denominations among one another—as, for example, with ecclesiastical superiority, Pentecostal-charismatic triumphalism or an egotistic vainglory in individual leaders. This makes it more difficult for others to accept the proclamation of the gospel and hinders evangelization. In the proclamation of the *evangelium* we must always distinguish between what is given to all and the charismatic gifts, which the Spirit imparts 'as God wills'. And so there is no universal requirement of 'baptism in the Spirit' in the specific sense of the word, and likewise no sign that is universally required. Charismatic signs are not in themselves the kingdom of God, but in each case a finger pointing to it. Mk 16.17 says that signs will follow the believer, and so they will happen from time to time—as God grants—not that the Apostles should cure all the sick or raise all from death or even could do so.[1] False teaching often leads to an unfortunate pressure, which frequently leads to frustration and ultimately makes the gospel message unbelievable.

From the point of view of the gospel message, charismatic signs are a confirmation. But the signs do not lead automatically to faith. That was already the case with Jesus. Where a person does not embrace the invitation that the signs contain, Jesus takes back the signs. God knows best how the individual can best find God. Therefore God often refuses to give us the sign, even when we may ask for it with 'perseverance and faith'. We should then learn not to hang on to the sign, but to hang on to God, so that the signs remain only a path to God and become secondary, in order that we may see our salvation in God alone and not in miracle-working or in physical healing.

4. *The Testing of Charismatic Signs*

The great care which the Catholic Church takes before confirming a miracle is not a sign of skepticism but of responsibility. For besides true signs, there are certain powers of nature and certain abilities that can easily be confused with some charisms. There are also spiritual

---

1. In the Greek text of Mk 16.18 there is no article in front of the 'sick', whereas 'the sick', as many translations have it, could be taken to mean all sick people. The mission of the apostles in Lk. 10.1-20 is a one-time affair for a definite time, after which they 'return'. Otherwise we would be sent to raise up all the dead (Mt. 10.8)! Like Jesus, the disciple is shown which work the Father bids him or her perform in each case.

illusions, which may often not be recognized as such, and there are demonic signs. An extraordinary phenomenon, which wears a pious face, is not infallibly a charismatic sign (see the so-called 'Ghost-healer'). The basic question is always: Does Jesus stand clearly in the middle or does one seek to justify it with much rhetoric? Signs must be tested according to content and spiritual quality.

The content must be good and must produce something good; in word-charisms this goodness consists in the correctness, which must been measured by their agreement with the Bible and the teachings of the Church. Moreover, the teachings involved in the charisms must also be examined. A present-day example: at the moment there are many prophecies that we are living in the 'last days'. If you mean by that, that since the first Easter we are living in the eschatological era and that we do not know when this last time will end, that is biblical. But people often mean that we are living in the last phase before the second coming of the Lord. Such exact determining of times has time and again occurred in the history of the Church, especially before the year 1000. Will something of the sort occur before the year 2000? The Abbot Joachim of Fiore proclaimed the year 1260 as the beginning of the 'Age of the Holy Spirit'. Do present day determinations of the times possess any better foundation? Moreover, when someone makes such prophecies, they should be not only messages for an individual group; but since they concern all Christianity, they must be presented to the whole of Christianity for testing. Finally, Jesus says that the son of man and the angels of heaven do not know the day or the hour (Mk 13.32). This biblical truth has not changed. The second coming may happen today or in a thousand years.

This example makes clear the Church dimension of all charismatic signs. They must fit into the growing ecumenical consensus. In what sense are they a confirmation of a doctrine? First of all they confirm that Jesus is saviour for that specific person or group (Mk 2.1-12). Moreover, the more central a truth to which they point, the more convincing it will be to all; the more specific the teaching to which a charismatic sign relates, the more it will need dialogue and a common testing.

Along with content one must consider the spiritual quality of the sign. Does the person involved, for instance the prophet, move 'in the way of the Lord' (*Did.* 11.8), and is dialogue part of his life? In large conferences the believing community must have an important say. The ecclesial community has an instinct for the faith and so it must consider whether the sign occurs in an atmosphere of anointing, felt in the 'peace and joy in the Holy Spirit', and finally it must consider what the effects of the signs are in the long run.

The determining criterion is, consequently, not the miracle in itself but its spiritual quality. Only thus can the signs find their evangelical and missionary dimension; they then point to the Saviour, and quietly step into the background after they have done their service and made possible for the individual a personal encounter with the bestower of all good.

5. *Our Mission*

By these considerations I do not intend to belittle or downgrade the charismatic signs, but through evaluation to remove all obstacles, so that the signs reach their goal. Let us pray 'that signs and wonders may be performed' (Acts 4.30).

To the protest of the disciples against the 'other exorcist', who drove out demons in the name of Jesus, Jesus answers: 'The one who is not against you is for you' (Lk. 9.50). Let us never abuse the signs of God to aggrandize our denomination or some miracle-worker, and let us rejoice when people are led to God by true signs worked by others.

Besides, the Lord gives us not only the striking signs evoking wonder but also simple signs in day-to-day life, which reveal the same God. Signs are so much the more valuable inasmuch as they point to the Lord, and therefore simple signs can be the most important.

Striking signs often occur at the beginning and have the function to shake people and awaken them to faith, and therefore are important for evangelization. But for the growth and strengthening of faith God often gives the quieter and less impressive signs and those mystical graces with or without their corporal manifestations, whose content is the personal love between God and his creature. Praise be to Jesus Christ!

MIRACLES AND MARTYRDOM IN THE EARLY CHURCH:
SOME THEOLOGICAL AND ETHICAL IMPLICATIONS

James E. Bradley

On the cover of the July issue of *World Vision Magazine* is the title 'Mozambique: A Suffering Church, A Growing Church'. In Mozambique today, profound suffering has resulted in people turning to God in unprecedented numbers. It was the third-century Church Father, Tertullian, who in the midst of the decimation of the early Church, said, 'The blood of the martyrs is the seed of the church'. Yet today, in 20th-century North America, the growth of the Church is often connected to the gifts of healing and the charismatic signs that relieve suffering; evangelization is hardly ever related to suffering itself. What is the relationship in the history of the early Church between miracles, martyrdom and evangelism? And how might we learn today from the Church's experience of suffering in the first three centuries?

The topic of the relationship between charismatic signs and early church growth has received careful scrutiny by Ramsey MacMullen in his widely acclaimed *Christianizing the Roman Empire.*[1] The

1. I wish to thank Cecil M. Robeck, Jr for directing me to numerous references cited in this study. Still one of the best accounts of supernatural phenomena in the early church is A. von Harnack's 'The Religion of the Spirit and of Power, of Moral Earnestness and Holiness', ch. 5 in *The Mission and Expansion of Christianity in the First Three Centuries*, I (New York: Harper Torchbooks, 1962, [repr. from the 1908 edn]), pp. 199–218. For more recent accounts, see H. Remus, *Pagan–Christian Conflict over Miracle in the Second Century* (Patristic Monograph Series, 10; Cambridge, MA: The Philadelphia Patristic Foundation, 1983); Remus does not focus on miracles in the post-apostolic period, but more broadly, the status of miracles in the ancient world; this book is valuable for its definition of miracles (pp. 3-94); see the extensive reviews of this book and other recent literature by W.R. Schoedel and B.J. Malina in *Religious Studies Review* 12.1 (1986), pp. 31–39; R. MacMullen, *Paganism and the Roman Empire* (New Haven: Yale University

church growth movement in the United States has referred to this book to defend the argument that there is indeed a historic basis for linking the healing gifts of the Spirit, or signs and wonders, to the growth and expansion of the Church. It is this particular use of early church history that this paper will address by a careful examination of those texts that refer to healing. Attention will be given to the social context in which the early Christians wrote, particularly persecution, and we will also look at other possible motives for evangelization that appear in the context of passages that refer to healing. This concentration on the specific context in which references to signs and wonders is found is designed to redress the imbalance found in MacMullen's account. First, however, we must give brief notice to the prominence of charismatic signs in the literature of the early church.

Continuity with the Period of the Apostles

Prophets were clearly active in the period of the Apostolic Fathers (AD 95–150), and the emphasis in this era falls particularly upon gifts of utterance rather than miracles of healing.[1] The 'miraculous' is therefore necessarily defined broadly in the second century. The first emphatic avowal of the presence of gifts of the Spirit in the church is found in the writings of the Apologist Justin Martyr, about AD 155, and he is self-consciously aware of the problem of the passage of time and continuity with the primitive church.[2] About a generation

Press, 1981); *idem, Christianizing the Roman Empire, AD 100–400* (New Haven: Yale University Press, 1984). McMullen is excellent on the secular literature but superficial and misleading on Christian sources. R.A.N. Kydd (*Charismatic Gifts in the Early Church* [Peabody, MA: Hendrickson, 1984]) surveys most of the sources.

1. See, for example, Ignatius, *Epistle to the Philadelphians* 7.1 (edition: Kirsopp Lake [ed.], *Apostolic Fathers* [LCL; 2 vols.; Cambridge, MA: Harvard University Press], I, p. 247); *Didache* 11.7-12 (K. Lake [ed.], *Apostolic Fathers*, I, p. 327); the *Shepherd of Hermas*, Mandate 11.7-16 (K. Lake [ed.], *Apostolic Fathers*, II, pp. 121–23. This article will not treat references to gifts of the Spirit and miracles which may be biblical only. See, for example, Athenagoras, *A Plea for the Christians* (about AD 177) 7 (A. Roberts and J. Donaldson [eds.], *The Ante-Nicene Fathers* [Grand Rapids: Eerdmans, 1979, hereafter, *ANF*], II, p. 132), and Clement of Alexandria (c. AD 202), *Stromata* 4.21 (*ANF*, II, pp. 433–34), where the gifts that are mentioned are not obviously contemporary.

2. *Dialogue with Trypho, a Jew*, 82, 88, 39 (*ANF*, I, pp. 240, 243, 214). See several additional references, including incidents of exorcisms in *Dial. Tryph.* 87;

removed from Justin Martyr, Irenaeus, Bishop of Lyon (AD 180), made observations similar to those of the famous Apologist.[1] In *Against Heresies* Irenaeus mentioned the contemporary practice of exorcism and added, 'Others have foreknowledge of things to come: they see visions and utter prophetic expressions. Others still heal the sick by laying their hands upon them, and they are made whole. Yea, moreover, as I have said, the dead even have been raised up, and remained among us for many years'.[2]

The Montanist movement (AD 170–230) will not be dealt with here in any detail, but it is important to observe in passing that Montanism, at least in its North African expression, did not prize an unusual display of power above other facets of the Spirit's work. Tertullian specifically said that the presence of the Spirit in the Montanist movement contributed to the direction of ecclesiastical discipline with an emphasis upon purity, to insight into the Scriptures, to the reformation of the intellect, and to an 'advancement toward better things'.[3]

The early Church's acquaintance with miracles, however, was not confined geographically to centers of Montanism. The Alexandrians and the Romans were as familiar with miracles as the North Africans. Writing about AD 245, Origen claimed to have been a eyewitness to the banishment of demons and to 'many cures' performed by the power of the Holy Spirit through Christians.[4]

and the *Second Apology of Justin* 6 (*ANF*, I, pp. 243, 190).

1.   *Against Heresies* 5.5.1 (*ANF*, I, p. 531); *Proof of the Apostolic Preaching* 99, (in J.P. Smith [ed.], *Ancient Christian Writers*, XVI [New York: Newman Press, 1952], pp. 108-109). On the text in *Against Heresies* and its interpretation, see C.M. Robeck, Jr, 'Irenaeus and "Prophetic Gifts"', in P. Elbert (ed.), *Essays in Apostolic Themes: Studies in Honor of Howard M. Ervin* (Peabody, MA: Hendrickson, 1986), p. 110.

2.   *Against Heresies* 2.32.4 (*ANF*, I, p. 409. On the dead being raised, see also 2.31.2 (*ANF*, I, p. 407).

3.   *On Veiling of Virgins* 1 (*ANF*, IV, p. 27). On the Spirit's aid in interpreting Scripture, see also *On the Resurrection of the Flesh* 63 (*ANF*, III, p. 594). D. Wright ('Why were the Montanists Condemned?', *Themelios* 2.1 [September 1976], pp. 15–22) provides a fine survey of Montanism. Karl Holl observed concerning the presence of miracles in the late second century: 'What the real state of things was at that time one may conclude from the fact that the Montanist prophets never made any attempt to prove the truth of their proclamation by means of miracles' (cited in H. Chadwick [ed.], *Contra Celsum* (Cambridge: Cambridge University Press, 1953], p. 402 n. 1).

4.   *Contra Celsum* 1.46; 2.8; 3.24; 42, 142; see also C.M. Robeck, Jr, 'Origen,

We find similar references to charismatic signs in the work of the out-spoken Roman presbyter and noted theologian, Novatian.[1]

One of the most neglected and yet most fascinating testimonies to the continued belief in God's miraculous intervention in healing is found in the various liturgies of the Church. Prayers for healing are not uncommon and they can be found in 1 Clement, the *Constitutiones Apostolicae*, and the *Sacramentary of Serapion*. In the latter, dated around AD 325, we find this prayer:

> Lord God of compassion, stretch out your hand and graciously grant all the sick to be healed, graciously grant them to be considered worthy of health, release them from the sickness which lies upon them, in the name of your only son let them be healed, let his holy name be to them a medicine for health and wholeness; since through him is glory and might to you in the Holy Spirit, both now and to the whole of the ages of the ages. Amen.[2]

These references are important because they reflect widespread usage and popular expectation at the broadest levels of the Church's life.

The widespread belief in miracles in terms of geographic extent is equally impressive with the uniform belief in miracles. The most prominent early Church leaders in Asia Minor, southern Gaul, North Africa, Egypt and Rome all attest to the conviction that miracles were part of the legacy of the primitive Church. The early Church apparently took the words of Jesus to the disciples, 'Heal the sick, raise the dead, cleanse lepers, cast out demons' (Mt. 10.8), as having broad implications for the ongoing ministry of the Church. If the end of Mark's gospel (16.15, 18) was written on the basis of the book of

Celsus, and Prophetic Utterance' *Paraclete* 11.1 (1977), pp. 19-23. It is true that in his homily on Jeremiah, Origen mentioned miracles as a thing of the past. On traces of miracles, see *Contra Celsum* 7.11 (Chadwick edn p. 404). But in 1.2, 8 Origen says 'traces' of 'prodigious miracles' still remain. See also 7.8 (p. 402, and Chadwick's note, p. 402 n. 1). C.M. Robeck, Jr ('Origen's Treatment of the Charismata in 1 Cor. 12.8-20', in C.M. Robeck, Jr [ed.], *Charismatic Experience in History* [Peabody, MA: Hendrickson Publishers, 1986], pp. 111-25) explains these apparent discrepancies in terms of Origen's use of allegory and the audience he is addressing.

1. *Treatise Concerning the Trinity* 29 (*ANF*, V, p. 641); see also R.A.N. Kydd, 'Novatian's De Trinitate, 29: Evidence for the Charismatic', *SJT* 30 (1977), pp. 313-18.

2. Cited and translated by D.R. Foubister, 'Healing in the Liturgy of the Post-Apostolic Church', *Studia Biblica et Theologica* 9.2 (1979), p. 143.

Acts, it nonetheless remains the case that the Church of the second and third centuries saw itself in continuity with the Church in the book of Acts on the issue of miracles. But if the gifts of the Spirit were viewed as important to the ongoing life of the Church, it is equally clear that not everyone exercised these gifts. They were given to some people and not to others, and their operation and exercise was carefully monitored by the leadership of the Church, since pagan magicians claimed the same powers as Christian presbyters. More importantly, the political setting of the early Church meant that God's intervention in history was viewed in an unusual and very sobering light.

Suffering and the Development of Critical Acumen

The same God who healed early Christians often led them to sudden, violent death, even in the flower of youth. The ever present reality of confessing Christ at the risk of one's life (confessorship) and martyrdom itself in relation to supernatural healing is a vital, but almost wholly neglected aspect of the early church's life.[1] The social and political context in which miracles were expected is thus of central importance in any attempt to understand them. Before the first empire-wide persecution of Decius in the mid-third century, the variety of approaches the state made to this so-called 'illicit religion' was as great as the diversity between the emperors themselves. But even though persecution was sporadic and mostly local in scope, it was often deadly, and it was a constant fact of life in the Christianity of the first three centuries.

It seems to be significant that in the very midst of the fathers' references to gifts of miracles, the crucifixion of Christ is often mentioned. Justin Martyr observed, 'For numberless demoniacs throughout the whole world, and in your city, many of our Christian men exorcising them in the name of Jesus Christ, who was crucified under Pontius Pilate, have healed and do heal...' In almost identical words Irenaeus said, 'It is not possible to name the number of the gifts which the Church scattered throughout the whole world has received from God, in the name of Jesus Christ, who was crucified under Pontius

---

1. Tertullian discusses the apparent contradiction in *Apology* 27 (*ANF*, III, pp. 40-41). C.M. Robeck, Jr pointed out to me that Cyprian also wrote on the subject of why Christians suffer, on the occasion of an outbreak of the plague.

Pilate'.[1] These references may suggest more than a predictable link between the cross and Christ's triumph over principalities and powers when discussing the subject of exorcism; they point toward the early church's concern to remind believers that any temporary relief from suffering found in healing in no wise exempted them from the setbacks, limitations, suffering, and possibly even death that were necessarily involved in following Christ. That this was a vital concern of the early fathers is proven by the frequent reiteration of the subject of persecution in their narration of accounts of healing.

We find, for example, that the manifestation of the Spirit in prophetic utterance was often given specifically to encourage people in the face of impending martyrdom. This is characteristic of the prophetic words found in Tertullian's treatise *On Flight in Persecution*, and we see the same thing in the account of the martyrdom of Perpetua.[2] Cecil M. Robeck, Jr has categorized the various types of visions Cyprian experienced, and one of the most prominent categories was that having to do with comfort in the face of persecution and threatened martyrdom.[3] It was quite impossible, at least in these cases, for prophetic utterances to contribute to a highly triumphalistic gospel that would claim to exempt one from the limitations and tragedies of this life. In the early church the power of the Spirit was intimately connected to one's identity with the cross of Christ.

The more spectacular demonstrations of the Spirit and power do

1.   *The Second Apology of Justin* 6 (*ANF*, I, p. 190); *Against Heresies* 2.32.4 (*ANF*, I, p. 409). Harnack noted the prominence of the crucifixion in Christian accounts of exorcism (*Mission and Expansion*, p. 134). In the *Sacramentary of Serapion* we find healing linked to the crucifixion in such a way that it appears to reflect a belief that healing is 'in' the atonement: 'the name of the one crucified and risen again for us, the one who carried our diseases and weaknesses and who is coming to judge the living the dead, Jesus Christ...' (cited in Foubister, 'Healing in the Liturgy', p. 145).

2.   *On Flight in Persecution* 9 (*ANF*, IV, p. 121); *Passio Perpetua* 7–8 (edition: P. Wilson-Kastner, *et al.* [eds.], *A Lost Tradition: Women Writers of the Early Church* [Lanham, MD: University Press of America, 1981], p. 23).

3.   C.M. Robeck, Jr, 'Canon, *Regulae Fidei*, and Continuing Revelation in the Early Church', in J.E. Bradley and R.A. Muller (eds.), *Church, Word and Spirit: Historical and Theological Essays in Honor of Geoffrey W. Bromiley* (Grand Rapids: Eerdmans, 1987), p. 71. See the *Epistles* of Cyprian 7.6; 8; 33.1; 78.1-2; 80.1-3 (*ANF*, IV, pp. 287, 288, 312, 377, 405-406, 406-408). Spiritual gifts are mentioned along with confessorship and martyrdom in Clement, *Stromata* 4.21 (*ANF*, II, p. 434), but see p. 229 n. 1 above.

constitute one—but only one—of the appeals the early fathers made concerning the genuineness of the gospel. Irenaeus did indeed note the impact of exorcism on evangelism: 'For some do certainly and truly drive out devils, so that those who have thus been cleansed from evil spirits frequently both believe [in Christ] and join themselves to the church'.[1] Similarly, Tertullian observed that 'the greater part' of the people have a knowledge of God through visions, though it is not clear that he meant converts to Christianity. Origen also said, 'many have come to Christianity as it were in spite of themselves, some Spirit having turned their mind suddenly from hating the gospel to dying for it by means of a vision by day or by night. We have known many instances like this'.[2] In several texts in Tertullian and Cyprian we find what can only be called evidence for 'power encounters' of the Mount Carmel variety.[3] But while these episodes are spectacular, what is most striking about the early fathers is that they found the greatest defense for the gospel not in the casting out of demons, nor in the physical healing of Christians, but precisely in their physical weakness.

Miracles of healing were considered of value simply for the benefit they brought to the recipient, and this beneficial aspect of direct divine intervention was mentioned almost as frequently as the apologetic value. Here the focus was not upon the power of the Christians, but upon their neediness. This emphasis was especially characteristic of Irenaeus. 'Those who are in truth His disciples, receiving grace from Him, do in His name perform miracles, so as to promote the welfare of other men, according to the gift which each one has received from Him'. Gifts of the Spirit were exercised 'day by day for the benefit of the Gentiles, neither practicing deception upon any, nor taking any reward from them...' Irenaeus was thus insistent that the church 'has been accustomed to work miracles for the advantage of mankind, and not to lead them into error'.[4] The same theme is also found in

1. *Against Heresies*, 2.32.4 (*ANF*, I, p. 409).
2. *A Treatise on the Soul* 47 (*ANF*, III, p. 226); *Contra Celsum* 1.46, 42. On the impact of prophecy on evangelism, see C.M. Robeck, Jr, 'Origen, Celsus, and Prophetic Utterance', *Paraclete* 11.1 (1976), p. 21.
3. Tertullian, *Apology* 22–24 (*ANF*, III, pp. 36-39); for Cyprian, see the lengthy quotation in Harnack, *Mission and Expansion*, pp. 142-43. MacMullen (*Paganism*, pp. 95-96, and *Christianizing*, pp. 28, 60-61) has additional illustrations of 'power encounter', but many of these are late third and early fourth century, and this is significant, in my view.
4. *Against Heresies* 2.32.4 (*ANF*, I, p. 409). In other places he said that

Tertullian, and he seems to have caught the balance that is characteristic of the literature when he observes that 'God everywhere manifests signs of His own power—to His own people for their comfort, to
strangers for a testimony unto them'.[1]

If one surveys the early literature in its entirety, simply in terms of
the frequency of references, the Christian's willingness to die for
Christ in martyrdom was an equally prominent apologetic theme as
miraculous displays of power. Justin Martyr argued that the true
power of the gospel was shown in the Christians' willingness to die
for their faith.[2] In Origen the willingness of people to die for their
convictions is at least as frequent an apologetic topic as the miracles
which Christians perform.[3] Tertullian was emphatic on this point:
'Hope in this resurrection amounts to a contempt of death'. It is a
well-known fact that he related martyrdom directly, if paradoxically,
to church growth. 'Nor does your cruelty, however exquisite, avail
you, it rather is a temptation to us. The oftener we are mown down by
you, the more in number we grow; the blood of Christians is seed'.[4]
Athanasius, too, believed that the martyrs were the grandest testimony
to the truth of the gospel: 'For many who were formerly incredulous
and scoffers believed and so despised death as to become martyrs for
Christ himself'.[5] It was, of course, not the bare miracles on the one

miracles are 'for the general benefit', and again they are done 'for the well-being of
men'; (*Against Heresies* 5.6.1; 2.31.2 [*ANF*, I, pp. 531, 407]). Remus hints that
this beneficial, or eleemosynary, characteristic of miracles is one way in which
miracles might be distinguished from magic, though he rightly underscores how
much this distinction depends upon one's point of view. See H. Remus, '"Magic or
Miracle?" Some Second Century Instances', *The Second Century* 2.3 (1982),
p. 145.

1.   *A Treatise on the Soul* 51 (*ANF*, III, p. 228). See the same treatise, ch. 9
(p. 188), where he refers to a woman in the church who exercises gifts of the Spirit
and adds, 'to them who are in need she distributes remedies', though this may have
to do merely with healing.

2.   *The Second Apology of Justin* 12 (*ANF*, I, p. 192); see also ch. 10
(p. 191).

3.   *Contra Celsum* 1.31; 3.27; 8.44 (Chadwick edn pp. 30-31, 145, 483-84).

4.   *Ad Nationes* 1.19 (*ANF*, III, p. 127); *Apology* 50 (*ANF*, III, p. 55). See
also, in the same vein, *To Scapala* 3 (*ANF*, III, p. 106); and *Scorpiace* 1 (*ANF*, III,
pp. 633-34).

5.   *On the Incarnation of the Word* 28 (E.R. Hardy [ed.], *Christology of the
Later Fathers*, pp. 82-83). All of these references are drawn from those who
advocated miraculous healing, so it cannot be said that some advanced one aspect of

hand, nor the martyrdoms on the other, that recommended Christianity. Speaking of miraculous powers, Harnack wrote, 'The fact that their Christian range included the exploits of moral heroism, stamped them in this field with a character which was all their own and lent them [the miracles] a very telling power'.[1]

Miracles were sometimes used by the early church to demonstrate the truth of Christianity, but never in a simple or unqualified way. The reason for this is patent: before the power of the Roman Empire the Christians were weak—indeed, in this they were like their Savior. Because of the relatively constant threat of persecution, Christians in the first three centuries who believed in God's miraculous intervention could not possibly have believed that he would alleviate their every affliction. It thus comes as no surprise that suffering and martyrdom were ranked by the early Christians as important as divine miraculous interventions for the 'proof' of the gospel. When miracles were used to validate the claims of Christianity, they were displayed in the context of a martyr church. This context of suffering provided an indispensable balance to the emphasis on the miraculous works of God. One finds the same tension in the early church as there was in the apostle Paul, who could say at the same time, 'the signs of a true apostle were performed among you', and 'If I must boast, I will boast of the things that show my weakness' (2 Cor. 12.12; 11.30). Some concluded that Paul was not an apostle precisely because he suffered as he did, but he made it clear that one mark of a true apostle was weakness. God appears to have allowed the first three hundred years of Christianity to be characterized by persecution and weakness so that the genuineness of its identity with its Lord would be placed beyond dispute. Pagans could and did compete with the miracles of the early Christians; they could not compete with the early Christians' willingness to suffer and die.

Ethics and the Development of Critical Acumen

Extraordinary manifestations of God's power were thus used as an apology for the gospel, but they were not viewed as the primary nor the only line of defense. In addition to martyrdom, it could be argued

---

power and others another. Athanasius, for example, also cites exorcisms as evidence of the truth of the gospel. See, especially, chs. 30, 32, 48.

1. Harnack, *Mission and Expansion*, 202.

that an emphasis on the transformed life-style and ethical behavior of
Christians was as prominent a defense of the truth of Christianity.[1]
What is striking about this fact is that once again, just as with martyrdom, the emphasis on ethics is found precisely in conjunction with
statements claiming miracles. It can be no mere coincidence that, in the
same texts that discuss miracles, the quality of the life of Christians is
often held forth as a testimony to the truth, almost as if the fathers
sensed the inadequacy of the former when standing independently. In
the same passage in which Justin Martyr emphasized the gifts of the
Spirit, he insisted that the quality of the life of Christians is a
testimony to the gospel. More was at stake here than 'personal' ethics,
for elsewhere he noted that the very people who once took most
pleasure in the means of increasing their wealth and prosperity now
brought what they had 'into a common stock and communicate to
everyone in need'.[2] The same balance between supernatural healing
and ethical concern is found in Irenaeus, who wrote, 'and inasmuch as
those who are cured very frequently do not possess the things which
they require, they receive them from us'.[3] Similarly, Novatian
discussed the charismata, the transforming ethical power of the Spirit,

---

1.   MacMullen fails to see the ethical appeal of Christianity. He clearly overstates
the case when he says, 'Indeed if we relied only on pre-Constantinian sources, we
would suppose that such supernatural acts accounted for very much the greater part
of conversions' (*Paganism*, p. 96). See also, *Christianizing*, pp. 29-30, 40. Remus
is far more positive on the importance of the ethical behavior of Christians (*Pagan–
Christian Conflict*, p. 149), as is E.G. Hinson (*The Evangelization of the Roman
Empire: Identity and Adaptability* [Macon, GA: Mercer University Press, 1981],
pp. 234-41). Harnack's chapter, 'The Gospel of Love and Charity', in *Mission and
Expansion*, pp. 147-98, must be read as a corrective to MacMullen.
2.   *Dialogue with Trypho* 82 (*ANF*, I, p. 240); *First Apology* 14 (*ANF*, I,
p. 167). It could easily be argued that the testimony of social-ethical transformation
is as prominent in Justin as miracles. On helping those in need, see *First Apology*
13, 15, 27, 29, 37 (*ANF*, I, pp. 166-67, 172, 175). Many people, once on his
opponent's side, observes Justin, 'have turned from the ways of violence and
tyranny, overcome by observing the consistent lives of their neighbors, or noting the
strange patience of their injured acquaintances, or experiencing the way they did
business with them' (*First Apology* 15, translation from the Library of Christian
Classics). Says Harnack, 'A whole series of proofs is extant, indicating that the high
level of morality enjoined by Christianity and the moral conduct of Christian societies
were intended to promote, and actually did promote, the direct interests of the
Christian mission' (*Mission and Expansion*, p. 210).
3.   *Against Heresies* 2.3 (*ANF*, I, p. 407).

and martyrdom, 'which shows forth the constant faithfulness of their religion', all in the same chapter.[1] Athanasius, who cites exorcism as evidence of the truth of the gospel, refers, in almost the same breath, to the moral character of the Christians: 'so that the adulterer no longer commits adultery, and the murderer murders no more, nor is the inflictor of wrong any longer grasping, and the profane is henceforth religious'.[2] In other cases where the ethical behavior of Christians and the allusion to miracles are not discussed together, it is a fact of some importance that the same authors who emphasized the apologetic force of contemporary miracles make much of the miracle of a transformed life. This is particularly true of Ignatius, Tertullian and Origen.[3] The balance the early church struck between supernatural gifts, changed lives and commitment even to martyrdom is well summarized by Justin Martyr. In the context of asserting that Christ has given gifts to the church and thereby fulfilled the prophecy of Ps. 68.18 (quoted in Eph. 4.8), he writes,

> Accordingly, we who have received gifts from Christ, who has ascended up from on high, prove from the words of prophecy that you... are foolish, and honour God and his Christ by lip only. But we, who are instructed in the whole truth, honour them both in acts, and in knowledge, and in heart, even unto death.[4]

Once again, spectacular supernatural intervention must be placed alongside of, but not over and above, ethical transformation. It appears that the early church gave as much attention to caring for the sick as they gave to praying for the sick.[5] In any case, in each of these facets (personal piety, social concern for others and martyrdom), there was either a dying to self, or an orientation toward others that has not always been characteristic of circles placing an emphasis on supernatural healing.

Ethical concern was also evident in the analytical approach the fathers took to the actual practice of miracles, particularly in their

1. *Treatise Concerning the Trinity* 29 (*ANF*, IV, p. 641).

2. *On the Incarnation of the Word* 30 (E.R. Hardy [ed.], *Christology of the Later Christian Fathers*, pp. 84-85).

3. On Ignatius, see *Smyrneans* 6.2; *Polycarp* 4 (K. Lake [ed.], *Apostolic Fathers*, I, pp. 259, 271-73); For Tertullian, *Apology* 39, 46 (*ANF*, 3.46-47, 50-51); *To Scapala* 4 (*ANF*, III, p. 107); Origen, *Contra Celsum* 3.15 (Chadwick edn p. 137).

4. *Dialogue with Trypho* 39 (*ANF*, I, p. 214).

5. So Harnack claimed (*Mission and Expansion*, pp. 122-23).

serious attention to the personal ethics of those who performed miracles. The fathers self-consciously eschewed an emphasis on technique for the purpose of avoiding any comparison to the practice of magic and pagan patterns of healing. The attention they gave to probing the nature of the reported miraculous event in order to determine the authenticity of claims of miracles was also a salutatory emphasis. Apparently there was no fear that a critical approach would somehow hurt one's faith or that it was incompatible with trust.

Simplicity, for example, was a prominent theme in the performance of miracles (understood broadly) among Christians in the first three centuries. This quality was thought by early Christians to be evidence for the claim that they were free from the desire to deceive. Irenaeus said of the church:

> Nor does she perform anything by means of angelic invocations, or by incantations, or by any other wicked curious art; but, directing her prayers to the Lord, who made all things, in a pure, sincere, and straightforward spirit, and calling upon the name of our Lord Jesus Christ, she has been accustomed to work miracles for the advantage of mankind, and not to lead them into error.

Origen also reveals acute discernment concerning the contemporary religious context. Referring to demons he observed that 'many Christians' drive them 'out of people who suffer from them, without any curious art or sorcerer's device, but with prayer alone and very simple adjurations and formulas such as the simplest person could use'. He insisted that power over demons is not by incantations or use of spells, 'but only of the name of Jesus with other words which are believed to be effective, taken from the divine Scripture'.[1] On the whole, the early Christians were free from popular superstitions concerning healing, but not entirely; and the problem of syncretism

1. *Against Heresies* 2.32.4 (*ANF*, I, p. 409). See also 1.13.3-4 (*ANF*, I, pp. 334-35), on the spurious preoccupation with technique; *Contra Celsum* 7.4; 1.6; see also 3.24 and 2.33. Harnack, quoting the pseudo-Clementine *de Virginitate*, observes the same: 'Let them exorcise the sick with fasting and with prayer; instead of using elegant phrases, neatly arranged and ordered, let them act frankly like men who have received the gift of healing from God, to God's glory' (*Mission and Expansion*, p. 133). On parallels to magical invocation, that overplays, I think, the similarities between pagan magic and Christian miracle, see Remus, '"Magic or Miracle"', p. 147.

would become overwhelming by the early fourth century.[1]

The fathers were concerned with criteria for judging the validity of claims of miracles, and they did raise the question of the authenticity of supernatural phenomena. Tertullian examined the nature of 'ecstasy', for example, by describing one's mental processes when one receives revelation. He claimed that such a state leaves a person in full possession of their mental faculties. Of a woman in his church who had visions, he said: 'for all her communications are examined with the most scrupulous care, in order that their truth may be probed'. Tertullian mentioned numerous 'men of rank' who had been 'delivered from devils, and healed of diseases', implying that their rank might contribute to the veracity of his account. 'Distinguished testimony', as alluded to in this text, was important to Tertullian, as he cites the healing of Severus, the father of Antonine, by anointing with oil.[2]

The early church was very sensitive to the fact that in the area of spiritual power the frailty of human nature was particularly vulnerable. The character of the prophet was constantly being appraised in two specific areas: vanity was seen to be a real temptation, but above all, the request for money was repeatedly viewed as the certain indication of a false prophet. Examples of concern for the life-style of the prophet or miracle worker can be found in the Didache, the Shepherd of Hermas, Irenaeus, Tertullian and Origen, with emphasis upon humility, purity and discipline.[3] Warnings about the request for

---

1.   *Scorpiace* 1 (*ANF*, III, p. 633); Origen, *On First Principles* 3.2.1 (cited in Harnack, *Mission and Expansion*). Remus (*Pagan–Christian Conflict*, pp. 183-84) discusses pagan and Christian presuppositions (cf. pp. 137-41). If the presuppositions of pagans and Christians concerning miracles were similar, as MacMullen insists (*Paganism*, 60, 75, 82, 96), much remains to be said concerning the differences in technique. But my sense at this state of research is that MacMullen has overstated the similarities in the pre-Nicene church. For a fine review of recent studies on exorcism, see P. Brown, *The Cult of the Saints: Its Rise and Function in Latin Christianity* (Chicago: University of Chicago Press, 1981), p. 108.

2.   *Treatise on the Soul* 45.9 (*ANF*, III, pp. 224, 188); *To Scapala* 5 (*ANF*, IV, p. 107). C.M. Robeck, Jr pointed out to me that in *Against Marcion* and in *A Treatise on the Soul* (45.3), Tertullian treats the experience of receiving revelation in terms of a 'dream state'.

3.   *Didache* 11.7-12; 13.1-7 (K. Lake [ed.], *Apostolic Fathers*, I, pp. 327, 329); *Shepherd*, Mandate 11.7-16 (*Apostolic Fathers*, II, pp. 121-23); *Against Heresies* 1.13.3-4; 3.11.9 (*ANF*, I, pp. 334-35, 429); *On Exhortation to Chastity* 10 (*ANF*, IV, p. 56), *Contra Celsum* 3.25; 7.8 (Chadwick edn, pp. 143, 402).

money are found in the Didache, the Shepherd of Hermas and Irenaeus.[1]

Some Modern Applications of the Early Church Materials

Today, the consciousness of suffering and martyrdom in any part of the world-wide body of Christ should mean that we cannot suppose miracles will deliver us from temporal suffering. But, sadly, this is not the case. Careful observers of the Church in the West, and particularly in the United States, have noticed how an emphasis on supernatural healing is often, paradoxically, a sign of secularization and naturalism—indeed, of materialism. Charismatic signs of healing are all too often appealed to as an attempt to remove the last vestiges of suffering in areas where modern medicine has not yet devised a means of granting relief. Healing is often linked with an overall preoccupation with material well-being, a preoccupation that most Christians in other times and other countries would have found scandalous. Moreover, the focus on healing is sometimes associated with a denial of the unwanted and unpleasant realities of physical traumas (e.g. cancer), and even, in extreme cases, of aging and dying. Astonishing as it may seem, the elderly are sometimes led to believe that the loss of their hearing or eyesight ought to be reversed, if only they had enough faith. Their physical affliction is then compounded by the mental affliction of guilt, and this guilt is applied by the very pastors who ought to be dedicated to strengthening them in their affliction.

In the late 19th century, one of the most phenomenal revivals in Europe centered around the healing ministry of Johann and Christoph Blumhardt. Signs and wonders were done at their hands that astonished Europe, and as eminent a modern theologian as Emil Brunner attributed much of the inspiration for his work to the prophetic witness to Jesus Christ in the person of the elder Blumhardt. But after some years of experiencing a continuous miraculous display of God's power of deliverance, the younger Blumhardt began to detect an unsanctified mentality in those who came to him for healing. In this context he wrote:

---

1. *Didache* 11.12 (K. Lake [ed.], *Apostolic Fathers*, I, p. 327); *The Shepherd*, Mandate 11.12; *Against Heresies* 4.33.6 (*ANF*, I, p. 508).

It is God's honor which we must now exalt in our own persons, both physically and spiritually. Not our own well-being must be in the foreground, but the one desire that God may come into His well-being, into His right on earth. His Kingdom must gain ground in us and in our lives before we can enjoy all the goodness through the miracle-working hand of our Savior Jesus Christ. Now, many people write us letters just as they used to, asking for our intercession. We should actually answer in each case: Leave for a time your begging before God and first find the way together with us. Let us seek how we can do justice to God in the recognition of guilt and the true striving for God's justice and His Kingdom on earth. Turn your inner being to the opposite direction, and do not look at yourselves and all your suffering. Look at the suffering of God, whose Kingdom has been held up so long because of the lying spirit in men...[1]

Is it not time for Christians to say with Blumhardt, 'Let us strive for God's justice and His Kingdom on earth; let us look at the suffering of God?' And if we are mindful of human suffering in the world-wide body of Christ, our prayers for healing will be not less, but more compassionate. We will not, however, allow ourselves the luxury of praying selfishly, or for petty grievances. Nor will we murmur or be discouraged when our prayers are answered with a firm 'No'. In Mozambique, the multitudes are turning to Christ because 'the Gospel of Christ meets their suffering on three key levels: offering healing from trauma, freedom from bitterness, and the strength to endure what must still be suffered daily'.[2] Today, we, especially those of us in the West, must strive for the pattern of reality we find in the early Church and live with the consciousness of the Church in Mozambique. We must unite prayer that God's Kingdom would be displayed in our midst by signs and wonders, with active concern for justice for the poor and the dispossessed, and a willingness to suffer ourselves when God, in his mercy, calls us to suffer.

1. Cited in K. Barth, *Action in Waiting* (Rifton, NY: Plough Publishing, 1969), p. 7.
2. T. Brenneman and G. Hope, 'Mozambique', *World Vision Magazine* 35.4 (1991), p. 6.

EVANGELISM AND ESCHATOLOGY

Paul Bechdolff

1. *There is no Evangelism without Eschatology*

Every missionary movement of the Church and every evangelistic movement is strongly linked to a revival or to a renewal of Christian faith: for example, over the centuries we have seen monasticism, the Franciscan friars, the Reformation, the Jesuits, and the Pietist and Pentecostal movements. Neither external circumstances nor political expansion, progress in the discovery of the world nor colonialism, can produce anything at all if there is not a revival or a renewal in the Churches—that is to say, a rebirth of living faith, a deepening and rekindling of love, and an ever deeper and enlivening hope.

It is hope in particular which provides the basis for evangelism and makes it urgent. This was the case in the first centuries of the Church. In the beginning of the first letter to the Thessalonians (1.2-10), the apostle Paul describes the coming of the gospel through his ministry: 'you turned to God from idols to serve the living and true God, and to wait for his Son from heaven, whom he raised from the dead, Jesus who delivers us from the wrath to come' (1 Thess. 1.9-10).

The Christian hope comprises two inter-related themes: a general global theme, the coming of the Son to establish the Kingdom, and a personal theme, to escape from the wrath to come and to receive eternal life, that is, to enter the Kingdom. The two themes of the imminence of the Kingdom and the necessity of salvation, that is, of accepting the gospel of Jesus, give an urgency to evangelism. This drives Paul further and further on, from city to city, to Rome and beyond, missing out those places (Rome excepted) where the gospel has already been preached. The declaration, 'Amen, I am coming soon' (Rev. 22.20) echoes the words of Peter at Pentecost: 'And in the last days it shall be...' (Acts 2.17) and his pressing appeal: 'Save yourselves from this crooked generation' (Acts 2.40). This eschatological urgency was maintained throughout the period of expansion in the first centuries of the Church, despite all opposition. Michael Green, in his book *Evangelism in the Early Church* has numerous illustrations of this in his chapter on the strategy of Evangelization: 'May grace come and this world pass away. Maranatha. Amen' (*Did.* 10.6); 'In truth, quickly and suddenly will His will be accomplished, as also the Scripture testifies when it says: Quickly will He come and will not tarry; and suddenly will the Lord come to His temple—the Holy One, for whom you are looking' (*1 Clem.* 23.5); 'The last epoch has arrived!...Obviously, we must either fear the gathering storm of anger, or else cherish the present time of grace' (Ignatius of Antioch *Eph.* 11.1). But the word which most strongly underlines the link between eschatology and evangelism is found in the *Letter of Barnabas*: 'Remember the day of judgment to bear it in mind day and night...Keep yourselves always at the ready, either in proclaiming the Word and in carrying to distant places your exhortations in your concern to save souls or in working with your hands to redeem your sins' (19.10).

Later the general theme of hope continued but became weaker, while the personal theme was reinforced: be ready for the hour of judgment, so as to attain heaven. The imminence has not disappeared, but it has been individualized to refer to the hour of death. The question is now the eternal destiny of each person, whether of perdition or of salvation. These alternatives have impelled Christians of faith and love to evangelize. In England in the 18th century William Carey, who counted up all the nations of the world and all the peoples discovered by the explorers, wept over all who would be lost if no one came to tell them about Jesus Christ, while the leaders of his Church regarded this as God's business and not theirs. In France in the 19th century Felix Neff and Jean-Frédéric Vernier approached their fellow-travellers on the coach with the question, 'Are you saved?' while the Brethren asked, 'Where will you spend eternity?'

In the 19th century various Churches and denominations, new and old, saw a rebirth of general eschatology and the expectation of the imminent return of Christ without this apparently having any effect on patterns of evangelism and missionary work. The 20th century has seen a reaffirmation of the hope of the Kingdom, in the face of the catastrophe of two successive world wars. When the French Reformed Church was reconstituted in 1938, its declaration of faith stated:

'Through evangelism, missionary work and the struggle against social evils, the Church prepares the way of the Lord for the coming of God's Kingdom and God's justice through the triumph of her Head'. This modern text re-emphasizes in a forceful way the link between eschatology, evangelism and mission.

2. *The Gift of the Holy Spirit, Evangelism and Eschatology*

The Pentecostal renewal is like a resurgence of what happened in the first century: on the one hand, the Holy Spirit is the dynamic behind an effective evangelism; on the other hand, the gift of the Holy Spirit confirms the Christian hope and brings it to life.

In the first century the charisms were the signs by which the Lord confirmed the Word (Mk 16.20). Among the proofs of his apostolic authority Paul presents as distinctive signs: patience in every trial, miraculous signs, wonders and acts of power (2 Cor. 12.12). To the Thessalonians as well as to the Corinthians he affirms: 'Our gospel came to you not only in word, but also in power and in the Holy Spirit' (1 Thess. 1.5). Similarly, in this 20th century, marked in the West by materialism, rationalism and positivism, in which the idea of eternal life seems to have disappeared, the reappearance of the charisms on a large scale, accessible in principle to all, provides a clear sign of the living God, active and attentive to human beings. It is not surprising that one of the sources of the Pentecostal movement was a Bible School training evangelists and seeking the secret of the power of the apostles. Their search was answered in the writings of Luke where the evangelization of the world is dependent on the gift of the Holy Spirit: 'You shall receive power when the Holy Spirit comes upon you; and you shall be my witnesses'.

However, in the New Testament, the gift of the Holy Spirit is strongly linked with eschatology. The gift of the Holy Spirit at Pentecost is the inauguration of the last days, the Messianic era: 'this is what was spoken by the prophet Joel: And in the last days, God declares, I will pour out my Spirit on all flesh' (Acts 2.16-17); 'Being therefore exalted at the right hand of God, and having received from the Father the promise of the Holy Spirit, he has poured out this which you see and hear... Let all the house of Israel therefore know assuredly that God has made him both Lord and Christ, this Jesus whom you crucified' (Acts 2.33, 36)

What is true at the level of general eschatology is also true of personal hope: 'In him you also... were sealed with the promised Holy Spirit, which is the guarantee of our final deliverance until we take possession of it, to the praise of his glory' (Eph. 1.13-14). The gift of the Holy Spirit as first fruits awakens the desire for the final and corporate fulfilment: 'we ourselves, who have the first fruits of the Spirit, groan inwardly as we wait for adoption as sons, the redemption of our bodies' (Rom. 8.23).

The same correlation between the gift of the Holy Spirit, manifestations of the Spirit and living eschatology is found again in the 20th century. Very quickly the Pentecostals insisted that this outpouring of the Holy Spirit is the latter rain, the sign of the last days, and that the coming of Jesus is near. The confession of faith of the Foursquare Gospel proclaims: 'Jesus saves, Jesus baptizes with the Holy Spirit, Jesus heals and Jesus is the coming Messiah'. In 1932, Louis Dallière, a pastor of the French Reformed Church, concluded after visiting the Elim Pentecostals in England: 'This demonstrates that the graces of the Holy Spirit which were so indispensable at the beginning may be so again today, because we are in the end times'. As a result of the charismatic revival of the 1930s in the Ardèche, where Dallière was one of the leading pastors, the Charmes Prayer Union[1] was born in 1947 and defined itself as a community of hope. Its fourth prayer subject, the most important and the one that determines the other three, is prayer for the coming of Jesus Christ and for the resurrection of the dead. It is also a prayer that Christians will want Christ to return (*Charter*, para. 57).

We find the same correlation between the gifts of the Holy Spirit and a lively eschatology with the Evangelical Sisters of Mary in Darmstadt, who lived through a deep repentance for all that the German people and they themselves had done, an experience of the gifts of the Spirit and an active waiting for the coming of Christ, being ready and waiting for the glorious goal of the wedding feast of the Lamb. In our time the baptism in the Holy Spirit and the accompanying manifestation of charisms not only demonstrate that God is alive, but that in Jesus God is coming. If God comes into our lives, God is coming in history. If God already reigns on earth to a certain extent, God is coming to establish the Kingdom. If there is hope in Jesus for this life, there is also hope for the end of time. The apostle

1. The official title is L'Union de prière de Charmes-sur Rhône.

Paul is not mistaken when, in ch. 8 of Romans, he links hope with the ineffable prayer of the Holy Spirit within us: the Spirit who knows what to ask. He is not mistaken when he links the overflowing of hope with the power of the Holy Spirit: 'so that by the power of the Holy Spirit you may overflow with hope' (Rom. 15.13). Finally Revelation makes it clear that the Spirit and the bride say: 'Come' (Rev. 22.17). It is the same today when the Holy Spirit acts with power. Wherever the Holy Spirit is at work, there the Christian hope is reborn in its general form. The well-known saying of Christ at the end of Revelation is lit up as a contemporary word: 'Yes, I am coming soon' (Rev. 22.20).

3. *Make no Mistake about Eschatology*

I wish to present here a summary of the teaching of M. Louis Dallière during the retreats of the Charmes Prayer Union since 1947.

1. *The Heart of Eschatology is Jesus Himself, and through Him God All in All*

Certainly Jesus' coming involves the destruction of sin, of Satan and of death (Rev. 20), but beyond that there is the presence of God and of the Lamb without any distance or veil; there is the wedding feast of the Lamb with his bride the Church, made worthy by him, perfect and without blemish. The Christian longing is above all the longing for Jesus, the desire finally to see Jesus, the crucified and risen Lord. 'I am coming.'

2. *The Goal of Eschatology is not Distant but Near: 'I am Coming Soon'*

The expression 'soon' or 'near' occurs eight times in Revelation, of which five are in ch. 22 alone. *tachu*, frequent elsewhere in the New Testament, means in haste, rapidly or more quickly (Jn 11.31; Acts 12.7; Mt. 5.25; Lk. 15.22; Jn 13.27; Mt. 28.7). What does 'I am coming soon' mean in 1991? The question had already been raised at the end of the first generation in 2 Pet. 3.5, with the first answer being: 'with the Lord...a thousand years [is] as one day' (2 Pet. 3.8). Two thousand years are like a few seconds of the day compared to the history of the earth. From that starting point, Christians became accustomed to the idea that they had plenty of time, and now we are approaching the third millennium of the Church. But the author of 2 Peter began with the affirmation that 'one day is as a thousand years'. By this expression, which is not in Psalm 90, Peter emphasizes that God's time is not measured by our standards, and that God can do in one day what we think will take a thousand years. So we have the constant theme of the suddenness of the coming of Jesus. 'I am coming soon' means that God hastens to accomplish the divine purpose, God's plan. In contrast to our human thinking, which imagines that God is not in a hurry, Jesus affirms that 'I am impatient to return; I am coming soon'. Time is in tension between the creation and the Kingdom on account of this haste, and even more between the death and resurrection of Jesus and his coming again. God's time is neither cyclical nor indefinite; it is in tension.

Human time can be indefinite: 'For you it is always the right time' (Jn 7.6) or cyclical (Eccl. 3.15). While it may be good to celebrate the birth of Jesus every year or the year 2000 in particular, remember that these anniversaries are cyclical. The really important feast for which we must prepare, the definitive feast, is the wedding feast of Christ and his Church, towards which both Christ and the Church are heading. This is why the word of Jesus, as yet unaccomplished, 'this generation will not pass away until all these things take place' (Mt. 24.34) has been carefully preserved by the Church together with another word: 'heaven and earth will pass away, but my words will not pass away' (Mt. 24.35). This is not only that it will be accomplished for a generation that will not see death, but because each generation must desire to be and consider itself to be that generation.

3. *We Can Neither Predict a Date, nor Establish a Calendar, nor Even an Order of Events for the Things to Come*

In the 19th century those circles which awaited fervently the return of Christ had many prophets who predicted the date of this event and were confounded in every case when nothing happened. This is not surprising since the entire New Testament repeats the message, 'no one knows the day nor the hour'. Similarly, I do not have the right to affirm categorically that Jesus will come back at the end of this generation, say 80 years from now. This would be to engage in more calculations. Other circles represented in France, especially the Evangelicals (Rene Pache *et al.*) or renewed Catholics who have rediscovered the Bible (such as M. & R. Chasles), without actually calculating dates have searched the Scriptures to see how the end times will unfold. For this purpose they have studied all the eschatological texts of the Old and New Testaments, have listed all the events announced and then sought to harmonize them. But no one text, not even the longest, the book of Revelation, contains all the elements and, to be honest, they are sometimes contradictory or impossible to correlate one with another. We are like the Jews at the time of Jesus faced with all the Messianic texts of the Old Testament: there were several irreconcilable images (the Messiah Son of David, the Son of Man, the suffering servant...) which forced them to make a choice or develop a new plan. And for that reason, most of them at least were prevented from recognizing Jesus as the Messiah. Those who recognized him belonged in one way or another to the poor, whose only trust was in God. We cannot organize in a coherent way all the prophetic data of the Old and New Testaments. Even the succession of visions in the book of Revelation faces us with the question: is it describing a chronological succession or are the same themes being taken up in a cyclical manner?

4. *The Bible Describes Events Which Serve as Signs for Those who Believe.*

Some of these signs are well-known, others have only recently been rediscovered. The apocalyptic passages in the Synoptics describe many *negative signs*: wars, rumours of wars, natural catastrophes, false prophets and false Christs, persecutions, general impiety and apostasy. All the passages indicate a mounting crisis, and in particular, the Johannine apocalypse is constructed according to this schema, although the texts also affirm that these events could be very limited in duration. All stretch through time from the resurrection of Christ, and we see many of them today. Have we now arrived at the final paroxysm? We cannot know. God alone knows. But we can pray that these times will be cut short, for God will shorten them (Mt. 24.22).

Among the *positive signs* there are: 1. *The gift of the Holy Spirit*, presented by Peter as the sign of the last days (Acts 2.16). 2. *The proclamation of the gospel to all nations* (Mk 13.10). Today the centrifugal movement from Jerusalem to the ends of the earth is almost finished. While there are still two billion people who do not know Jesus Christ, there are no more countries without a Christian Church, even if the Christians only form 2% or 3% of the population (as in the

Moslem countries and some other countries in Asia). If we count tribes and languages there are no more than 350 ethnic groups yet to be evangelized, and without a translation of the Bible in their native tongue. The Wycliffe Bible Translators, dedicated to this work, claim that at the present speed of translation this could be completed by 2035! 3. *The centrifugal missionary movement is replaced by a movement 'from everywhere to everywhere'*, for it is no longer just a question of evangelizing individuals. This is the slogan of the Evangelical Community of Apostolic Action founded in 1972. Now there is a centripetal movement towards Jerusalem (The Ascents to Jerusalem etc.). 4. *Since 1968 Jerusalem is no longer trodden under foot by the Gentiles.* According to Lk. 21.24, this is the sign that the time of the Gentiles is coming to an end. Moreover the collapse of Christendom can be dated to the first world war (August 3, 1914) in which officially Christian countries led the nations of the world in a fratricidal war. 5. *Since the last century evangelical authors have prophesied the return of Israel to the land*, but they were not much heeded. The events of the years 1930–45 have led several theologians to re-read Romans 9–11 more attentively (Karl Barth, Louis Dallière in 1941), abandoning the thesis of the definitive rejection of Israel and replacing it with a temporary setting aside of Israel awaiting the turning of the whole people to Jesus. Since 1967 many Jews have turned spontaneously to Jesus as their Messiah, independently of any evangelization by the Churches or missionary societies. 6. *There is a particular aspect of the gift of the Spirit in the 20th century.* Not only has God poured out his Spirit on all the Churches, whatever their denomination, but often the gifts have been ministered from one Church to another, as if the Lord did not want us to receive them just for our own Church. It is thus that God is preparing a united Church for the return of Jesus, confirming the importance of all the ecumenical progress already made.

The Word of Jesus, which we have received by faith, which has been impressed on our hearts by the Holy Spirit, brings light to these signs in the same way as it is enlightened by them. In the same way, the second petition of the Our Father, 'Thy Kingdom Come', is also made clear. As in the first three phrases of the Lord's prayer, we are called to associate ourselves with the desire and the will of the Father and to the prayer of the Spirit, 'Come, Lord Jesus, Maranatha'.

This prayer of the Charmes Prayer Union is also taken up in a complementary prayer: that the whole Church may pray with fervour 'Come, Lord Jesus' so that this will happen speedily. If we cannot fix a precise date, we can at least take hold of the Word by faith: 'We shall not all die' (1 Cor. 15.51), and truly desire to be part of this last generation. This desire is then broken down into prayers so that the preliminary steps before the Lord's return may be realized: the revival of the Churches and the evangelization of the world, the illumination of Israel and the visible unity of the Church. This is the first way of hastening the return of Christ, for we must not just wait passively, turned in on ourselves, but we must commit ourselves to the plan of God to save all people (2 Pet. 3.9). The Christian hope is active: 'waiting for and hastening the coming of the day of God' (2 Pet. 3.12). The second way of hastening the day of the Lord is to participate actively in the plan of God 'so that all people may come to conversion' (2 Pet. 3.9), that is to say, to evangelize all the people of the world.

4. *Make no Mistake about Evangelism*

1. *To Remain Within the Movement and the Dynamic of the Holy Spirit*

This ideal is not the same as going back to an evangelism of speeches and apologetics, nor to an evangelism of charity based on human abilities (medicine, technology). I am not saying that there should be no speech, but that the Holy Spirit equips us with intelligence to understand people and to speak to them about God, this speech being confirmed by signs. I am not saying that there should be no charitable work—quite the contrary; however this activity should be neither a condition nor a method, nor an alibi for evangelism, but rather the Holy Spirit making us act in love for the whole person, for the power of the Holy Spirit is that of love and hope in action. In evangelism in the power of the Spirit the evangelists are led by the Spirit and remain submitted to the Spirit. For powerful evangelism let us fully put into action what the Spirit gives us, or rather let us allow the Holy Spirit to put us to work as the Spirit desires.

2. *To Bring to an End the Proclamation of the Gospel to the Gentiles*

There are still something like twenty nations without an indigenous Church, even if there are a handful of Christians who have come from elsewhere. There are 350 ethnic groups who do not have the Scriptures available in their own language. How can this work be hastened? We can pray that the Lord of the harvest will send out workers. Like William Carey we can inform ourselves about these nations and ethnic groups. We can call a halt to the competitive evangelism of the 19th century when Protestants were sent to areas where the Catholics were already present, and vice versa. I dream that the parallel missionary congresses (ecumenical, evangelical, Catholic) might disappear to give way to one sole missionary congress, in which all participate so as to work together in this task of God. May this at least be a fruit of this congress in Brighton and may there also spring up from here evangelistic teams to go and complete the evangelization of the nations.

3. *To Permit the Illumination of All the Jewish People*
The situation of the Jewish people in regard to the gospel is not the same as that of other peoples. There is no need to reveal to the Jews both the one God and Jesus the Christ. The Jew already knows the Eternal Lord, the only God. Certainly, each Jew, like each pagan, or rather like each one born into Christianity, needs to discover personally the gospel of Jesus. May God be blessed for all the Jews who over the course of time have accepted Jesus as the Messiah and have become Christians. But each time this has been at the expense of a break with their people, a break which we Christians have enforced by our failure to understand the true status of Israel, and by our rejection of Judaism as if God had rejected it, forgetting God's philosemitism: 'God loves them on account of their ancestors' (Rom. 11.28). The age of the Gentiles will end with the conversion of Israel *en masse*, by a divine *coup d'état*: when God will baptize the whole people of Israel with the Holy Spirit, in order that this people can fully recognize their own essence and mission, and that their eyes may be opened concerning him whom they have pierced.

In order for this to be possible, we must come alongside the people of Israel, and before Israel be witnesses to the grace of God, in abandoning all anti-Semitism to share in God's philosemitism. May the Christians of the West be reconciled with Israel following the horrors of the Shoah, which are not yet effaced. May the Christians of the whole world recognize what they owe to Israel and reserve for Israel the place of the elder brother in the parable of the prodigal son. May our lives as renewed Christians led by the Spirit be a sign that the hour of the Messiah has already come: in particular may the Christians of the Holy Land be united, despite the diversity of their human origins, despite their divisions and mutual hatred, so as to proclaim the gospel to all, Christians, Jews and Arabs. And if we proclaim the gospel to a Jew, may this be to offer the possibility of becoming a completed Jew and not a renegade.

4. *To Preach the Gospel to Every Person to Prepare them to Meet the Lord who is Coming Soon*

The age of Christendom is over. Before us is the Kingdom. Like John the Baptist, we must preach to every person to prepare them for the return of Christ, whether this is in countries that are Christianized, post-Christian or those not yet reached and transformed by the gospel. If we believe that Jesus is coming soon, it is a completely mistaken perspective to evangelize in order to reproduce a form of Christendom, for this would mean that our hope is still distant, and not the hope renewed by the Holy Spirit. We do not preach to establish people in a Christian world, but so that they can be disestablished and ready for Christ's return. This 'disestablishment' involves a relationship to human power, to money and to riches, in line with what is taught in the Sermon on the Mount. The rise of covenant communities[1] expresses this simplicity, as well as adopting a priority for the poor, whatever kind of poverty it may be, so that the poor may experience the love of God for them.

5. *Preaching the Gospel to Prepare the Church of the Parousia*

The Church born of this evangelism will be ready for Christ's return and be a united Church. Evangelism always leads to the raising up of the Church, the body of Christ. But today this Church cannot be distinguished from the existing Churches. It is not a question of a new Church, of the nth denomination. It is an object of faith and longing. It is necessary then to evangelize in the perspective of this united Church. To fragment each existing Church to constitute a new Church is an aberration, in opposition to the spirit of unity. That is why it is right that those who are touched by the gospel should join one or other of the existing Churches, whether that of their own upbringing, or that of their spiritual father, but always in a way that does not

1.   In French, 'communautés de vie'.

further divide the body of Christ, already so fragmented. This united Church of the return of Christ should always be more important than my particular Church. In waiting for (in the double sense of being patient and of desiring) the ecumenical labours to produce decisive results for Christian unity, let us live prophetically. Let us recognize that each Church, and mine in particular, is not coextensive with the Church that is waiting for the return of Christ. Let us rejoice unreservedly in the radiance of each local Church, of each denomination; let us pray for their revival, and that they may grow through an extensive evangelism; let us stop advancing as a motive for evangelism the expansion of 'my Church', of 'my denomination'. The making of converts is the natural fruit of the preaching of the gospel, but it cannot be the primary motivation, except when it is seen in this context of the united Church ready for the Parousia.

6. *Proclaiming the Gospel Together*

Until now each Church has organized its own evangelism around its distinctive confession: Orthodox evangelism, Catholic evangelism, Protestant evangelism, Anglican evangelism. Certainly non-confessional missionary societies have existed in the Protestant and Evangelical world since the 19th century, but theirs was an exclusively Protestant evangelism. We are always tempted to do it this way. Can we maintain a common message when we are not in agreement on all points without reducing the gospel to the lowest common denominator? Do we not, some say, have the responsibility to present the full riches of the gospel? Are we not obliged, say others, to preserve the purity of the gospel? How can we speak together when, for some, others are impoverished, and for the latter the former are unbelievers? Is the solution that each continue to evangelize separately? This is unacceptable today if we are to be faithful to what the Holy Spirit is doing among us.

God has in fact blessed us all in the same way, whatever our denominations. God has enabled us to rediscover life in Christ, the calling that is in him; by the Spirit we have renewed contact with the Father and the Son, and our lives have changed through repentance and conversion. All of us have received gifts for the service of all, and we have become capable of benefiting from any ministry given by the Spirit, irrespective of the denomination of the minister. What exchanges, what riches there are when we are together! What we share is truly great, is vast, and is what every person needs: the living knowledge of the Father, the Son and the Holy Spirit, salvation and life in God. Here lies the power of our evangelism. We still differ on doctrine and on the right way of doing things, but these questions can no longer keep us apart. If today we continue to evangelize separately, we contradict our own experience.

If we evangelize separately we also contradict our hope, our eschatology. It is a united Church, ready for his return that will welcome the Christ. Yet we continue to behave as though our divisions were more important than the Church of the Parousia. By contrast, when we evangelize together, we perform at one and the same time an act of faith and an act of hope. Our contemporaries must see with their own eyes the reality of the unity of the children of God. Both our unity and our love in our diversity will be more of a sign than any tendency to uniformity in our initiatives. To be sure, they must also sense that this evangelistic unity is not just organizational, but that it flows from a growing unity of life. Evangelizing together can only be the result of an already existing common life, or it will quickly oblige us to adopt one.

Certainly, evangelizing together is difficult, for it requires a *metanoia*, a radical ecclesial conversion. It requires that we offer to God the very existence of our own Church, our own denomination, being ready for it to disappear so that there may appear the united Church ready for Christ's return.

In the last resort, is it possible for the Holy Spirit to be incoherent? Can the Spirit unite us on the one hand and divide us on the other? Can safeguarding the confessional nature of evangelism come from the same Spirit that has blessed us all in the same way? The Holy Spirit has united us for the work of world evangelism. Let us remain united to accomplish it.

Understand well that I do not wish other Churches to die. On the contrary I pray for their development, their growth, their deepening, their sanctification, their empowering. But in these last days, the Holy Spirit unites us to proclaim to the world the love of God of which our mutual love is a sign despite our differences.

Evangelism is first of all a proclamation of the saving act of the living God and an invitation to live it out. Evangelism is thus an act of salvation and not an indoctrination, an act of love and not an act of power or domination, an act of hope and not of resignation. We must not resign ourselves to our divisions. Let us allow ourselves to be led by the Spirit.

EVANGELIZING TOGETHER:
ECUMENICAL ISSUES IN EVANGELIZATION[*]

1. *Philippe Larère*

Fr Larère described the work of an association for inter-confessional evangelization in France, called La Tente de l'unité (the Tent of Unity), founded by Pastor Thomas Roberts. In this association, teams made up of Catholics, Protestants and Evangelicals[1] conduct evangelistic missions under a large tent. This evangelistic community is not strictly speaking an 'ecclesial community', but is rather a group of Christians, belonging to different Churches and confessions, but all committed to the person of Jesus Christ, all sharing the same love of God and of neighbour, and all 'baptized in the Holy Spirit'.

1. The initial proclamation of the Gospel, the *kerygma*, is common to all the Churches, because it is biblical. It has:

   a. A *content* (see Lk. 24.46-50); it consists in proclaiming
       the death and the resurrection of Jesus
       repentance for the forgiveness of sins
       the gift of the Holy Spirit to be a witness.

   b. A *form* (see 1 Cor. 15.3-5); it is
       the story of a witness, who communicates an experience,
           like the apostles Peter and Paul
       the witness of an evangelist who invites others to have
           the same experience.

---

[*] Editor's Note: Space limitations permit only summaries featuring highlights of the above papers.

1. In France, the term 'Protestants' may refer as here to the historic Protestant bodies, the French Reformed Church in most of the country, and the Lutheran Church in Alsace, while the term 'Evangéliques' (Evangelicals) then refers to those who belong to 'les Eglises libres' (the Free Churches), that is to say, Baptists, Methodists and independent Evangelical assemblies.

2. Can the initial proclamation of the gospel be fully realized independently of a Church? The audience of this ecumenical evangelization is invited to share in the fellowship of the Tent of Unity during the mission. But this ecumenical community, which only offers prayer and a warmth of fellowship, will only last as long as the mission. It is not possible to live the full Christian life at present in an inter-confessional community, because we do not all have the same way of reading the Scriptures, the same idea of baptism and the Lord's Supper, or the same understanding of the Church.

In conclusion, a shared proclamation of the gospel is possible, but only up to a certain point. It is only possible up to the moment at which the new convert must enter into a local church, in which he or she will live all the dimensions of the Christian life. How can such a local church really exist without each Church being challenged by all the other Churches to be converted itself to the gospel? 'Restore us to thyself, O Lord, that we may be restored!' (Lam. 5.21).

2. *Theodore Jungkuntz*

How can Christians separated by denominational lines, but brothers and sisters nonetheless, actually cooperate in evangelistic activities,[1] since that includes baptizing and teaching all that which Jesus commands to be observed? How can we do that, when all too often we disagree over what Jesus taught, including baptism?

Some denominations make the distinction between cooperation *in sacris* (i.e. the means of grace, Word and sacraments) and cooperation *in externis* (e.g. works of mercy). Unfortunately, this distinction has frequently become an excuse for satisfaction with the *status quo*. Ecumenical communities such as the Word of God Community in Ann Arbor, Michigan, with which I have been involved for eight years, have taken steps such as the following to 'maintain the unity of the Spirit…until we all attain to the unity of the faith and of the knowledge of the Son of God' (Eph. 4.3, 13):

---

1. A biblical basis for 'cooperative ecumenism' is set out in S.B. Clark, 'Orthodox, Protestants, Roman Catholics: What Basis for Cooperation?', in P.S. Williamson and K. Perrotta (eds.), *Summons to Faith and Renewal: Christian Renewal in a Post-Christian World* (Ann Arbor: Servant Books, 1983), pp. 87-105.

1. Pastors and lay leaders from representative churches meet regularly to seek opportunities for joint ministry which will not compromise denominational convictions, for example, an evangelistic canvass of a given area or joint sponsorship of an evangelistic event where the simple Gospel message is proclaimed; time is also spent in intercession for unity.
2. Members of the participating churches share in ecumenical prayer services which are open to the public. Rather than fighting over new people being evangelized, we trust the Spirit to show the connection most likely to succeed in reaching the person in his or her circumstances.
3. The leadership seeks to develop a theology which supports ecumenically cooperative evangelism; our focus is on lifting up in proclamation and worship the one who was 'lifted up from the earth' (Jn 12.32).
4. We remain committed to love each other as we encounter the many snags which could again drive us apart into sectarianly operating segments of the body of Christ.
5. We sense that God is encouraging us to foster in other locations the formation of ecumenical charismatic covenant communities.

What are the limits that we have experienced? While evangelism according to the New Testament is primarily evangelism to Jesus, it is secondarily but necessarily evangelism into the body of Christ (Acts 2.41, 47; 4.4, 32; 5.42–6.7; Eph. 2.11–3.10; 3.20-21). We cannot avoid dealing with the scandal of the divided body. We must admit to new converts that until now we have failed as Churches to 'attain to the unity of the faith'. This scandal has the potential to scatter what the proclamation of Jesus has just gathered, but in humility we evangelize people into this broken body and help them to choose that expression of the body which the Holy Spirit seems to be most powerfully using in their case. At the same time, we show them how the various denominational expressions of the Church can 'maintain the unity of the Spirit in the bond of peace'.

3. Roger Cabezas

Evangelization is an ecumenical *task*: 'you shall receive power when the Holy Spirit has come upon you; and you shall be my witnesses in

Jerusalem and in all Judea and Samaria and to the end of the earth' (Acts 1.8; cf. also Jn 1.12; Gal. 3.28).

Likewise, evangelization has an ecumenical *purpose*: 'Go therefore and make disciples of all nations, baptizing them in the name of the Father and of the Son and of the Holy Spirit' (Mt. 28.19); 'through him to reconcile to himself all things, whether on earth or in heaven, making peace by the blood of his cross' (Col. 1.20); 'All this is from God, who through Christ reconciled us to himself and gave us the ministry of reconciliation' (2 Cor. 5.18; cf. also Gen. 1.27-31; Rom. 6.18; Eph. 1.22).

It is necessary to clarify these two words: evangelization and ecumenism. Dr Julio de Santa Ana characterizes three levels, three stages and three instances of ecumenism.[1]

In the first instance, ecumenism is manifested as *ecumenical dialogue*, in which the main emphasis concerns matters of order and doctrine. This dialogue takes place at an academic level, it is formal, it is composed of experts, generally representing their Churches, and has an official purpose. Examples would be the Faith and Order Commission of the World Council of Churches, and the Anglican–Roman Catholic International Commission (ARCIC).

A second level, *fellowship ecumenism*, involves cooperation, and the promotion of interpersonal relationships among leaders, ministers, pastors and priests from different Christian Churches. This is found especially at the intermediate level in Church structures, and also has an official purpose.

A third level may be called *missionary ecumenism*. The main emphasis is common action for social justice, the many forms of work for the poor who live in misery. Basic elements are faith experience, Bible study and witnessing, bringing together Christians of different Churches and often those without a Church connection. This practical ecumenism is usually unofficial.

It is important to distinguish evangelization as a means of proselytism from evangelization as an integral service of the Church to the community.

Evangelization as a Means of Proselytism
The main goal of this would be to organize congregations—generally

1. J. de Santa Ana, *Ecumenismo y liberacion* (Madrid: Ediciones Paulinas, 1987).

those that are strong economically, politically and socially—so as to multiply the initial experience and add new converts. Thus, proselytizers constantly look for individuals in other Christian organizations with the purpose of adding them to their own congregation by the preaching of Jesus as Savior and healer, using any effective means.

An historical example can be found in Latin America, not only in missionary ventures of the last 100 years, but also in the conquest and submission of the land south of the Bravo river (the Rio Grande). In 1492, a Genoese, Christopher Columbus, came across a land in which 'flows milk and honey'. The aborigines found there (Mayans, Aztecs, Toltecs, Incas and many other races) were called Indians; the land discovered was baptized with the name of America and upon this land and its peoples was imposed the force of the sword, a culture and a religion. That sin has continued for 500 years, and so the traces, the purity and the hospitality of those people have continued to be destroyed. Nevertheless, they still resisted and tried to survive. They kept on looking for solidarity, for new horizons, for a new land in which there might be justice and peace. It is being proposed to celebrate the 500 years of evangelization: 1492–1992. This time will be one of great rejoicing for the conquerors, but of great sorrow in the kingdom of God.

Evangelization as an Integral Service of the Church to the Community
This occurs through concrete actions in the perspective of the kingdom of God (Rom. 14.17; 2 Pet. 3.13). A deeper experience of conversion to Jesus Christ, as the only and sufficient Savior, is emphasized. The new life, a community life of faith and hope, of Christian camaraderie and solidarity, in which the fruits of the Holy Spirit are manifested (Gal. 5.16-25; 2 Cor. 6.14-18) is lived more intensely. An ecumenical and missionary effort seeks better living conditions for the poor and marginalized, for victims of discrimination on account of race, beliefs or customs. The purpose is to serve God by serving the person nearest to you, especially the little ones. Each new believer, male and female, becomes a servant totally committed to the cause of Jesus and the kingdom.

Therefore, we believe that all Christians should work for this cause, especially Pentecostals and charismatics. That is what the three of us Latin American Pentecostals do as representatives of a spiritual force that energizes the mission of the Church in the power of the Holy

Spirit.[1] We practice a missionary ecumenism through an integral evangelization mission and service to the community. May God help us to fulfill this ministry, so that we may be able to give 'liberty to the Spirit of God' so that the Father can do a marvelous work in us and in all who will believe. Amen.

1.   Cf. G.O. Vaccaro, *Identidad Pentecostal* (Quito, Ecuador: Consejo Latinoamericano de Iglesias, 1990).

THAT THE WORLD MAY BELIEVE

Brighton '91—An International Congress on World Evangelization,
July 8–14, 1991

(Theological Stream)

July 9

The Most Revd George Carey, Archbishop of Canterbury, 'The Importance of Theology for the Charismatic Movement'.

Dr Jürgen Moltmann, Professor of Theology, Universität Tübingen, Evangelisch Theologisches Seminar, Lutheran, Germany, 'The Spirit of Life: Spirituality and New Vitality'. Respondents: Dr Miroslav Volf, Professor of Systematic Theology, Evangelical Theological Faculty, Pentecostal, Yugoslavia; Fr Raniero Cantalamessa, OFM Cap., Official Preacher to the Papal Household, Roman Catholic, Italy.

Dr Norbert Baumert, SJ, Professor of New Testament, Philosophisch-Theologische Hochschule St Georgen, Roman Catholic, Germany, 'Evangelization and Charismatic Signs'; Dr James Bradley, Professor of Church History, Fuller Theological Seminary (CA), American Baptist, USA, 'Miracles, Martyrdom and Evangelization in the Early Church'. Chair: Dr Tokunboh Adeyemo, General Secretary, Association of Evangelicals of Africa and Madagascar, Pentecostal, Kenya.

Dr Kilian McDonnell, OSB, President, Institute for Ecumenical and Cultural Research (MN), Roman Catholic, USA, 'A Catholic View of the Relationship between the Holy Spirit and the Church'. Respondent: Revd David Daniels, Assistant Professor of Church History, McCormick Theological Seminary (IL), Church of God in Christ, USA. Chair: Revd Dr Hans Haselbarth, Pastor, Lutheran, Germany.

July 10

Lic. Juan Sepulveda, Pastor, Servicio Evangelico Para El Desarollo, Pentecostal, Chile, 'A Pentecostal Perspective on Liberation Theology'. Respondents: Brian G. Hathaway, Pastor, Open Brethren, New Zealand; Dr Hubert Lenz, SAC, Philosophie-Dozent, Roman Catholic, Germany.

Canon John Gunstone, County Ecumenical Officer of Greater Manchester, Anglican, England, 'Evangelization in the Power of the Holy Spirit in an Urban and Multicultural World'; Lic. Luis Segreda, Seminaro Biblico Latinoamerica, Foursquare, Costa Rica, 'Evangelization and the Holy Spirit in an Urban and Multicultural Society: The Existence of the Pro-Human Rights Ecumenical Committee'. Chair: Dr Edith Blumhofer, Institute for the Study of American Evangelicals (IL), Assemblies of God, USA.

Dr Ioan Sauca, Press Officer for the Patriarch of Bucharest, Orthodox, Romania, 'Poverty, Persecution and Deprivation in the Light of Jesus' Cross and Resurrection'; Anthony Lim, Light of Jesus Christ Community, Roman Catholic, Malaysia; Dr Ronald Sider, Professor of Theology, Eastern Baptist Theological Seminary (PA), Mennonite, USA. Chair: Ven. R.A. Torrey III, Archdeacon of Kangwondo, Anglican, South Korea.

July 11

Dr Karla Poewe-Hexham, Professor, Department of Anthropology and Dr Irving Hexham, Associate Professor, Department of Religious Studies, University of Calgary, Anglican, Canada, 'Charismatic Churches and Apartheid in South Africa'. Respondents: Dr Robert Mapes Anderson, Professor of History, Wagner College (NY), USA; Dr Wynand de Kock, Academic Dean, Cape Evangelical Bible Institute, South Africa; Dr Nico Horn, Lecturer in Theology, University of Namibia.

Fr Philippe Larère, OP, Roman Catholic, France, 'Ecumenical Issues Concerning Evangelization'; Dr Theodore Jungkuntz, Pastor, Cross &

Resurrection Church (MI), Lutheran, USA; Lic. Roger Cabezas, Presidente, Mision Pentecostal Fe y Santidad de Costa Rica, Costa Rica.

Dr Cheryl Bridges Johns, Assistant Professor of Christian Formation and Discipleship, Church of God School of Theology (TN), Church of God (Cleveland), USA, 'Women in the Church'; Regine Maire–Besser, Editor of *Tychique*, Roman Catholic, France; Aida Luz Beltran de Gaetan, United Methodist Church, USA. Chair: Dr Trevor Grizzle, Associate Professor of New Testament, Oral Roberts University School of Theology (OK), Church of God (Cleveland), USA.

July 12

His Grace Bishop Antonius Markos, Bishop, Coptic Orthodox, Kenya, 'The Orthodox Understanding of the Role of the Holy Spirit in the Birth and Growth of the Church'. Respondents: Fr Matthew Vellanickal, Professor of New Testament, St Thomas Apostolic Seminary, Syro-Malabar, Catholic, India; Canon Michael Green, Regent College (BC), Anglican, Canada.

'From Here, Where?', moderated by Dr Russell P. Spittler, Professor of New Testament, Fuller Theological Seminary (CA), Assemblies of God, USA.

Dr Clark H. Pinnock, Professor of Systematic Theology, McMaster Divinity College (ON), Baptist, Canada, 'Evangelism and Other Living Faiths'; Rt Revd Anthony Gbuji, Bishop, Roman Catholic, Nigeria. Chair: Dr J.A.B. Jongeneel, Professor of Missions, University of Utrecht, Netherlands Reformed Church, The Netherlands.

Dr Cecil M. Robeck, Jr, Associate Professor of Church History and Ecumenics, Fuller Theological Seminary (CA), Assemblies of God, USA, 'Pentecostal Origins in a Global Perspective'; Revd Desmond W. Cartwright, Official Historian, Elim Pentecostal Church, England. Respondents: Dr James Goff, Assistant Professor, Appalachian State University (NC), Pentecostal Holiness, USA; Dr Japie J. Lapoorta, Principal, Sarepta Teologiese Kollege, South Africa. Chair: Dr David E. Harrell, Breeden Eminent Scholar in the Humanities, Auburn University (AL), USA.

July 13

Dr Martinus L. Daneel, Professor of Missions, University of South Africa, Shona Independent Churches, Zimbabwe, 'African Independent Church Pneumatology and the Salvation of All Creation'. Respondents: Dr James D.G. Dunn, Professor of Divinity, University of Durham, England; Revd Derek Mutungu, Pastor, Baptist, Zambia.

Pastor Paul Bechdolff, French Reformed Church, France, 'Evangelization and Eschatology'. Respondent: Dr Barry Chant, President, Tabor College, Australia. Chair: Rt Revd Godfrey Ashby, Bishop, Anglican, United Kingdom.

Graham Perrins, House Churches, United Kingdom, 'This Worldly Realities and Progress in the Light of the Eschatological Kingdom'; Dr Tormod Engelsviken, Senior Lecturer in Missiology, Free Faculty of Theology, Lutheran, Norway; Dr Guillermo Cook, Associate General Secretary, Fraternidad Teologica Latinoamericana, Costa Rica, 'The Church, the World, and Progress in Latin America, in Light of the Eschatological Kingdom'. Chair: Dr Paul Toaspern, Hauptgeschaftsfuhrer der Arbeitsgemeinschaft missionarisch Dienst, Lutheran, Germany.

INDEX OF NAMES